What Leaders Are Saying about *The*

"A book for people who want to develop their potential as transformative leaders, full of stories that show what wonderful things happen when one's inner life merges with an outward mission and how just such a development is necessary to meet the challenges of the 21st century."
—**Bill Bradley, former US Senator**

"An important and persuasive alternative view of leadership. Carol Pearson has brought together an impressive range of contributions into a coherent and highly readable account that is deeply relevant to today's world."
—**Michael Walton, Lecturer in International Development, Kennedy School of Government, Harvard University, and former Chief Economist, The World Bank**

"A comprehensive guide to the latest thinking in leadership communications that explores new ways of thinking about leadership, building charisma, and entering rich interactive relationships with listeners."
—**Steve Denning, former Program Director, Knowledge Management, The World Bank, and author of *The Leader's Guide to Radical Management*, *The Secret Language of Leadership*, and *The Leader's Guide to Storytelling***

"The challenges the world faces in the 21st century can't be addressed with traditional policy and management practices...Pearson has assembled some of the best minds in the field to examine how transformational leadership models can help us update the structures of our thinking, optimize innovative capacity, and harvest the wisdom of groups we lead."
—**Kenneth S. Apfel, Professor of the Practice and Director, Management, Finance, and Leadership Program, University of Maryland, and former Commissioner, Social Security Administration**

"If you've wondered how to successfully transform leadership to meet the emerging issues of today, look no more. Pearson and her colleagues have imbued each chapter with inspiration and examples that offer hope and simultaneously demand the heavy lifting required to transform leaders. Leading *is* rocket science, a science that is growing and changing. This book is a must-read for all who aspire to the work."
—**JoAn Knight Herren, former Chief of Training and Technical Assistance, Office of Head Start, US Department of Health and Human Services**

"We are reminded daily that leadership strategies that worked in the past are generally inadequate for 21st-century challenges. *The Transforming Leader* offers leaders—and those who develop and support them—new insights about personal and organizational leadership approaches and pathways to achieving positive and lasting change."
—**Shelly Wilsey, Director, International Leadership Association**

"*The Transforming Leader* is an important book. It is brilliant and insightful and speaks to our future. I highly recommend it to my friends, associates, and others who want to engage in crafting a new and better world."

—**Harvey Bottelsen, Chairman of the Board, James S. Bower Foundation**

"Ours is an age of cascading threshold crossings. *The Transforming Leader* is the field guide to this kaleidoscope landscape, where leadership emerges as a property of our interdependence."

—**Matthew J. Rezac, Director of Rural Community Partnerships, Sherwood Foundation**

What Leadership Educators Are Saying about *The Transforming Leader*

"From helping the reader to think through what transformational leadership is in its many forms, to integrating psychological, spiritual, cultural, and scientific perspectives about our deepest sense of being and purpose, to discussing the art of applying leadership from individuals to societies, this valuable book expands the territory of transformation and what it means for leaders to deeply engage in leadership for our interdependent world."

—**John B. McGuire, Senior Faculty Member, Center for Creative Leadership, and coauthor of *Transforming Your Leadership Culture***

"Steeped in nature, poetry, and music, the gatherings in the beautiful, wooded Fetzer Institute provided a perfect setting for the germination of ideas on the transforming leader in this book. It reads like a symphony. Read it. Enjoy it. Live it, and become the transforming leader."

—**Cynthia Cherrey, Vice President for Campus Life, Princeton University, and President, International Leadership Association**

"A must-read for individuals or groups starting or deepening their inner journey to the authenticity that becomes leadership that transforms. Reading this book is a gift to your head, heart, soul, and spirit."

—**Susan R. Komives, Professor of Student Affairs, University of Maryland, and former President, American College Personnel Association**

"*The Transforming Leader* illuminates, transcends, provokes, and enhances much of what has been said, written, and thought about leadership. Dr. Pearson and her colleagues provide a way to see leadership from the inside out—building on the ever-increasing understanding of what it means to be leaders who are aware and mindful not only of the skills, knowledge, and experience they need but also of the sense of purpose and meaning they need to bring to their worldview. It is a must-read for all who are, plan to be, and have been leaders of their time."

—**Donna Shavlik, former Director, Office of Women in Higher Education, American Council on Education, and board member, National Council for Research on Women**

"*The Transforming Leader* should be required reading for every leader, leadership scholar, and leadership consultant because of its scope and depth. The many brilliant contributors help us think anew about models of transforming leadership, as well as plumb the depths of our own consciousness as leaders. Then, if that weren't incredible enough, they show us how to use this powerful 'inner/outer dynamic' to transform the world."
>   —**Jean Lipman-Blumen, Thornton F. Bradshaw Professor of Public Policy and Professor of Organizational Behavior, Claremont Graduate University, Peter F. Drucker and Masatoshi Ito Graduate School of Management, and author of *Connective Leadership* and *The Allure of Toxic Leaders***

"Packed full of the latest research and ancient wisdom, *The Transforming Leader* honors the past while creating great vision. It is simultaneously scientific and spiritual, full of intuition and deeply practical!"
>   —**Valerie Shangreaux, Director of Leadership, Blandin Foundation**

"I wish I had this book to read for my first experience as a leader—and each one thereafter! Fortunately, Carol Pearson and her colleagues have provided this remarkable set of essays in time to help current and future leaders in organizations and in the classroom transform their inner thoughts and emotions into powerful leadership actions in the service of others."
>   —**Robert J. Thomas, Professor of Marketing and former Dean, School of Continuing Studies, Georgetown University**

"The current leadership discourse seems to agree that a big change, a transformation, is required for 21st-century leaders. This refreshing book brings together creative thought and artistic science to offer a hopeful model for the leaders of the future."
>   —**Eliat Aram, PhD, CEO, The Tavistock Institute of Human Relations**

"*The Transforming Leader* is a comprehensive and elegantly integrated guide to the latest thinking in the study of leadership. It offers opportunities for deep exploration within a clear, accessible structure and can be used by leaders to deepen their humanity while developing their efficacy."
>   —**Hélène Smit, Program Director, National Diploma in Facilitation, South African College of Applied Psychology, and author of *Beneath***

"Carol Pearson and her colleagues give us the inspiration, the confidence, and the tools to bring our leadership visions and skills to the fore. These essays are so insightful and imaginative that readers will want to turn to them again and again to inform their leadership practice as it evolves in new contexts and with new challenges."
>   —**Julie L. Ramsey, EdD, Vice President for College Life and Dean of Students, Gettysburg College**

"There has been much discussion on transformational leadership since Jim Burns wrote his tome in the 1970s. Much of it is structural and theoretical with little application to ordinary businesses and people's lives. This book changes that. If you are serious about transforming your business or yourself…read this work."

—**Mark Grandstaff, PhD, co-editor of *Strategic Leadership* and former Clinton appointee to the leadership team, Commission on National Service**

"Carol Pearson has assembled a collection of innovative thinkers and writers who present new, refreshing, and challenging ideas about leadership. Engaging and actionable—this is not your 'flavor of the month' volume."

—**Hile Rutledge, President, Otto Kroeger Associates**

What Psychologists Are Saying about *The Transforming Leader*

"This compelling recount of historical and contemporary narratives of transformative leaders will inspire, educate, and enlighten anyone who may seek to lead others through the valley of shadows and fears."

—**Dexter Freeman, DSW, LCSW, Director, Army–Fayetteville State University Master of Social Work Program**

"The synthetic scope of this collection brings the spiritual and the scientific into dialogue in a manner that will carry us deeply into the 21st century. A must-read for all who recognize the importance of true leadership."

—**Joseph Cambray, PhD, President, International Association for Analytical Psychology**

"Carol Pearson, a leading light in fusing the psychological and the corporate, has once again done us all a favor. Gathered together in this insightful book is a wide array of authors who shed light on the complexities and nuances needed for leadership. Their insights are eagerly welcome at a time when we are hungry and searching for new leaders."

—**Aryeh Maidenbaum, PhD, Director, New York Center for Jungian Studies**

"There are rare moments in time when truly pioneering spirits emerge. Through their work, insights, and the vastness of their vision and nature, we suddenly become aware of a world far greater than what we have previously experienced, and at such moments, a new paradigm is created. Such is the work, life, and influence of Carol Pearson."

—**Michael Conforti, PhD, Jungian analyst and founder and Director, Assisi Institute**

THE
TRANSFORMING
LEADER

BOOKS AUTHORED OR COAUTHORED BY CAROL S. PEARSON

The Hero Within: Six Archetypes We Live By

Awakening the Heroes Within: Twelve Archetypes That Help Us Find Ourselves and Transform Our World

Magic at Work: Camelot, Creative Leadership, and Everyday Miracles (coauthored by Sharon Seivert)

The Hero and the Outlaw: Building Extraordinary Brands Through the Power of Archetypes (coauthored by Margaret Mark)

Mapping the Organizational Psyche: A Jungian Theory of Organizational Dynamics and Change (coauthored by John G. Corlett)

What Story Are You Living? (coauthored by Hugh Marr)

THE
TRANSFORMING
LEADER

NEW APPROACHES TO LEADERSHIP
FOR THE TWENTY-FIRST CENTURY

Carol S. Pearson, PhD
EDITOR

Published in Partnership with the Fetzer Institute

Berrett–Koehler Publishers, Inc.
San Francisco
a BK Business book

Berrett-Koehler Publishers, Inc.
235 Montgomery Street, Suite 650
San Francisco, CA 94104-2916
Tel: (415) 288-0260   Fax: (415) 362-2512   www.bkconnection.com

Ordering Information
QUANTITY SALES. Special discounts are available on quantity purchases by corporations, associations, and others. For details, contact the "Special Sales Department" at the Berrett-Koehler address above.
INDIVIDUAL SALES. Berrett-Koehler publications are available through most bookstores. They can also be ordered directly from Berrett-Koehler: Tel: (800) 929-2929; Fax: (802) 864-7626; www.bkconnection.com
ORDERS FOR COLLEGE TEXTBOOK/COURSE ADOPTION USE. Please contact Berrett-Koehler: Tel: (800) 929-2929; Fax: (802) 864-7626.
ORDERS BY U.S. TRADE BOOKSTORES AND WHOLESALERS. Please contact Ingram Publisher Services, Tel: (800) 509-4887; Fax: (800) 838-1149; E-mail: customer.service@ingrampublisherservices.com; or visit www.ingrampublisherservices.com/Ordering for details about electronic ordering.

Berrett-Koehler and the BK logo are registered trademarks of Berrett-Koehler Publishers, Inc.

Printed in the United States of America

Berrett-Koehler books are printed on long-lasting acid-free paper. When it is available, we choose paper that has been manufactured by environmentally responsible processes. These may include using trees grown in sustainable forests, incorporating recycled paper, minimizing chlorine in bleaching, or recycling the energy produced at the paper mill.

Library of Congress Cataloging-in-Publication Data

    The transforming leader : new approaches to leadership for the twenty-first century / edited by Carol S. Pearson. — 1st ed.
        p. cm.
    "Published in Partnership with the Fetzer Institute."
    Includes bibliographical references and index.
    ISBN 978-1-60994-120-8 (pbk.)
    1. Transformational leadership.   I. Pearson, Carol, 1944-
    HM1261.T734 2012
    303.3'4—dc23

                                                                        2012005725

First Edition
17 16 15 14 13 12   10 9 8 7 6 5 4 3 2 1

BOOK PRODUCED BY: Westchester Book Group
COVER DESIGN: Cassandra Chu
COPYEDITOR: Karen Fisher
INDEXER: Robert Swanson
AUTHOR PHOTO: Cheryl Van Scoy

To Donna Shavlik and Judith Touchton
for their pioneering work transforming
leadership in higher education

CONTENTS

PART TWO
Being the Change: Inner Work for Transforming Leaders
Setting the Context for Part Two *85*

Deepening and Expanding Inner Capacities for Becoming the Change *85*

PART THREE
The Art of Working with and Transforming Groups
Setting the Context for Part Three *151*

Shifting Perspectives on Inner/Outer Connectivity *151*

FOREWORD

The mission of the Fetzer Institute is to foster an awareness of the power of love and forgiveness in the emerging global community. And a core guiding principle is the importance of the connection between one's inner life of mind and spirit and one's outer life of service and action in the world. Leadership for transformation speaks directly to this connection. When we do the work we do in the world—whether it be teaching, managing the business operations of a Fortune 500 company, preparing meals for others, or whatever we might do—from a place of connection to and expression of our innermost values, we unleash our tremendous potential to be the love we wish to see in the world.

We are delighted to observe how the Leadership for Transformation Project has served this work. Through the dialogues, a remarkable group of participants shared their insights, experiences, and wisdom and we all grew from the interactions and rich conversations. It is heartwarming to see how the seeds from that project have grown beyond the planning stage, to the retreats, and now to this book of essays by an extraordinary group of authors who represent a wide range of experience and backgrounds.

The Institute continues to look for ways to seed conversations that can have such rich harvests. To that end, we have convened sixteen international advisory councils, each representing various sectors of work in the world. Each council is exploring its domain, looking for existing examples of love and forgiveness in action. From these examples, we seek to learn: What are the conditions that made this possible? What can we do to help inspire others toward love and forgiveness in their work? How can we demonstrate leadership for transformation and help foster even greater awareness of the power of love and forgiveness in the emerging global community?

As we think about what goes into being a leader for transformation, particularly in a global community, the insights and messages conveyed throughout this book offer great guidance. There are formal leaders, and informal leaders, in every sector of work, and every dimension of our community. Becoming more aware of and nurturing our capacities to be leaders for transformation, in every aspect of our lives, can help bring about a more loving and forgiving world.

DEBORAH HIGGINS
Director of Programs, Fetzer Institute

Deborah Higgins is director of programs for the Fetzer Institute, a private operating foundation with a mission to foster awareness of the power of love and forgiveness in the emerging global community. Particular areas of interest include leadership, organizational well-being, and whole-systems approaches to community engagement. She also is interested in evaluation and how organizations harvest, synthesize, and share learnings from their work. Prior to Fetzer, Deborah worked for twenty years at Western Michigan University, where she held a number of administrative leadership positions. She earned baccalaureate and master's degrees in sociology from Western Michigan University.

PREFACE

The Leadership for Transformation Project

The ideas about transformation offered in this book themselves grew out of an unexpectedly transformational process. They emerged from an inquiry and curiosity about leaders—at all levels—who have an appetite for, and skill at, helping organizations turn corners toward a more vibrant future. This natural and emergent process changed shape and focus as it evolved, and no doubt also changed many of us who were involved in it. We invite the reader to join us on that extraordinary journey.

It began, in a sense, as a walk in the park. On one such outing, Carol Pearson and Judy Brown, neighbors of many years and then both leadership scholars at the University of Maryland, found themselves wondering out loud about transformational leadership: Who are exemplars of this kind of leadership? How do they do it? What frameworks shape their ways of thinking? What practices do they employ in their work?

Carol and Judy mentioned these walking questions to the staff of the Fetzer Institute at an unrelated meeting, and were startled when the foundation expressed interest in joining the project as an active partner and funder. That itself was a transformational idea.

So Carol and Judy became principal investigators in a several-year exploration to create a deeper understanding of leadership that transforms. Their intention was to do this by drawing together experienced leaders, leadership theorists, and others who study and teach various practices that strengthen leadership.

After an initial planning retreat, it became apparent to Carol, Judy, and Michael Jones, a longtime colleague and musician who became a consultant to the project, that we were not so much investigators or facilitators as part of the very story of transformation we hoped to tell. We realized that assembling various communities of theorists, practitioners, and exemplars to examine the nature and dynamics of leading for transformation wasn't going to work for us if we were talking about transformation as an abstract concept "out there." Instead, we needed to bring ourselves into the discussion and explore what leading for transformation meant for us during the process of which we were stewards.

Then, almost without our noticing, what might have remained a traditional research project transformed into an effort led not by three people but by an extended group that also included poet and Fetzer Institute program officer Mark Nepo and his colleague Deb Higgins; collaborative leadership scholar Gil Hickman; International Leadership Association President Cynthia Cherrey and ILA's energetic director, Shelley Wilsey, and editor and wise counsel Megan Scribner. This stewardship team designed the meetings that, in turn, expanded this community of practice.

We hosted three gatherings at Seasons, Fetzer's conference center tucked into the side of a hill near Kalamazoo, Michigan, and built of native Michigan materials—limestone and huge timbers. The vast window that opened out into the woods carried its own messages about the nature of things. In autumn and springtime, through brilliant sunshine and surprise thunderstorms, we gathered in circles, large and small, to share stories and insights about transformation.

One might expect that such deliberations would have had a singularly academic framing. But somehow the setting, the structure of the conversations, the tone setting of Michael's keyboard artistry, Mark Nepo's poetry and teaching tales, the gentle, welcoming facilitation, and the fresh thinking and stories of so many who joined us made them more like campfire retreats.

At the time of the Seasons gatherings, our team also was participating in the annual conferences of the ILA—first in Vancouver, then Los Angeles, Prague, and Boston. In Vancouver, we invited attendees to engage in an informal conversation about our work. We were startled at the

large turnout and the deep interest in the questions we were exploring—
and in the way we were exploring them.

In the beginning, we thought that making sense of and sharing what
we heard from others would be the key outcome of the leadership retreats. And, of course, that is in part the purpose of this book. Carol
Pearson, as only someone with her range of interests and expertise can,
has created a full, integrated understanding of leadership for transformation, drawing on the ideas and writings of those who joined us in
person at Seasons and others who were our colleagues in spirit.

But we also suspect that the Seasons retreats, by bringing us together
and fostering such rich discussions, changed the lives and leadership
practices of those on the stewardship team and many of the participants. Our hope is that this book will give you a similar space to explore
these questions and ideas and welcome you into this virtual community of transformational and regenerative leadership.

JUDY BROWN AND MICHAEL JONES

Judy Brown is an educator, speaker, poet, and writer, whose work in
organizations revolves around themes of leadership, transformation,
learning, dialogue, creativity, diversity, and renewal. Her books include
A Leader's Guide to Reflective Practice and a collection of her poetry, *The
Sea Accepts All Rivers*. Dr. Brown teaches leadership at the University of
Maryland. A native of a small fishing village in northern Michigan, her
heritage is that of agriculture and cooperative extension, which has
given her a commitment to the practical use of ideas, research, and
science as a way to transform our lives and our work.

As a pianist, composer, leadership speaker, writer, and creative facilitator, **Michael Jones** integrates creative artistry with personal transformation and organizational learning. He is the author of *Artful Leadership*
and *Creating an Imaginative Life* and has composed and produced
fifteen recordings of original compositions for piano, which have been
distributed worldwide. Michael was a consultant with the Fetzer
Leadership for Transformation Dialogues and a Senior Fellow with the
James MacGregor Burns Academy of Leadership. He also is a regular

session leader at the International Leadership Association annual conference, where, with the support of the Fetzer Institute and other Fetzer colleagues, he has been facilitating dialogues exploring the power of metaphor, poetry, and story as languages for transformational learning. His website is http://Pianoscapes.com.

| Introduction |

The Transforming Leader

New Needs for New Times

> Everything changes. Everything is connected. Pay attention.
> —Classic Buddhist teaching

Most of us want to make a difference, but doing so is not as simple as it sounds. Whether you hold a major leadership position or are just setting out to be a positive force for change, you likely know that good intentions are not enough. Many of us have had experiences where we meant well and tried hard, yet the changes we wished to see eluded us, were short-lived and unsustainable—or things actually got worse.

This book is written for people like you, who care about the quality of your life and your impact on the world around you. In it, we present leadership thinking and practices that can help you meet the challenges of today's world. You may be a practicing leader; an educator, coach, workshop leader, or consultant who develops leaders; a scholar who writes about leadership; or just beginning your career, not yet even thinking of yourself as a leader. We are called to lead in many different ways and it is important that we take the responsibility to do what is ours to do for the good of those around us and the larger world.

The ideas and practices in this book are based on the notion that modern challenges require our total commitment. This means three things: First, we must respond to these challenges by developing our capacities to think and lead in transformational ways. Second, to accomplish the first, we must access all our faculties—mental sharpness, emotional depth, body sensations, imagination, and creativity, as well as a connection to our souls and spirits. And third, we need to harvest

1

the full capacities of those around us, because we all have different experiences, gifts, and perceptions to offer, which collectively are greater than what any one of us has alone.

Transformational change also requires that we close the gap between what we want, what we are, and what we do. Thus, if we want to make significant and long-lasting changes, we must look within before we look without. By bringing our inner world (our thought processes, perspectives, self-awareness, emotional intelligence, capacity for staying centered in the midst of turmoil) into alignment with our outer world (our actions, how we lead, how we live the work, how we work with people), we are better able to transform our leadership and bring about the change we seek.

As leaders are transformed, so is their work and those with whom they work. For example, you may have witnessed settings where morale had plummeted, but then a new transforming leader (possibly you) comes in. Soon people start sharing responsibility for improving processes and outcomes, get things done without unnecessary drama, are curious and open to new ideas, learn from setbacks, and seem unusually fulfilled, having a sense that their labors are meaningful because their work supports values and a vision that they believe in. After a time, people working in such places may themselves become transforming leaders who create ripple effects as they practice what they have learned wherever they go.

Why Leadership Is So Difficult Today

Although making a difference is not easy, it is well worth the challenge. If you feel confused or frustrated by the trials of leading in a time of global uncertainty, interdependence, and unexpected difficulties, you are not alone. No matter how high up you go in leadership, and whether or not you aspire to be a transformational leader, today's realities are daunting, as the future is unpredictable. For example, President Barack Obama ran for office with a vision of what he wanted to accomplish but got hit, even before he was inaugurated, with the global financial meltdown. Before Obama, President George W. Bush was blindsided by

9/11, an event orchestrated from far away that was so unthinkable that neither he nor the CIA anticipated it. Both presidents had to grapple with intractable problems that were not even in their areas of primary expertise or on their agenda for change.

Few enterprises, however big or small, are exempt from the impact of national and global interdependence. International businesses worry about competitors rendering one of their products or a whole product line obsolete. To add to the complexity, many now buy materials and manufacture products in a variety of regions around the world, so that natural disasters anywhere, not to mention warfare and political unrest, become business challenges. On a more local scale, small businesses are vulnerable to shifting prices of essential items or to a global conglomerate moving into their neighborhood and creating price competition they cannot meet. The health of the international economy affects us all. For instance, unrest in the Middle East drives up gas prices, the cost of travel, and other aspects of doing business. And so on.

This level of interdependence makes it difficult to figure out how to solve problems, leading many people to retreat into survival mode or strive to maximize their own advantage regardless of long-term costs. Some, sensing the urgency of the situation, react in knee-jerk fashion, blaming others for their troubles and ending up making things worse.

When I taught at the University of Maryland School of Public Policy, my graduate students—mostly professionals in government, the military, businesses with government contracts, and nonprofit organizations—quickly identified a gap between the expectations of what leaders should be able to do and the immensity of the problems they face. They noted that most people imagine that a good leader will be informed, decisive, and able to steer the ship in every situation. People also believe leaders should be able to identify problems and energetically solve them, guided either by best practices or new scientific data. In addition, leaders should create strategic plans, sell them to their followers in a rational, scientific manner, and then implement them with excellent results in a timely fashion, in the process making the world better for us all. In short, they should be in control and achieve on a heroic scale.

The graduate students complained that such idealistic and, we began to believe, anachronistic models of leadership were unrealistic and unachievable in the situations they faced. Yet they felt pressured to at least pretend to fit this model. As we continued discussing the gap between the expectations to which they were subject and their actual ability to effect change, the students began to evince a "can we talk?" level of frankness concerning their reservations about how easy it is to describe leadership and how difficult it is to put it into practice. This was true at all levels of leadership and in all types of situations. For instance, soldiers who had returned from Iraq and Afghanistan spoke earnestly about what it was like to live in constant fear—even of groups of women and children, who might be holding a grenade or a bomb, or hiding a sniper ready to shoot—while being expected to make friends with the local populace. Government managers complained about the obstacles to accomplishing anything in a massive bureaucracy; some recounted situations where politicians who did not understand the science related to their bureau's mission passed laws requiring the agency to implement inadequate or even counterproductive polices. Executives of for-profit companies told of the tension produced by the constant pressure for quarterly profits, especially if meeting the goals conflicted with their values or undermined safety, quality control, or customer service. College and university administrators emphasized the impediments to getting things done in a context that requires collegial governance but with faculty who are resistant to needed change, while nonprofit leaders described being squeezed by mounting needs and expectations and shrinking donations and grants.

The students then began to tease out some common issues that made it difficult for them to succeed. They realized that although the examples they cited were very different, they all shared a Catch-22 quality, required unrealistic Superwoman or Superman powers, and/or led to results that themselves were counterproductive. Then there were challenges they all identified as problematic: employees, citizens, and customers today expect to have a voice, so leaders have to consult (and often please) them, but the leaders alone are held responsible for the results. Information overload and complexity means no single individual is likely to have the ultimate answer to any problem—yet they will be asked to supply one. As with any truly major issue, no one organization or even sector can address it alone, so leaders need to collaborate with others and incorporate diverse views, yet few have the skills or experience in this style of working. Finally, given the present pace of change and innovation in the world, even doing strategic planning is difficult because just about the time the plan is complete, it is no longer relevant.

These students' wide range of experiences and backgrounds—yet common challenges and struggles—made it clear that we need to think about leadership in a manner that works within a variety of contexts and that addresses what is happening on the ground in real groups, communities, and organizations. The specifics of what leadership requires, my students concluded, keep changing with varying circumstances and in different milieus. Thus, it makes no sense to focus primarily on teaching leaders particular skills, approaches, or fad-of-the-month organizational interventions. Instead, we should build their core capacities, so that they are able to meet unanticipated challenges and tailor their responses to specific situations. But what are these capacities, and how are they developed?

Learning from Transformational Leaders

My University of Maryland colleague, Judy Brown, and I agreed with our students about the need to foster such capacities. As leadership scholars and educators, we, of course, had our own hypotheses about what ideas and practices might fulfill this need. However, we wanted to explore these ideas and expand our knowledge by engaging with other leaders who were making a truly transformational impact in the world. We knew they were out there. We were familiar with some, had heard of others, and wondered what they had in common. We wanted to know what it was they drew on—what images of the world, what communities of thought, what personal practices. Our goal was to learn from other successful contemporary leaders what leadership capabilities made the difference. We also wanted to provide a platform to bring transformational leaders together to pool their knowledge for the betterment of all concerned.

This desire gave rise to the Fetzer Institute Leadership for Transformation Project, cosponsored by the James MacGregor Burns Academy of Leadership and the International Leadership Association (which was incubated by the academy). In this project, we were inspired by James MacGregor Burns's work on transformational leadership, but used the term "leadership for transformation" to distinguish our inquiry from expectations that transformational leadership was a particular school of thought that would seem to be in competition with other approaches. We wanted to learn more broadly, from any and all ways of thinking about leadership that were working today. We invited leaders who had accomplished positive, transformational change, as well as educators, coaches, and consultants who assisted them, and scholars who studied them, to join us in a series of three relatively lengthy dialogues over a three-year period.

As described in the preface, something magical happened at these retreats. It was not just what the participants shared with us. It was how they shared, what they focused on, and the way they were with us and with one another—indeed, what they modeled in all these ways taught us as much as what they said.

We saw none of the usual posturing or competitiveness you often get in groups of high achievers. From the beginning, participants spoke from a collaborative and authentic place. Instead of claiming credit for their accomplishments, they typically attributed their success to an inspiration, a sudden sense of calling, divine help, or a synchronous event. Instead of speaking in abstractions, they told stories, used metaphors, shared images, or invited us to engage in an experience with them and with each other. The pace of conversation slowed; pauses were pregnant rather than uncomfortable; and voices became deeper. Our project stewardship team—consisting of Judy Brown and Carol Pearson; Fetzer Institute program officers Mark Nepo and Deborah Higgins; ILA president Cynthia Cherrey, director Shelly Wilsey, and board member Gil Hickman; consultant Michael Jones; and editor Megan Scribner—and participants in the dialogues soon recognized that something profound was happening in the space we were jointly creating. Our team became aware that we were starting to collaborate even more seamlessly in the service of the group. We observed a ripple effect, with energy emanating from individuals to encompass the entire group, which then was reflected back to the individual members, creating a wonderfully healthy feedback loop that deepened our mutual inquiry. This effect also intensified over the three-year period, so that it was more pronounced in the last dialogue than in the first. And while it was somewhat less present in the related short dialogues we conducted at ILA conferences, those sessions were always filled to capacity and seemed to satisfy an intense hunger for such open sharing.

Some consensus began to emerge from the Fetzer and ILA sessions. The participants emphasized the importance of individuals connecting with their deeper and wiser selves, so that they could embody the change needed around them. They held up as exemplary leaders people who are authentic, connected with an internal source of wisdom, and also feel deeply connected to other people and the natural world. Such exemplars, they noted, show nonjudgmental curiosity and openness to what is emerging in any situation, as well as a capacity for contemporary types of thinking and ways of making meaning, some of which come from emerging paradigms in the new sciences and social networking theory as well as depth and positive psychology. Indeed, these leaders combine deep self-awareness with real-world savvy and are consciously striving to grow and learn on both dimensions.

Listening to the participants and observing their behaviors gave rise to the major sections of this book. Part One focuses on transformational models of leadership and how to think in ways that support transformational ends. Part Two offers practices that help leaders to embody the qualities of consciousness needed in leaders today. And Part Three centers on how these inner changes result in enhanced abilities to lead groups so as to bring out their best and most transformational efforts.

Or to be more concise, the three parts focus on modes of thinking, being, and relating that together constitute a new model for successful leadership practice.

This Book: Its Purpose, Design, and Content

In bringing these three elements—thinking, being, and relating— together, *The Transforming Leader* has the form of a Möbius strip, outlining the dynamic interrelationship between a leader's inner life, which affects behaviors; the effect of those behaviors on the outer world of people, events, and structures; the impact of experiences in the outer world on the leader's attitudes and emotions; and so on and on. This inner/outer dynamic is foundational to the flow of the book and provides its fundamental point of differentiation from books that focus on only one or two elements of this flow.

All this being said, *The Transforming Leader* complements various current leadership approaches or can stand alone as a source for learning and exploring the basic leadership capacities needed today. Because it is divided into sections with brief essays, each of which can be read in a short time, it can fit into very busy schedules. In fact, reading part of the book and taking time to integrate its lessons before moving on can support personal capacity building.

The essays, written by recognized leaders and experts in their own unique voices and styles, weave together insights from the Fetzer retreat participants and others to elucidate this dynamic interplay between the inner life of leaders and their outer actions, as informed by emerging knowledge in a variety of fields and from many different perspectives. They also provide powerful assistance in unlearning unhelpful and anachronistic approaches and replacing them with empowering ways of thinking, being, and relating that are congruent with the needs of this time in human history. Because today's challenges require leaders who can bring not just their heads but their hearts, souls, and spirits to the table, and who can recognize unconscious as well as conscious motivations, the essays also draw heavily from psychology and other disciplines that take the whole person into consideration.

Each essay is powerful in its own right, but a synergy occurs when complementary ideas from different fields are integrated into a more holistic approach. For this reason, introductions to each section provide important background to contextualize the essays that follow. Between essays, you will find brief transitional bridges that show how each builds on the other and identify the leadership competencies explored in the one that follows. The conclusion offers a brief summation and then provides information about how to anchor your learnings through consciously reframing the stories you tell in both formal and informal communication.

At the close of the book, in Appendix A, you will find exercises that foster the development of the capacities outlined in the essays and provide accessible ways to translate the powerful concepts described in the introductions and essays into empowering practices. Appendix B offers additional resources, followed by references and a bibliography.

The book begins, in "Part One: Transformational Thinking for Twenty-First-Century Leaders," with a context-setting introduction that focuses on the ideas of James MacGregor Burns, the founder of the transformational leadership school of leadership practice. It then briefly traces the development of his thinking, from emphasizing the transformational impact of individuals to that of whole groups or nations. The essays in Part One provide an overview of emerging modes of thinking that guide important elements of transformational leadership in action. They illustrate what transformational leadership is, how it works, and how it is evolving, and they offer guidance for updating conceptual paradigms to reflect the kind of transformational leadership thinking needed now. Part One includes:

- "Transactional and Transformational Leadership: Their Foundations in Power and Influence," by Michael Lovaglia, Jeffrey Lucas, and Amy Baxter. This exploration of research findings demonstrates the efficacy of James MacGregor Burns's ideal of transformational leadership and shows how you can be more effective in promoting change through inspiring others than by more transactional means.

- "Leadership in Action: Three Essential Energies," by Betty Sue Flowers. This case study of how President Lyndon B. Johnson cooperated with Martin Luther King Jr. and worked skillfully with Congress to pass civil rights legislation presents an inspiring real-life example that makes theories about transforming leadership come alive.
- "Leadership and Organizational Networks: A Relational Perspective," by Philip Willburn and Michael Campbell. This explanation of social networking theory shows how you can conduct a strategic analysis of groups and organizations through better understanding of natural social influence processes to communicate your transformational message more successfully.
- "Positive Power: Transforming Possibilities through Appreciative Leadership," by Diana Whitney and Amanda Trosten-Bloom. This exploration of positive psychology, strength-based leadership, and appreciative inquiry insights helps you know what to do to build confidence and bring out the best in yourself, other people, and social systems.
- "Dancing on a Slippery Floor: Transforming Systems, Transforming Leadership," by Kathleen Allen, describes new paradigms in science and systems analyses in organizational development theory to help you shift your thinking to be able to lead more effectively in complex adaptive systems.
- "On Mattering: Lessons from Ancient Wisdom, Literature, and the New Sciences," by Barbara Mossberg, shares insights from ancient myths and modern science to help you fully realize how much you do matter and how important it is to explore your own complexity and the complexity in the world in order to use your influence wisely.

"Part Two: Being the Change: Inner Work for Transforming Leaders" delves into the psychological and spiritual dimensions of the inner work needed to be a transformational leader. It provides guidance about various modalities of inner work, each of which serves to enhance leadership presence and help the leader become a catalyst for transformational change. The introduction to this section, highlighting the work of educational psychologist Robert Kegan, provides context on the pressing need for individuals to develop their full cognitive capacities. It then shows how recognizing the wisdom of the unconscious as well as the conscious mind can enable you to have greater success in fulfilling your transformational goals. The essays that follow reflect insights from psychospiritual theory and practice for developing cognitive capacities. Part Two includes:

- "The New Basics: Inner Work for Adaptive Challenges," by Katherine Tyler Scott, offers examples from organizational leadership to show how and why it is essential for you to do your inner work if you are to lead effectively in contemporary organizations.
- "Integral Leadership: Opening Space by Leading through the Heart," by Jonathan Reams, shares findings in integral psychology and neuroscience as an aid in connecting with your full self and with a greater sense of options and possibilities.
- "Mindful Leadership: Discovering Wisdom beyond Certainty," by Susan Szpakowski. Buddhism and neuroscience agree that the primary human impulse to fabricate certainty short-circuits the potential for creativity and intelligence. This essay shows how, when harnessed, this impulse becomes a doorway to leadership growth and transformation.
- "Leadership as a Spiritual Practice: Vocation and Journey," by Matthew Fox, explores four archetypal spiritual paths as frames for viewing leadership as a vocation and leadership experiences as learning opportunities that foster wisdom, resilience, and flexibility.
- "Transmuting Suffering: A Leadership and Advising Perspective," by Arthur Colman and Éliane Ubalijoro. It is very difficult to face suffering, loss, scapegoating, or a confrontation with one's own or a cultural shadow. This essay explores how a trusted and able advisor can help you do so. Most important, it provides support for facing one's shadow and the shadow of the world in order to become a healing presence.

- "Shapeshifter Leadership: Responding Creatively to the Challenges of a Complex World," by Carol Burbank, provides a mythic model of an archetypal Shapeshifter and examples from exemplary innovators to awaken your capacity to innovate and flow with continual change.

"Part Three: The Art of Working with and Transforming Groups" recognizes that leadership is a complex, interactive process. No leader can succeed alone. Leadership is about the intricate relationship of leaders with the groups they inspire, listen to, and awaken into transformational possibilities. The context-setting introduction to this section explores how experiences of synchronicity help us move beyond seeing the external and internal worlds as separate. It then discusses the ways our unconscious minds—which process information faster than can our conscious minds—are always tracking new information from our environment, socializing us without our conscious knowledge. This background helps us recognize why connecting unconscious with conscious knowledge is so important. It also helps us begin to understand that leaders of teams or other groups are in dynamic interconnection—influencing and being influenced—with the people led. Moreover, in times of information overload and fast change, leaders need access to the unconscious simply to keep up. The essays that follow describe ways of leading in relationships that bring out the group's most transformational efforts. Part Three includes

- "Depth Entrepreneurship: Creating an Organization Out of Dream Space," by Stephen Aizenstat, shares depth psychological insights that can help you access imaginal guidance balanced with sound management practice to build and sustain a thriving organization.
- "Deep Dialogue: Harvesting Collective Wisdom," by Alan Briskin, describes dialogue principles and practices, as well as stances or frames of mind, to inspire you to discover and harvest group intelligence and wisdom, and gives you tools for doing so.

- "New Approaches for Leadership: A Psychospiritual Model for Leadership Development," by Karin Jironet and Murray Stein, discusses strategies for establishing empathic connection in dyads and groups that provide space for transformational insights to be received and nurtured.
- "It's All a Dream: Depth Approaches to Understanding and Withdrawing Projection," by Jeremy Taylor. This analysis shows us why we need to recognize and withdraw projection in the interest of decreasing conflict in and among groups and seeing reality more clearly. It also suggests strategies for doing so, with an emphasis on group dream interpretation and other active imagination approaches that foster an understanding of how ubiquitous projection is.
- "Hearing the Music: Leadership and the Inner Work of Art," by John Cimino and Robert Denhardt, offers musical analogies and examples to provide a powerful metaphor for what it is like to lead in ways that attune to the rhythm of the group while also letting loose its capacity for improvisation.
- "Unleashing Possibilities: Leadership and the Third Space," by Zachary Green, Omowale Elson, and Anjet van Linge, describes group relations concepts that show you how to move out of "us/ them" dualities to live in a third space where attention moves from discrete parts to the relationship between them. Doing so can resolve inner and outer conflict, not with compromise, but with foundational, transformational change.

"Conclusion: Reinforcing Change through Transformational Communication" explores the power of narrative to help you ground new awareness about transformational thinking, being, and relating in a reframed conversation that encourages shifts in consciousness and habits in you and in those you influence.

PART ONE

TRANSFORMATIONAL THINKING FOR TWENTY-FIRST-CENTURY LEADERS

Setting the Context for Part One

Evolving Thinking about Transformational Leadership

Thinking clearly about leadership in ways relevant to our times and individual situations is essential to success today. This first section of the book begins with the work of James MacGregor Burns, a scholar who revolutionized how we imagine what leaders should be and do by introducing the concept of transformational, as opposed to transactional, leadership. This introduction provides background on his work. The first two essays in this section demonstrate the efficacy of his theories in current practice. The ones that follow explore the work of other scholars and theorists who provide new ways of thinking that enhance our ability to promote various elements of transformational change.

I was privileged to lead the James MacGregor Burns Academy of Leadership before taking my current position at Pacifica Graduate Institute. Through my work at the Burns Academy, I got to know Jim well. He combines the best of forward-looking attitudes with old-school graciousness, and is as thoroughly good and kind a man as he is a tough-minded, rigorous thinker. Being with Jim was a bit like my experience at the Fetzer Institute dialogues—somehow, everything seemed more possible when he was around, just as the dialogues continually opened up possibilities for how to lead with joy and ease even in these difficult times.

Although Burns coined the now widely used term "transformational leadership," he subsequently preferred the term "transforming leadership" because he thought it better captured the complexity of leadership that transformed the leader, his or her collaborators and followers, the process of leading, and the outcomes it produced. In biographies of great leaders, including his Pulitzer Prize–winning volume about Franklin Delano Roosevelt, he observed and then described a transformative quality in the leadership legends he studied. Such leaders as Gandhi and FDR, he argued, achieved structural change in ways designed to advance not only their own self-interest and that of their group, but also the larger common good (Burns, 1970b).

In contrast, transactional leadership, which Burns sees as still the prevailing mode, is motivated by self-interest on the part of both leaders and constituents. (For example, I support a particular leader because it is in my interest to do so. The leader helps me because then I'll support him or her—tit for tat.) The transactional leader gains cooperation through bargaining, the transforming leader by inspiring others with a larger vision that brings out the best in them and produces positive transformational outcomes (Burns, 1970a).

In a time of enormous uncertainty, I find Burns's work energizing and hopeful, and I know others do, too. It reminds us that we can work toward a future we believe in and that, to do so, we need to bring our better selves to leadership. Some may find this idealistic, even naive, so it reassures me to know that, being involved in politics himself, Burns understood the rough-and-tumble world he was writing about. Indeed, he formulated his theories by studying political figures who led in difficult times and had to deal realistically with unforeseen events and adversaries who very much wanted them to fail. Such leaders often balance transactional and transformational strategies in working toward transformational ends, and although they prefer to promote change through inspiration, when necessary they also use power, authority, and tough bargaining to get things done.

Transformational leadership ushers in radically positive possibilities so needed today to release the potential within situations and people, including the leader. Much of Burns's work as a biographer focused on individual leaders. But in recent years, the emphasis on individuals as agents of historic change has been attacked by many who argue the opposite: that leaders are products of the movements and ethos of the time. For a while, there was a standoff between those who emphasize the power of social and cultural movements and those who stress the impact of individuals. More and more, however, the interaction between individuals and their environments is viewed as complex and interdependent. For example, people are socialized by the time and place in which they live and have different advantages and disadvantages based on their station in life, their gender, race, and so on. Yet it is also true that the choices they make and the actions they take change their lives and create ripple effects that change others. They are then resocialized by the new reality they have created. All of this is an ongoing process.

Burns's work was inspired by his own desire to help people, and the more he explored how this could be done, the more attentive he became to the power of social movements, not just of individual leaders. He also very much saw his work as being within the philosophical tradition of the Enlightenment and credited the thinking of this movement as important to his writing. Burns (2003) began his book *Transforming Leadership* by citing the American Declaration of Independence, with its focus on "life, liberty, equality, justice, community . . . and intertwined with them—the pursuit of happiness" (p. 240). Referencing Abraham Maslow's (1943) "hierarchy of needs," he argued that to make happiness genuinely possible, we must eradicate poverty. As a witness to not only the civil rights movement but also other progressive movements, he began to stress the role of leadership in all of society and the need to view leadership as a complex, interactive process involving many actors.

Thus, Burns's *Transforming Leadership* ends with an appeal to move beyond what any individual leader can do. "In the broadest terms," Burns (2003) argued, "transformational change flows not so much from the work of a great man who single-handedly makes history, but from the collective achievement of a 'great people.'" While leadership by individuals is necessary at every stage, beginning with the "first spark that awakens people's hopes" (p. 240), its vital role is to create and expand the opportunities that empower people to pursue happiness for themselves.

This edited volume builds on the notion that individual leaders and leadership teams have a power to shape history, and that leaders also are riding the waves of enormous changes in an organization or society that they help steer but do not actually control. We see this illustrated in Betty Sue Flowers's essay later in this section, in the way personal leadership qualities and historic social movements came together to achieve the landmark Civil Rights Act of 1964 and the Voting Rights Act of 1965. The massive cultural revolution begun by the civil rights movement, and the changes in attitudes it produced, led in turn to the election of Barack Obama as the first African American U.S. president. Whatever history concludes about the Obama presidency, his personal qualities and his inspiring message helped a majority of American voters get behind the idea that an African American could lead the country. But without the historic achievements of the abolitionist and civil rights movements, the election of an African American president would have been unthinkable.

A similar interactive process takes place between individual leaders and the groups they lead. In a very practical way, we need to realize that we cannot lead successfully unless people want to follow or collaborate with us. Groups choose leaders based on a match with their own values and priorities: politicians are nominated by their party and elected by the public. Organizational leaders are selected by boards, search committees, or managers who, if they are smart, consider the needs of the group to be led. Citizens emerge as community and organizational leaders because of the faith others have in them. In all such cases, we, as leaders, are expected to achieve the ends the citizens or stakeholders desire. And, generally, we are deposed if those who chose us lose faith in our ability to deliver on our promises.

But leadership requires more than just acting to implement the will of the group. Leaders who become slaves to market forces, opinion polls, focus groups, or the self-interest of their constituents are not truly transformational. For transformation to occur, leaders need to educate, inspire, and motivate groups to have higher aspirations. This means that whether or not we have positional power, we have the responsibility to use whatever power we do have in the service of a positive vision of the greater good. Finding the right balance between truly listening to others, even those who disagree with us, and actually fulfilling the hefty responsibility to speak and act courageously to bring about such a vision is a challenge. Several of the essays in this book suggest specific strategies that can help us get this balance right.

Burns (2003) stressed the need to find this balance, saying that leaders should create "the links that allow communication and exchange to take place . . . and . . . address ourselves to followers' wants, needs, and other motivations." At the same time, leaders also must "serve as an independent force in changing the makeup of the follower's motive base." He saw that this balance can shift, based on what is required by particular situations. There are times, he noted, that require very strong, assertive leadership, and times when leaders are so attuned to their followers, and they to them, that the two become "virtually interdependent" (Burns, 2003, pp. 20–21).

Historically, ways of leading have evolved rather slowly. In ancient Rome, emperors rewarded their friends and cruelly punished anyone who got in their way (remember crucifixion). Transactional leadership is an improvement on this, but it is failing us now because it is based on a trust in self-interest that the world no longer can afford. Its single-minded focus on the self-interest of businesses and individuals leads to environmental devastation and economic crises. Adam Smith's (1759) idea that an "unseen hand" will make everything work out if we follow our individual interests does not appear to be working today. Both coercive and transactional modes of leadership remain in evidence around the world. The coercive mode, where it still exists, is horribly reductive, pulling people back into anachronistic ways of being with one another and themselves, while the transactional mode takes away our power by reinforcing an immature level of self-involvement and shrinking our sense of options.

Transformational leadership as Burns defines it has long been accessible to human consciousness (e.g., King Arthur legends). Now, because of twenty-first-century challenges, it needs to become common practice. Becoming conscious of what we want our leadership to be like, rather than just unconsciously enacting old patterns, can speed up our participation in a paradigm shift that is taking place in virtually all fields today.

Thinking in more transformative ways can free us from being freaked out by continuous change and the impact of global interdependence and allow us to recognize these realities as opportunities. Yet, in the process, we are forced to let go of many old beliefs, which is why deconstructionism has been a major focus of academic thought. Still, older paradigms often continue to be enacted long after new, more effective ones come into use. Sometimes this is because an older paradigm remains functional in practice. For example, quantum physics augments, but does not replace, Newtonian physics. Unfortunately, people are inclined to continue in old ways even when they no longer work well, which is the case today with the continued expectation that our leaders can save us single-handedly. If ever it were true, it is not true now.

On a personal level, we can better accept the necessary losses of our time if we recognize that new situations demand new capacities, just like when we let go of being children to take on adult responsibilities. Burns is, himself, a wonderful example of someone who is always learning and growing. Perhaps for this reason, while Burns has always been appreciative of followers who apply his ideas, he has the greatest enthusiasm for work that breaks new ground. Motivated by a powerful passion for justice and a sharp, insightful mind, he has little or no interest in adulation. After I left as director, the University of Maryland School of Public Policy phased out the Burns Academy of Leadership as a separate unit, but kept its many externally and self-funded programs. Burns accepted this change graciously, saying he cared only about the good work, not the recognition of having a prestigious institute named for him.

The essays in this section focus first on transformational leadership theory and then augment this theory with emerging ideas in positive psychology, organizational development, social networking theory, and contemporary science. This developmental sequence is designed to help you experience greater ease and mastery in leading today. If, at the end of this section, you would like to apply what you have learned to specific leadership situations, visit the Application Exercises for Part One included in Appendix A.

Transactional and Transformational Leadership

Their Foundations in Power and Influence

Michael J. Lovaglia, Jeffrey W. Lucas, and Amy Baxter

While Burns's work has focused primarily on political leaders, others—initially and most notably Bernard Bass—have expanded his ideas and applied them to organizational leadership. The first essay in this section, by Michael Lovaglia, Jeffrey Lucas, and Amy Baxter, integrates transformational leadership theory with power theories, reporting findings from contemporary research that tests the efficacy of various philosophies when actually practiced in workplace settings or simulated situations. Although they conclude that transformational leadership is, in fact, more effective than transactional leadership, they also show how other models of leadership can support transformational leadership success. Overall, they provide research data that can build confidence that transformational leadership does work, even in settings where power and status are highly valued.

One of the most influential theoretical developments in the study of leadership has been James MacGregor Burns's (1978) distinction between transactional and transformational leadership. *Transactional leadership* motivates through the measured application of promised rewards and threatened punishments, while *transformational leadership* motivates by transforming the identities and goals of individuals to coincide with those of the group. Burns not only researched the ways that leaders pursued their goals but also envisioned an ideal of leadership that minimized the use of coercive power and brought out the best in followers. Transformed by good leadership, followers would strive to accomplish goals that perhaps even the leader had not fully realized. Followers, then, might both be led by and push leaders to a greatness that had not before been contemplated. Both followers and leaders would be transformed.

A parallel stream of research in social psychology builds on French and Raven's (1959) theory of the bases of power that leaders can use to influence followers. Recent social psychological research has made progress analyzing not only the ways that leaders can wield influence but also the processes that produce such power and influence. These streams of research now converge to explain the distinction between transactional and transformational leadership and how understanding the processes of power and influence can help leaders to more effectively motivate their followers.

Relating Transactional Leadership to Research on Power

French and Raven (1959) launched a study of how power influences the behaviors of others. They delineated five bases of power useful to leaders:

1. Reward power based on a leader's ability to reward
2. Coercive power based on the ability to punish
3. Legitimate power based on a leader's authority to direct followers
4. Referent power based on a follower's identification with the leader
5. Expert power based on a leader's access to special knowledge

The bases of power are interrelated in complex ways (Raven & French, 1958), for example when a police officer legitimately uses coercive power to make an arrest or when expert knowledge is made available as a reward contingent on a transfer of resources.

French and Raven's typology of power bases stems from their broad conception of power as the *power to* influence others. Parsons (1963) identified a related use of the term as *power over*, the power that one person has to control another. Power over others is captured by Weber's (1968) definition of power as the ability to enact one's will despite others' resistance. Similarly, in political science, power is conceived as the ability to wrest resources from one person or group and bestow them on another (Lovaglia, Mannix, Samuelson, Sell, & Wilson, 2005). Power over is included in the five bases of power to influence and is related to them in complex ways that have proven useful in understanding transactional and transformational leadership.

Emerson (1962) noted that the power of one person over another is profoundly social in that this power resides not in an individual but rather in the relationship between individuals. The power of Person A over Person B is equal to the dependence of Person B on Person A. Power over another person derives from a person's ability to reward or punish, bringing together two of French and Raven's (1959) five bases of power: reward and coercive power. Note that the difference between a promised reward and threatened punishment often rests on expectations. The withdrawal of an expected reward feels punishing, for example, when a stockbroker accustomed to living on substantial year-end bonuses finds the bonus suddenly curtailed.

Emerson's work shifted research on power from identifying types of power to analysis of power processes, from the bases of power to the transactions of power. Thus we might term a person's power over another as *transactional power* to distinguish it from French and Raven's (1959) broader conception of power as all of the means used to influence others. Recent research has similarly narrowed the definition of influence to indicate changes in attitudes and behavior not brought about directly by the use of transactional power but, for example, by identification with another, or reliance on another's expertise and expected competence (Rashotte, 2006).

The Limits and Negative Outcomes of Transactional Power

Social psychological research on transactional power confirms the drawbacks of transactional leadership that Burns (1978) noted. Transactional power can produce public compliance without altering private attitudes (Raven & French, 1958), which are key to long-term engagement. An employee might work extra hours on a project to earn a reward without coming to see the project as worthwhile. Perhaps the most robust finding is that the use of transactional power creates resistance (Willer, Lovaglia, & Markovsky, 1997). Those subjected to power seek ways to circumvent it. Workers find ways to get bonuses without accomplishing the goals those bonuses were meant to incentivize. People might prefer rewards to punishments, but even rewards fail to motivate followers to pursue group goals if they lack a sense of ownership of the goals.

Research shows that extrinsic motivators such as rewards and punishments—including praise and criticism—can decrease intrinsic motivation, the desire to accomplish something personally important (Deci & Ryan, 1985). The decrease in self-motivation produced by rewards and punishments is most pronounced in work that requires creativity and initiative, exactly those activities most important for successful organizations today.

The impact of intrinsic versus extrinsic motivation on performance can be seen in research developed by Lovaglia (1995), where participants bargained with a partner, represented by a computer program, that had a power advantage over them and would only accept more than an equal share of available resources. For example, a participant might successfully bargain to earn 45 cents out of a dollar but not more. The computer would insist on receiving 55 cents. Participants were told that it was important to reach an agreement and earn as much as they could in every round. But if no agreement was reached, the participant received nothing. They then bargained with the computer in a number of rounds, which meant they could earn about $5.00 in a few minutes. But few participants would accept less than a 50-50 split with the computer. In postexperiment interviews, participants reported that they felt that taking less than an equal share was unfair and they could not bring themselves to reach such an agreement. That is, they willingly gave up 45 cents in profit to avoid giving their bargaining partner an extra nickel. Their intrinsic motivation to gain a fair outcome overwhelmed the extrinsic rewards offered. Increasing the amount of potential reward had little effect. In one version, participants were offered a bonus that would double their total reward if they would reach a profitable agreement in every round. Not one participant could bring him or herself to comply. Intrinsic motivation trumped extrinsic.

Lucas's (1999) research illuminates the cause-and-effect relationship between extrinsic and symbolic rewards and motivation. In this experiment, some members working on a group task were given a title indicating that they were at a higher level than other group members. No pay or other benefits came with the title. It could be seen as a purely symbolic reward. When working on the task, group members with titles performed better, contributed more to group success, and felt better about the group and their job than other group members. The group members who were given a title seemed to identify more with the group and its success than did the others. They worked hard because it complemented their view of themselves as valued group members. Such symbolic rewards would appear to be an inexpensive way for managers to motivate productivity. Readers, however, gave examples from their own experience where such symbolic rewards were soon devalued by workers as meaningless, suggesting that rewards, whether symbolic or material, have limited motivational impact over time.

Transactional power can also be problematic because its impact and use can often be unintended and out of a leader's control. As Emerson (1972) noted, transactional power lies not with the powerful person but in the relationship between two people. When people perceive themselves at a power disadvantage, they respond as if the powerful person had intentionally wielded transactional power. Skvoretz, Willer, and Fararo (1993) designed a bargaining experiment in which some positions had a transactional power advantage over others. When those in power bargained aggressively, they gained substantially more resources than those in low-power positions. But surprisingly, when the high-power position was a computer program that bargained passively—merely accepting the best offer available—the computer gained as much as the people in that position who bargained aggressively.

Leaders can find it difficult to accept the idea that promised rewards and threatened sanctions have limited and often negative effects on performance. But as pointed out in the *Economist* review (2010) of Daniel Pink's (2009) book, *Drive*, "carrots and sticks are not only outdated, but can also be counterproductive—motivation killers and creativity dampeners" (p. 62). There are good reasons to pay high-performing employees well, especially with an ownership stake or share of the profits; people crave appreciation for their accomplishments and bonuses can show that appreciation. The mistake is thinking that the bonuses caused those accomplishments (Deci & Ryan, 1985).

Transactional power is required in most managerial positions. Managers hire, promote, confer bonuses, and fire workers. The goal is not to avoid using transactional power but to use it sparingly while seeking other ways to motivate that do not produce resistance as a negative side effect.

Positive Outcomes of Transformational Influence

Transformational leadership seeks to motivate followers by transforming their conceptions of self and their private goals to coincide with the larger purposes of the group. Rather than working for money, employees work to be part of the success of a larger mission. Recent research shows how leaders can use their influence to produce such transformation in their followers and to engender private acceptance (Rashotte, 2006). We use the term *transformational influence* to distinguish this idea from French and Raven's (1959) broader conception of influence that includes public compliance without private acceptance.

Research on the social psychology of work groups begun by Joseph Berger at Stanford University links a person's relative status in a work group to the respect and honor given to her or him by others (Berger, Fisek, Norman, & Zelditch, 1977). A leader's high status results in prestige and transformational influence, the ability to get people to do things to help the group whose mission they have adopted as their own. When leaders use their high status, their prestige and honor, to lead, they step beyond transactional leadership toward transformation.

President John Kennedy's statement "Ask not what your country can do for you—ask what you can do for your country" is an example of transformational influence. Kennedy promised no reward, threatened no punishment. He pulled the American people with him by appealing to their aspirations to become better people and to join a great cause. Burns (1978) called this influence that leaders have on followers, using their prestige and honor to inspire others toward a higher goal, transformational leadership. A brief example shows how effective transformational influence, totally devoid of promises and threats, can be.

In the early 1900s, Charles Schwab took over Bethlehem Steel. Production at one of the steel mills was chronically low. The mill manager had tried threats, encouragement, coaxing, and promises to motivate steelworkers. Nothing seemed to work. At the end of the day shift, Schwab toured the plant with the manager but said little. As night shift workers arrived and day shift workers started to leave, Schwab asked one of them how much steel the day shift had produced. The worker replied that they had produced six heats (units of steel production). Schwab asked for a piece of chalk, wrote a big 6 on the mill floor, and walked away. Workers from both shifts were intrigued. The big boss had chalked 6 on the floor; what could it mean? The next morning when Schwab and the manager returned to the plant, they noticed that the 6 had been replaced by a 7, the number of heats produced by the night shift. The informal competition between shifts continued and soon that mill was one of the high producers in the company (Carnegie, 1981). Schwab had made neither promises nor threats. Workers could expect no reward beyond personal satisfaction for winning the competition. Schwab had used his high status, his prestige as head of the company, to influence workers, dramatically altering their productivity.

From Transactional Power to Transformational Leadership

Effective leadership requires both transactional power and transformative influence. Research has found that those positions with the most transactional power are also those with the most transformational influence. The correlation between the power and the influence of specific occupations is extremely high (Rogalin, Soboroff, & Lovaglia, 2007).

Being a judge is a good example of an occupation high in both transformational influence and transactional power. Effective judges, however, restrain their use of power, using only as much as a particular case requires. Rather than surrender transactional power, effective leaders restrain their use of it; they use transformational influence to the extent possible and transactional power when necessary.

Leaders who rely on transactional power assume that they know the specific behaviors employees need to perform for the organization to reach its goals. But in complex, rapidly changing organizations, that assumption lacks validity. In contrast, a leader can use transformational influence to inspire followers to commit to finding ways to help the organization succeed, while refraining from directing their behavior. When leaders use transformational influence, they share control of their organization with their followers. Thus, transformational leadership can harness all of the abilities of followers to innovate and produce in ways that no leader, no matter how competent, could have foreseen.

Michael J. Lovaglia is professor of sociology at the University of Iowa. His research investigates power, status, and identity and how those social processes can be applied to problems of educational achievement, leadership, and the abuse of power. He is past president of the Iowa Sociological Association, editor of *Current Research in Social Psychology*, and a member of the National Academy of Sciences Committee on Incentives and Accountability in Education. He can be reached at michael-lovaglia@uiowa.edu.

Jeffrey W. Lucas is associate professor of sociology at the University of Maryland. He operates a group processes experimental laboratory in which he and collaborators carry out research on status, power, and leadership in groups. His research has been funded from sources including the National Science Foundation, National Institutes of Health, National Oceanic and Atmospheric Administration, and the Spencer Foundation. In addition to his research, he teaches a course on leadership each year to U.S. Navy and Marine Corps officers preparing to assume leadership positions at the U.S. Naval Academy. He can be reached at jlucas2@umd.edu.

Amy Baxter is a PhD student in sociology at the University of Maryland. Her focus areas include power and status hierarchies, gender, and group identity. Her most recent research examines relationships between status processes and the salience of group identities. She can be reached at abaxter@socy.umd.edu.

Leadership in Action

Three Essential Energies

Betty Sue Flowers

To illustrate what such transformational leadership looks like in practice, Betty Sue Flowers offers a lively and touching example of how President Lyndon B. Johnson collaborated with Martin Luther King Jr. and persuaded members of Congress to pass groundbreaking civil rights legislation. Flowers shows how LBJ, whom she acknowledges was in some ways a flawed leader, nevertheless fully utilized his power as president to transformational effect. At the same time, King ably led and collaborated with the multitudes of people (and leaders at many levels) within the civil rights movement—all of whom were essential to its success. Flowers's essay is a wonderful vehicle for providing an image for us of what leadership as a complex, interactive process looks like. It also contributes to leadership thinking about how to free up energy to get worthy things done, even in situations where success requires cross-sector cooperation and collaboration. Finally, it shows us that transformational leaders can be tough as well as inspiring in the interest of socially desirable ends.

One of my greatest joys as director of the Johnson Presidential Library was the opportunity to understand more deeply how some of the most significant social transformations of the twentieth century were achieved. During those years, I continually pondered a number of questions, including: How is it that President Johnson was able to sign into law over 1,000 landmark bills in fewer than five years? These bills transformed America: Medicare, Medicaid, Clean Air, Clean Water, the bills founding the National Endowment for the Humanities and the National

Endowment for the Arts and what later became PBS, Job Corps, Head Start, forty bills connected with the War on Poverty, sixty education bills, including the student loan program, 300 conservation and beautification bills, the Immigration Act that removed quotas on non-European immigrants, bills supporting career opportunities for women, bills improving children's health and safety, and the transformational Civil Rights Act of 1964, Voting Rights Act of 1965, and Open Housing Act of 1968.

But I also had other, more troubling questions: How could this transformational president lead us more deeply into the tragedy that was Vietnam—a war that he hated and that his secretary of defense was unconvinced we could win? As early as May 1964, President Johnson said to his national security advisor, "I don't think it's worth fighting for, and I don't think we can get out. . . . What is Vietnam worth to me? . . . What is it worth to this country?" (Johnson, L. B., Bundy, M., 1964).

Over the years at the Johnson Library, I also developed questions about public discourse and public memory. Why is it a truism that Johnson's War on Poverty failed? President Reagan (1988) famously quipped, "the Federal Government declared war on poverty, and poverty won." And yet, during the Johnson administration, the poverty rate declined from 22.2 percent to 13 percent—"the greatest one-time reduction in poverty in our nation's history" (Califano, 2008, p. 7).

In the decades following these achievements, it has seemed almost impossible to dream a big public dream. The ideal of a "Great Society" is inconceivable in our current public discourse—naive, grandiose, maybe even absurd. It is one of those conversations, like world peace or global citizenship or universal human rights, that serious policymakers would be embarrassed to sponsor. Yet President Johnson not only conceived such an ideal, he acted on it, and, in doing so, transformed our world.

As a poet and student of world religions and mythology, I pondered these questions not as a historian would but from what might be called "the subjective empirical" point of view. Historians use facts on which to build a story; poets use observations from inner life and from the wisdom literature that humans have treasured since before facts became our dominant foundation for truth. From this "poetic" perspective, I concluded that President Johnson worked effectively by evoking three significant energies:

- The energy of a big dream
- The energy of "inside-outside"
- The energy of working at every level

Perhaps the clearest example of how he worked with these energies can be seen in the passage of the Civil Rights Act of 1964 and the Voting Rights Act of 1965.

The Energy of a Big Dream

In 1963, racial equality was a very big dream indeed.

In response to increasing pressure from the civil rights movement, President Kennedy introduced a "carefully limited" bill (Rosenberg & Karabell, 2003, p. 129) but had not pressed forward to pass the bill, being "a pragmatist who would not sacrifice his administration on the altar of civil rights" (p. 115). What he might have done had he not been assassinated, no one can know. But Martin Luther King once said, "I'm not sure that Kennedy could have done this for us" (Young, 2008).

Hours after Kennedy's assassination, Johnson was already talking to his inner circle about the need for civil rights, telling them "he would not compromise, for this was going to be a fight to the finish and he had no qualms about the outcome" (Valenti, 1975, p. 152). And when introducing his voting rights legislation to Congress in 1965, Johnson (1966) spoke about his experience teaching Hispanic schoolchildren on the Texas border:

> I never thought then, in 1928, that I would be standing here in 1965.
> It never even occurred to me in my fondest dreams that I might
> have the chance to help the sons and daughters of those students
> and to help people like them all over this country. But now I do have
> that chance—and I'll let you in on a secret—I mean to use it.

The bigger the dream, the more energy it is capable of evoking. When a vision is large enough, it appeals to dimensions other than personal ambition. Johnson, whose personal ambition was certainly greater than most, understood that something larger had to be evoked. Almost all his major efforts were couched in visionary language, not in the partisan language of winning. In his "Special Message to the Congress on Conservation and Restoration of Natural Beauty" in 1965, Johnson (1966) said:

> Our conservation must be not just the classic conservation of protection and development, but a creative conservation of restoration and innovation. Its concern is not with nature alone, but with the total relation between man and the world around him. Its object is not just man's welfare but the dignity of man's spirit.

Johnson worked incessantly to pass the bills that would make up the Great Society—and he overworked his staff in the process. Yet, in spite of the brutal demands, those who worked for Johnson remained loyal and committed because they felt that both he and they were engaged in a great cause.

Small dreams are often bounded by the egos of their creators. But a big dream is larger than any one leader, so the flaws or weaknesses of the leader do not obscure the dream. The light shines on the dream, not the leader, allowing followers to use the dream as their major guide and to continue to pursue the dream even if their leader fails or disappoints them.

At the same time that President Johnson was pursuing the big dream of racial equality, another transformational leader was dreaming the same dream.

The Energy of "Inside-Outside"

During the early 1960s, the Reverend Martin Luther King Jr. led marches and protests to highlight the need for a transformation that would make real the equality that African Americans supposedly enjoyed under the U.S. Constitution. "I have a dream," he famously said—but such a dream needed federal legislation before it could begin to be realized. King needed Johnson—and Johnson also needed King.

The degree to which Johnson used King's actions on the "outside" to pressure lawmakers on the "inside" is clearly seen in the telephone conversations that Johnson secretly taped from both the Oval Office and the LBJ ranch. In May 1964, Johnson called Republican Senator Everett Dirksen, who was the Senate minority leader, and asked him to persuade Republicans to vote for the passage of the Civil Rights Act. Alluding indirectly to the young protesters, he warned Dirksen that the schools were "coming out at the end of this month, and if they're out, and we haven't got a bill, we're in a hell of a shape" (Johnson & Dirksen, 1964).

To some extent, Johnson and King collaborated in this inside-outside strategy. Johnson urged a moratorium on mass demonstrations until after the 1964 elections—and King agreed (Kotz, 2005, p. 185). Johnson talked to King of getting "our heads together on the things that are ahead" (Kotz, 2005, p. 228), and he consulted with King on judicial appointments (p. 231). During the delicate negotiations, the "two men were careful not to embarrass each other. King did not criticize the president for inaction, and Johnson was careful to deny that King had made a deal with federal authorities regarding the [march on Pettus bridge]" (p. 300), in which King had agreed to halt the second march and turn it into a kind of prayer service—thus giving time for a judicial ruling on the legality of what would become the third, successful march to Birmingham the following Sunday.

Like Johnson and King, transformational leaders use the energy aroused by those who oppose them or who are outside to forward the realization of their own dream. The use of energy in this way is a little like aikido, in which the master uses the aggressive energy of the opponent to actually help propel the opponent's fall. You take the energy and move it in the direction you want it to go. Johnson took the energy of the protests and the outrage aroused by pictures of dogs and fire hoses being unleashed on well-dressed and apparently well-behaved young protestors in Birmingham and turned it into pressure on individual lawmakers to vote in favor of his civil rights legislation. Without the energy of King's movement, it is unlikely that the civil rights bills ever could have passed. In this way, both Johnson and King were right about each other when King told the president, "You have created a Second Emancipation," and Johnson replied, "The real hero is the American Negro" (Kotz, 2005, p. xi).

Sometimes Johnson made explicit the necessity of the inside to join the outside. Introducing his voting rights legislation to a joint session of the Congress, the president alluded to "Bloody Sunday," when the marchers attempting to cross the Pettus Bridge in Selma, Alabama, had been tear-gassed and many of them had been brutally beaten. The president said, "Their cause must be our cause too." Embedded in his speech were the words of the rallying song of the marchers—"we shall overcome"—to which he added an emphatic "And we *shall* overcome" (Johnson, 1966). In using this adopted phrase, Johnson turned the "we" of protest into the "we" of "all of us"—the ultimate inside-outside aikido. And in Alabama, where civil rights leaders were watching the newscast of the speech, tears streamed down the face of Martin Luther King. (For John Lewis's moving account of his and others' reaction to the speech, see the video, "Media and the Voting Rights Act of 1965.")

The Energy of Working at Every Level

We sometimes assume that leaders effect a transformation through simply inspiring it. They are so charismatic or speak so eloquently that they inspire us to do the right thing. But we forget that transformations are not the automatic by-products of charismatic leadership, but the result of continuous discipline and incredibly hard work.

When working on a big dream, Johnson pressed every argument and inducement he could muster on every lawmaker who could possibly influence the outcome. As his young aide, Tom Johnson (2010), would later recall, the president would constantly be on the phone with congressional members ("not just the leaders") as well as key staffers, arguing that the bill would be good for the country—and not only the country but "good for your wife, your children, and your grandchildren. They will be so proud that their granddaddy voted for this, because it will mean a better life for them."

Before it [was] over, he would have completed a phone call or would have an in-person visit with every member individually or in a small group. He would use charts, graphs, coffee, tea. He would keep the coffee and tea flowing without giving anybody a chance to get up to go to the bathroom before they gave him their support. . . .

They would get "the Johnson treatment" like nobody else could give it. If he knew something about a sick wife, a secret girlfriend, a long ago embarrassing moment, he likely would use it individually to remind a congressman that he would do anything "to help."

He would be willing to horse-trade with every member. A "yes" vote for a post office, for example. . . .

He would have Dr. Billy Graham calling Baptists, Cardinal Cushing calling Catholics, Dr. King calling blacks, Congressman Henry Gonzales of San Antonio calling Hispanics, George Brown and Perry Bass calling oilmen and construction company executives, and George Meany and Lane Kirkland calling all AFL-CIO and union leaders. . . .

He would walk around the South Lawn of The White House with a flock of reporters—telling them why this bill was important to *them* and to *their* families. . . .

He would flatter, threaten, cajole, flirt, hug, and get the bill passed. (Johnson, 2009)

In his telephone conversation with Senator Everett Dirksen, Johnson not only warned about what might happen (protests and unrest) when school was out (the energy of "inside-outside"), but also argued for Dirksen as party leader to support the bill because "we don't want it to be a Democratic bill, we want it to be an American bill." And then he piled on the flattery, saying, "I saw your exhibit at the World's Fair, and it said 'Land of Lincoln.' You're worthy of the Land of Lincoln, and a man from Illinois is going to pass the bill, and I'll see that you get proper attention and credit" (Johnson & Dirksen, 1964).

He kept the promise, handing over the first signing pen for the Civil Rights Act not to Dr. King but to Senator Dirksen. And later, at the signing of the Voting Rights Act, he gave the second pen to Dirksen. When his daughter, Luci Johnson, asked him why he had given the pen to

Dirksen instead of to "one of the great civil rights leaders who was there," he told her:

> Because all of those great civil rights leaders were already for that legislation. They had already made that commitment. We could stand in our corner and espouse the righteousness of doing it, but if we hadn't been able to get Everett Dirksen to step across the aisle and bring our foes with us, we would have had a great bill, but we wouldn't have had a great law. (as quoted in Smith, 2008)

Johnson's conversation with his daughter illustrates the point that "working at every level" includes working with the outside forces that are part of one's own inside world. Just as Dr. King had to work with those in his own movement, such as Stokely Carmichael, who thought he was focusing too much on integration and not enough on black power, President Johnson had to work not only with his own party but also with the opposition party—and not only with the opposition party but with the opposition (the Southern Democrats) within his own party. Every inside has its own outside.

Within a few days after Bloody Sunday, Johnson met with George Wallace, the governor of Alabama, in the Oval Office—a meeting that Attorney General Nicholas Katzenbach characterized as "the most amazing conversation." One of Johnson's speechwriters, Richard Goodwin, also was there and described how Johnson seated the 5-foot 7-inch Wallace on a low sofa, "so he's now about three feet tall," while Johnson sat on the edge of a rocking chair "leaning over him." (Young, 2008)

Johnson suggested that he and Wallace could end the demonstrations by simply going out in front of the television reporters and announcing that every schoolhouse in Alabama would be integrated :

> George, you and I shouldn't be thinking about 1964, we should be thinking about 1984. We'll both be dead and gone then. . . . Now in 1984, George, what do you want left behind? You want a great big marble monument that says "George Wallace—He built?" Or do you want a little piece of scrawny pine laying there on that

harsh caliche soil that says "George Wallace—He hated?" (Young, 2008)

Wallace agreed to ask for help in protecting the Selma marchers, and when he did, the president was able to federalize the Alabama National Guard without provoking a states' rights crisis.

A few days later, President Johnson spoke to Congress, saying:

> Rarely in any time does an issue lay bare the secret heart of America itself. Rarely are we met with a challenge, not to our growth or abundance, our welfare or our security, but rather to the values and the purposes and the meaning of our beloved Nation.
>
> The issue of equal rights for American Negroes is such an issue. And should we defeat every enemy, should we double our wealth and conquer the stars, and still be unequal to this issue, then we will have failed as a people and as a nation.
>
> For with a country as with a person, "What is a man profited, if he shall gain the whole world, and lose his own soul?" (Johnson, 1966)

At the end of my term as director of the LBJ Library, I still had not solved the conundrum of how such a transformational leader, who dared so much, had not dared to walk away from a war he didn't want. But I am haunted by a little piece of paper in the library archives—a note from Ho Chi Minh, leader of North Vietnam, with whom we were at war. It had been sent indirectly, through France. The note simply thanked President Johnson for a picture of the earth rising over the moon—*Earthrise*, it was called. The picture had been taken in December 1968 by the Apollo 8 astronauts, the first humans to escape earth's gravitational field, and the first to see the dark side of the moon. As one of his last acts as president, Johnson had sent *Earthrise* to all the world's leaders—even to those, such as Fidel Castro and Ho Chi Minh, with whom we had no diplomatic relations. From the transformational perspective of the earth as seen from space, all of us, even our enemies, travel together.

Betty Sue Flowers, PhD, served as director of the Johnson Presidential Library and Museum from 2002 to 2009. Before that appointment, she was Kelleher Professor of English and a member of the Distinguished Teachers Academy at the University of Texas–Austin and served as associate dean of graduate studies and director of the Plan II Honors Program. Her recent publications include *Presence: Human Purpose and the Field of the Future* (with Senge, Scharmer, and Jaworski); "The Primacy of People in a World of Nations"; *The Partnership Principle: New Forms of Governance in the 21st Century*; and *The American Dream and the Economic Myth* (monograph in the Fetzer American Dream series).

| 3 |

Leadership and Organizational Networks

A Relational Perspective

Philip Willburn and Michael Campbell

The more we grasp the kind of complex interaction Burns, Lovaglia/
Lucas/Baxter, and Flowers write about, the more important it is to
understand not just leaders, but the groups and social networks they
lead. Philip Willburn and Michael Campbell employ insights from social
networking theory to do just that. This knowledge can help you get your
vision out effectively to a large number of people that you communicate
with directly. In the following essay, they provide a model that you can
use to analyze the social networks you influence. As leaders, we often
believe that if we develop a plan and share it, the people who report
to us will implement it because it is their job to do so. But people act
like people, and not necessarily according to an organizational chart.
Their energy to implement any plan is dependent on (1) whether the
communication gets to them in a way that is motivating and sparks
their imaginations, and (2) who they listen to and what those people
say about the plan.

Every day in our work life, we are creating, developing, maintaining, or
neglecting informal relationships and organizational networks. These
informal networks can be anything from the people we have lunch
with, to the mentors we choose at work, to the people who help us get
work done outside the "formal" work procedures. Once considered a
nuisance by traditional management, these informal networks are now
being used to leverage creativity and talent within the workplace.

Two main principles have emerged from the research on leadership and organizational networks regarding the role of leaders and their relationships to these networks:

1. The ability to lead is directly affected by the networks a leader builds.

    The structure of a leader's network affects how a leader shares and receives new ideas, who a leader trusts for information, and how leaders can locate resources outside their traditional roles. Leaders should be aware of their relationships. Building a diverse network (not just a big one) of associates can greatly influence the success of a leader.

2. A leader's behavior influences the type of network structure that develops in organizations, which consequently impacts organizational performance.

    Transformational leaders are aware of the network they are reinforcing and its impact on their organization. For example, is a leader reinforcing hierarchy or promoting collaboration? Is a leader creating decision bottlenecks that restrict information flow, or connecting information hubs across the organization? Is a leader encouraging a robust network that can withstand changes in the environment, or creating a brittle network that breaks with the slightest change? Creating the conditions for robust relationships to develop is critical for the twenty-first-century organization.

Awareness of Organizational Networks

A leader must be aware of the organization's informal networks to understand how the organization is truly working, not just how it is supposed to work on paper (Cross & Parker, 2004). Communication rarely flows like it does in an organizational chart. Instead, it moves through informal communication networks, which may have nothing to do with how the organization is structured. A leader must understand and leverage these informal organizational networks to avoid network insularity, promote network diversity, and facilitate organizational communication. Leaders must avoid network insularity to ensure that their perceptions of the organization are not biased toward only one set of opinions. Having a biased or "insular" network leads to poor decision making and potentially negative consequences for organizations. Some of the original research on leadership and insularity discussed open versus closed systems (see Meyer [1975] for insight into some of the first studies). For example, would Ken Lay, former CEO of Enron, have acted differently if he had received perspectives and ideas outside his inner circle of executives who were part of the Enron scandal? The case of the Enron executive committee is one of the extreme instances of network insularity that unfortunately had very bad consequences for its shareholders and the American people. Even if leaders avoid network insularity, they often assume communication and work flows in their organization based on their personal networks. This assumption, however, is often false and can produce a skewed sense of how the organization functions. A leader receiving communication from only one informal network will receive only the generalized opinions from that network, which may be very different than another informal network. A leader with insight into multiple organizational networks will have a more accurate understanding of the organization.

> **CASE EXAMPLE** · A Great Vision Going Nowhere
>
> One of the authors, Philip Willburn, recently worked with an executive committee struggling to disseminate its vision throughout the organization. A recent climate survey showed the organization was in the top quartile in customer focus, core values, and creating change, but in lowest quartile in vision and strategic direction. The organization's senior leader recognized that communication was not getting down to the employees but didn't understand why. She communicated her vision frequently with her executive team, did a few town halls each year, and sent a number of organization-wide emails. She assumed the members of her executive team were using their channels to communicate the vision as well. After speaking to her,

Wilburn decided to do a quick diagnostic test on the executive committee's social network.

In his network assessment, he asked two questions: "Who did you receive the organization's vision from?" and "Who do you then communicate the vision to?" After compiling network analysis results, he could see multiple channels of vision statements and many interpretations of the visions (Figure 3.1). Seventy percent of the executives reported that they received the vision from the senior leader. However, 60 percent reported they also received the vision from the chief technical officer, 50 percent from the director of strategic initiatives, and 50 percent from the director of operations. With the exception of one executive (a key broker), most of the

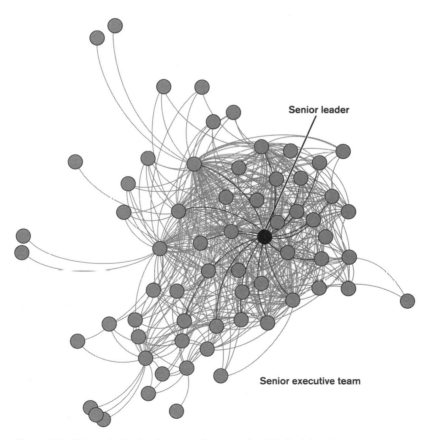

Figure 3.1 Network of who the executives received their vision from.

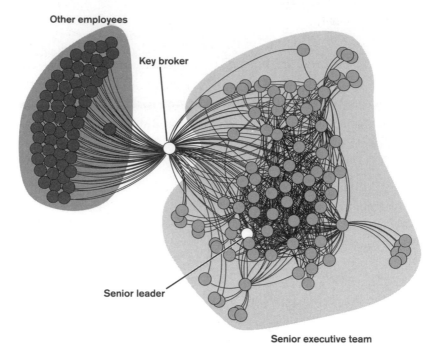

Figure 3.2 Network of who the executives communicated the vision to.

executives spent their time communicating the vision to each other (Figure 3.2). The senior leader was completely unaware of this communication insularity.

Interviews with the senior leader's team revealed that the leader prided herself on creating a clear and compelling vision, and was put off by people who could not articulate it exactly the way she wanted it articulated. In one instance, a division manager asked the senior leader why the services segment of the business was not included in the vision. She quickly responded that it was included, and then berated the division manager for not appropriately listening to the vision. The fear of being criticized for miscommunicating the vision kept the executive team from getting the vision out to the organization and admitting this to her. The organization was suffering, not from a lack of a clear vision, but from the lack of effective openness, inclusiveness, and dissemination. The senior leader did not have a communication problem, as she originally thought. She had a network insularity problem.

Network Insularity

In the case study above, the senior leader was unable to get her vision out to the organization because her executives told her what she wanted to hear, not what was actually going on. And because of her network insularity, she did not have a way of finding out what was going on. The issues of insularity can be counterintuitive, because leaders want to surround themselves with trusted, competent people (often people like themselves). Insular networks also occur as people work with each other. They become more like-minded and develop similar perspectives. But as leaders create an insular network, they shed other relationships that might give them different, more helpful perspectives.

Network Diversity

The opposite of network insularity is network diversity. The senior leader in our case example was unaware that her vision was not getting out and that the executive team was the choke point. By examining her individual relationships, we discovered that she had a large network of relationships, with many ties to her customers and subject matter experts across her organization, but that's where her network stopped. She did not have insight into the executive team's fear of communicating her vision incorrectly, nor did she have insight into what her middle managers were receiving about the vision. Her general lack of relationship diversity kept her from seeing what was "really happening" in her organization. For leaders, increasing network diversity and fighting off insularity is one of the most challenging tasks. It is difficult for a leader to forge new relationships, but the downside can be a lack of organizational perspective.

Leadership Positions in Organizational Networks

When you receive information from a corporate mass email about future organizational changes, do you believe the message outright, or do you verify that information with a friend or trusted advisor? Whom do you believe more, the mass email or your friend who has worked at the company for ten years? If the number of people who go to your friend for the same advice is large, your friend is the network's "opinion leader," and he or she can have a big impact on whether employees believe what management is saying.

Through research on organizational networks, four leadership network positions have been identified as critically influential (Balkundi, & Kilduff, 2005). These leadership positions are often not occupied by leaders formally identified in a company's organization chart, but by an informal leader. Conflict, miscommunication, and organizational confusion can arise when the formally recognized leader is not aware of or does not work with the informal network leader. Both informal and formal leaders must be aware of these four positions and understand how to work with each other to avoid detrimental outcomes.

Popularity

A person filling the popular position in a network will have numerous relationships (incoming and outgoing ties) within an organization or team. The person has influence because of the sheer quantity of interpersonal relationships maintained and managed on a daily basis. This person is often the lifeblood of an organization, a rallying point, and someone who can either help the organization achieve its mission or undermine its success. Formally recognized leaders who are also popular have high-performing teams (Balkundi & Harris, 2006; Brass, 1992; Fielder, 1955). The opposite can be true as well; team performance decreases when formal leaders are not the popular network leaders.

Being the popular leader, although appealing, also has its drawbacks. A popular leader is popular in the informal network because she is able to respond to people and maintain relationships with even the lowest-level employees in the organization. The most difficult part of being the popular leader is managing the reciprocity of ties. When teams and organizations become large, the popular leader must manage a larger number of relationships, requests, and communications on a daily basis.

Prestige

Prestigious leaders are those who have valuable information that other people in the network want. A person in this position might be a trusted mentor whom everyone knows they can depend on to give good advice, or the information technology support person who goes the extra mile to make sure everything is working. When the number of different people coming to a leader for advice is much larger than the number of people the leader asks advice from, then that leader is considered the prestigious leader in the network (Balkundi, Barsness, & Michael, 2009). Prestigious leaders are also known as information hubs, experts, and consultants. These leaders rarely want to be in the center of the flow of information, but because of their known expertise, they become centralized in the organization. In small teams, when the formal leader is also the prestigious leader, these teams experience less conflict and better overall team performance. However, when the formal leader is also the prestigious leader in large networks, he or she may quickly become a communication and decision-making bottleneck to the organization.

Facilitation

To avoid the bottleneck phenomenon, many leaders try to "borrow" prestige or popularity by becoming facilitators of information. These network facilitators try to limit the total number of relationships they have and just focus on getting to know and develop the trust of the few prestigious and popular leaders in the network. This allows a leader to gain social capital through intermediaries, without becoming a bottleneck (see Bonacich, 1987; Bonacich & Lloyd, 2001; Moody, McFarland, & Bender-DeMoll, 2005). This type of network leader leverages "ghost" influence over an organization by having the trust and ear of the popular leaders. When the formal leaders are not facilitators, it is critical that they work to find this person, because the facilitator has the trust of the popular leaders and can either energize or undermine the formal leaders' goals.

Brokerage

Brokerage is the ability of a leader to bridge fragmented groups within networks. Fragmentation is caused by various organizational conditions, such as different functional areas, geographic locations, social identities (e.g., ethnicity, race, gender), and hierarchal positions. Brokers connect fragmented subgroups by acting as a bridge between them and are sometimes called the "go-between" people in an organization (for a more detailed description of the betweenness-centrality metric, see Freeman, Roeder, & Mulholland, 1979/1980). This position yields the greatest amount of influence in a network and has been the best predictor of future leadership promotions (see Balkundi, Kilduff, Barsness, & Michael, 2007; Burt, 1992; Krackhardt, 1990).

When the formal leaders are also the brokers, they work as coordinators and information conduits across multiple groups and are shown to help integrate specialists, avoid redundant uses of resources, and connect people. There is a downside, however, to the formal leader being the broker. Leader brokers can distort information between groups, increase intragroup conflict, and decrease team viability. The formal leader in this position must be cognizant of the potential distortion of information between subgroups and work to uphold the highest integrity when performing this function. The broker must be adept at translating between significantly different subgroups.

Regardless of who holds these network leadership positions, the formal leader must understand how to leverage these positions within the organization. Table 3.1 provides advice to formal leaders when dealing with network leadership positions.

Conclusion

People are communal beings who naturally create social networks that largely determine the collective attitudes and behaviors of their culture. Trying to fight this or circumvent it is as pointless as trying to control the weather. Transformational leaders, therefore, consciously work with networks to foster transformational change that does not engender great resistance but is in alignment with the norms, values, and shared

Table 3.1. Advice for Formal Leaders in Dealing with Network Leadership Positions

		Formal Leader and Network Leader	Formal Leader but Not Network Leader
Network Leadership Positions	**Popularity**	*When you are a formal leader and popular:* be careful not to abuse your position. Popularity in networks is a fleeting resource.	*When you are a formal leader and not the popular leader:* reach out to the popular leader and gain his or her trust. This person has the best view of what is really going on.
	Prestige	*When you are a formal leader and prestigious:* mentor others to take your place. You will soon become overwhelmed with requests.	*When you are a formal leader and not the prestigious leader:* recognize the prestigious leader, but don't be too anxious to formalize the position. He or she may not want it, or may not possess broader skills.
	Facilitator	*When you are a formal leader and the facilitator:* step out from behind the popular leaders and embrace your position in the open; otherwise people will think you are aloof.	*When you are a formal leader and not the facilitator:* identify the facilitator and ask for advice. He or she can provide good insight into the major decisions of the organization.
	Broker	*When you are a formal leader and a broker:* be careful not to distort messages between subgroups for political gain. Others may develop relationships around you and your subterfuge will be uncovered.	*When you are a formal leader and not a broker:* guide brokers to bridge the boundaries that will be most beneficial for your group or organization. They can help get your message out and get external information in.

ways of living together that are the basis for the network's culture and way of seeing the world.

Since 2006, **Philip Willburn** has been the director of network sciences at OE Consulting, a leadership and network analytics firm based in Arlington, Virginia. He is a social network analysis expert with formal training in dynamic network analysis and computational organizational theory. Willburn specializes in identifying and characterizing leaders and emerging leaders within organizational and social networks. He provides consulting services to Fortune 500 companies and governmental organizations and hosts workshops on leadership and social network topics in the United States and abroad. He holds an MA in organizational communication from the University of Colorado at Colorado Springs.

Michael Campbell is a research associate at the Center for Creative Leadership (CCL), a nonprofit educational and research institution dedicated to the understanding and practice of leadership. As a member of CCL's Research & Innovation division, Campbell's work focuses on research and client solutions in talent management and senior executive leadership. His work on social networks focuses primarily on how network development influences the effectiveness of leaders and the behaviors that lead to the creation of high-functioning networks. He holds a BS in business administration and an MA in communication from the University of Colorado at Colorado Springs.

| 4 |

Positive Power

Transforming Possibilities through Appreciative Leadership

Diana Whitney and Amanda Trosten-Bloom

Much of leadership success depends on working with, not against, natural processes—whether social, as illustrated by Willburn and Campbell, or psychological, as addressed in this essay. In his seminal article on appreciative inquiry, "Positive Image, Positive Action: The Affirmative Basis of Organizing," David L. Cooperrider (2001) built a scientific case for the power of positive images to inspire energy for change. Examples of this kind of "placebo effect" —that is, a healing immune response— include (1) the Pygmalion effect, whereby people live up to the positive images others have of them; (2) the power of imaging in athletic success; and (3) the phenomenon of learned helpfulness as the antidote to learned helplessness, triggered by images and stories of figures like Mother Teresa. Cooperrider argued that leaders can evoke similar power by providing images that reinforce a desired outcome. Diana Whitney and Amanda Trosten-Bloom have been primary cocreators with Cooperrider of the appreciative inquiry community of practice. In the following essay, they provide a history of the development of positive psychology, the strengths movement, and appreciative inquiry as an organizational intervention, with practical applications for enhancing your capacity for bringing out the best in yourself, other people, and entire organizations.

Research into positive psychology (Fredrickson, 2009) suggests that people flourish and perform at their best when surrounded by positive emotions and positive communication. Teams, departments, and entire organizations thrive in a positive emotional environment. Strengths-based research makes the case for viewing human learning and development in areas of strength rather than weakness (Buckingham & Clifton, 2001). Taken together, these growing fields point to the relational model and innovative practices of Appreciative Leadership (Whitney, Trosten-Bloom, & Rader, 2010). The global success of the affirmative, high-engagement process of Appreciative Inquiry (Whitney & Trosten-Bloom, 2010; Cooperrider & Whitney, 2005) provides a compelling approach that leaders can use for creating large-scale alignment, innovation, and positive change in organizations and communities worldwide.

The Birth of Positive Psychology

In 1996, Dr. Martin Seligman, then the new president of the American Psychological Association, posed a powerful question to the field of psychology. "What," he asked, "has the field of psychology been studying for the past thirty years?" A review of literature and research answered his question: there had been approximately 45,000 studies of human malaise, neurosis, or distress in some form, and only 300 studies of human well-being, joy, happiness, or success. Believing that the field had gotten off track, he dedicated his tenure as president to leadership in the area of positive psychology. He issued a call for psychological science and practice to be as concerned with strengths as with weaknesses; as interested in building the best things in life as in repairing the worst; and as committed to making the lives of normal people fulfilling as with overcoming pathology.

Among other things, the field of positive psychology explores the sources and benefits of positive emotions (Fredrickson, 2003), the relationship between inner dialogue and performance (Seligman, 1998), and the nature of character strengths and virtues (Peterson & Seligman, 2004).

Peterson and Seligman's work focuses on the development, measurement, and cultivation of character strengths such as wisdom, courage, humanity, justice, temperance, and transcendence. In the development of the Values in Action Inventory of Strengths (VIA-IS) strengths assessment, Peterson and Seligman systematically synthesized philo-sophical, religious, and scientific discussions of good character and identified the core virtues and specific character strengths that represent virtues in action. The VIA-IS is an online (35-minute) self-administered assessment tool that offers a rank ordering of twenty-four character strengths. Scores from the VIA survey are valid, reliable, and stable (see http://www.viacharacter.org). Those taking the VIA receive a printout of twenty-four character strengths in rank order, as well as a delineation of their top five signature strengths. Peterson and Seligman described sig-nature strengths of character as strengths that a person owns, celebrates, and frequently exercises. Recent research findings suggest that the pro-cess of defining and embodying your strengths, or putting your strengths into action, leaves you feeling connected, enlivened, competent, and with a strong sense of being in community (Fialkov & Haddad, 2010).

Fredrickson's research established what she calls the "broaden and build" theory. It suggests that humans flourish when they are in an en-vironment of positive emotions. Specifically, she finds that when people are surrounded by emotions such as hope, joy, optimism, love, confi-dence, trust, and happiness, they become more open to and capable of learning. Their capacity for new experiences and knowledge broadens, as does their resiliency to uncertainty and change (Fredrickson, 2009).

Positive emotions support organizational and community success as well as human flourishing. Indeed, many of the organizational qual-ities that leadership seeks to foster—collaboration, achievement, and innovation—are a natural by-product of positive emotions.

To contribute constructively to human, organizational, and societal well-being, leaders need to develop and enhance vocabularies of joy, hope, optimism, care, compassion, and health along with positive prac-tices that foster human flourishing. Key among these practices is main-taining what Fredrickson calls a 5:1 "positivity ratio." This means saying and doing five things with positive impact for every one negative, which seems to be the optimal determinant of an overall positive emotional environment and success for couples (Gottman, 1994) and teams (Losada, 1999) as well as in organizations. It can be said that positive emotional environments are created one conversation at a time.

The Strengths Movement

In their book *Now Discover Your Strengths*, Buckingham and Clifton (2001) describe the term "strength" as "consistent near perfect performance in an activity" (p. 25). They suggest that strengths—which are a composite of talents, knowledge, skills, and *use*—are things we do with ease. When we work from our strengths there is a sense of joy, flow, energy, and fulfillment; and operating from strengths increases people's success, productivity, and performance.

The strengths-based assumptions about learning and performance challenge the very foundation of more traditional leadership development and human resources (HR) practices, which assume that growth stems from improvement in areas of weakness. Thus, traditional leadership development identifies competencies for a position or a role; assesses people in relation to the competencies; identifies weaknesses; and puts together a plan to develop people in their area of weakness. The same process is followed for much organizational development: conduct a survey; identify areas of weakness; and hold managers accountable for planning improvements and measurable change.

Strengths-based change and development is based upon the following ideas:

- Each person's greatest room for growth is in his or her greatest areas of strength—not weakness.
- Excellent performers are rarely well rounded. They capitalize on their strengths and avoid or minimize their weaknesses.
- To help people capitalize on strengths, give people opportunities to identify and understand them—then reinforce them with practice and learning, and find roles (jobs, projects, classes) that draw on them (Buckingham & Clifton, 2001, pp. 25–35).

The notions of strengths-based learning and performance have tremendous implications for leadership, HR processes, and team building. Success in these endeavors comes through articulating and organizing around what people are good at, finding ways to enable each and every person to shine.

What Is Appreciative Inquiry?

Appreciative Inquiry is both a philosophy and methodology for positive change. It is founded on the simple assumption that human systems—teams, organizations, and people—move in the direction of what they study, what they focus on, and what they talk about with regularity. Appreciative Inquiry focuses on what "gives life" to organizations, teams, and people when they are at their best.

Appreciative Inquiry does not assume that any person or organization is always at its best. It does posit, and both research and experience confirm, that people learn, and organizations change, most readily when they focus on, study, and engage in dialogue about strengths, patterns of success, and who and what they are at their best.

For this reason, the Appreciative Inquiry process engages large numbers of people in dialogue and deliberations about their individual and collective strengths and their hopes and dreams for the future, as well as opportunities and plans for collaborative action.

The process generally follows what is called the Appreciative Inquiry 4-D Cycle (Figure 4.1).

Lessons about Leadership Using Appreciative Inquiry

We have worked with dozens of leadership teams to help them introduce Appreciative Inquiry to their organizations and communities and to use it successfully for significant transformation. We have noticed that the leaders who chose Appreciative Inquiry as their vehicle for positive change have the following four things in common (Whitney et al., 2010):

- *First, they were willing to engage with other members of their organization or community to create a better way of doing business or living.*
- *Second, they were willing to learn and to change.* They did not simply expect it of others. They were all open to learning from employees and stakeholders and to changing themselves as well as their organizations in the process.

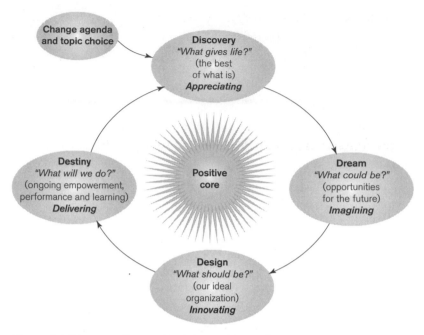

Figure 4.1 Discovery, Dream, Design, and Destiny (Whitney & Trosten-Bloom, 2010, p. 6).

- *Third, these leaders truly believed in the power of the positive.*
  When faced with low levels of employee morale and engagement,
  they chose positive approaches to change. They understood that
  by studying what was successful and promising in their organizations, people would gain confidence and hope, but also that
  morale and performance would improve.
- *And fourth, these leaders cared about people, often describing the
  work of their organization or business in terms of helping people
  learn, grow, and develop.* Carolyn Miller, executive director of the
  Community Development Institute, is an exemplar of this kind
  of leadership. Leading from a stance of coach and mentor, she
  actively solicits people's hopes and dreams for their future, and
  then supports them in taking on work that is consistent with
  those dreams. Her commitment to personal development is also
  reflected in the company's robust training budget, as well as the
  regular, ongoing coaching that she and her fellow leaders engage
  in with their staffs.

Peter Drucker has been quoted as saying that the primary task of leadership is to create an alignment of strengths toward a goal, in such a way that weaknesses are irrelevant. In many ways these leaders live this philosophy and practice. They seek to understand and learn what works well and to build the future upon it.

Appreciative Leadership: Putting Appreciative Inquiry into Practice

Appreciative Leadership articulates and organizes around what people are good at, finding ways to enable each and every person to shine. Appreciative HR processes such as performance management systems, succession planning, and career development are designed so that people can learn and leverage their personal strengths and high-performance patterns. And finally, appreciative team building ensures that the diverse strengths of team members are aligned and complementary (Whitney, Trosten-Bloom, Cherney, & Fry, 2004, pp. 9–15).

Appreciative Leadership is: "The relational capacity to mobilize creative potential and turn it into positive power—to set in motion positive ripples of confidence, energy, enthusiasm, and performance—to make a positive difference in the world" (Whitney et al., 2004, p. 3).

Embedded in this definition are four formative ideas about appreciative leadership: (1) it is relational; (2) it is positive; (3) it is about turning potential into positive power; and (4) it has rippling effects. Each of these four ideas represents a paradigm shift, a clear movement away from the habitual, traditional, individualistic, command-and-control practices of leadership toward a "new normal": the positive, socially generative principles, strategies, and practices of Appreciative Leadership.

Five Core Strategies of Appreciative Leadership

The five core strategies of Appreciative Leadership point to key areas of relational practice. Each is a means by which Appreciative Leadership successfully unleashes potential and elevates positive performance.

The Wisdom of Inquiry: Asking Positively Powerful Questions

Positive questions are Appreciative Leadership's most powerful tools. Inquiry lets people know that you value them and their contributions. When you ask people to share their thoughts and feelings—their stories of success or ideas for the future—and you sincerely listen to what they have to say, you are telling them, "I value you and your thinking." Such inquiry requires daily practice: to ask more and tell less; to study the root causes of success rather than the root causes of failure; and to wonder why people do what they do rather than judge and berate them.

The Art of Illumination: Bringing Out the Best of People and Situations

The art of illumination requires the willingness and ability to see what works rather than what doesn't, the interest and capacity to discover peoples' strengths, and the appreciative intelligence to sense the positive potential in every person and situation.

Success breeds success. Stories of strengths, high performance, and success create momentum and pave paths forward for ongoing high performance and success. When leaders discover and pass along stories of success, they are implicitly saying, "this is the way to do things around here if you too want to be successful." Through the practices of illumination you can help people learn about their strengths and the strengths of others. You give them confidence and encouragement to express themselves, take risks, and support others in working from their strengths.

The Genius Inclusion: Engaging with Others to Cocreate the Future

The practice of inclusion gives people a sense of belonging, which in turn opens the door for collaboration and cocreation. When people feel they are a part of something, they care for it. Imagine you are planning for the future of a school. Who would you include on the invitation list? Faculty, administrators, parents, students, and who else? One school included cooks, janitors, board members, bus drivers, and graduates in their strategic planning process. Or imagine a meeting to consider alternatives for community health care. Who would you include? Yes, physicians, nurses, administrators, politicians, and patients are among the many voices that need to be invited and engaged. How about pharmaceutical companies, social workers, educators, laboratory technicians, and local media? In every situation there is a myriad of people, groups, and organizations with a stake in the outcome, all of whom can make a valuable contribution, whose voice matters, and who will be enlivened through participation.

The Courage of Inspiration: Awakening the Creative Spirit

Appreciative Leadership unleashes latent potential—great ideas, strengths, capabilities, and skills—by inspiring creativity, confidence, and hope for the future. Through inspiration, people get a sense of direction. When you put into place a vision and path forward, you give hope and unleash energy and the action needed to realize the vision. Inspiration gives people hope and courage to shed habitual ways of living and working and move in new, innovative, and more life-affirming directions. Inspiration, hope, and creativity—three essential ingredients for personal and collective transformation—go hand in hand.

Do you know what inspires the people around you? It's easy to find out. Just ask them: "Tell me about a time when you were at your best. What inspired you?" Or watch them. When people feel inspired, they show excitement, enthusiasm, and high energy. Or listen to them. When people say things like, "I don't know where this idea comes from but what if we . . ." or "I have a creative idea that I need your help thinking through" or "I would love to . . ." they are expressing their creative spirit. An inspired workplace hums with the sounds of creative collaboration, synergy, and the surprise of collective wisdom unfolding.

The Path of Integrity: Making Choices for the Good of the Whole

Appreciative Leadership begins and ends with integrity. When you are on the path of integrity, people know it. They follow your ideas and ideals, model their ways of working after yours, and contribute their best to the ideals you put forth. When you practice integrity, you let people know that they are expected to give their best for the greater good, and that they can trust others to do the same.

When you are off the path of integrity, people sense it. They see it in your actions: when the way you relate to people minimizes them, belittles them, or even harms them. They hear it in your words and the tone of your voice when you make promises you cannot deliver upon. They feel it when you are short on emotional intelligence, avoid conflict, blame others, or express anger inappropriately. When you are off the path of integrity, people move away from your ideas and your way of working.

Conclusion: Appreciative Leadership for Today's World

The world has changed. We have crossed a threshold to a new era: one that demands a radical shift in leadership strategies and practices. With the help of technology, we have discovered, as if for the first time, that we are all related. Acknowledgment of this interdependence leads us to profoundly shift what we wish for and expect from leadership. To meet this challenge, leadership must be aware of and respond to trends currently defining the social milieu of organizations and communities.

Today, people want to be engaged and heard. They want to be involved in decisions that affect them and to be acknowledged for a job well done. Diversity is the norm. Whether local or global, small town or corporate, organizations and communities are composed of people with a wide variety of ethnic and cultural backgrounds, of differing ages and preferences. People in today's organizations need leadership that is collaborative and just. The most pressing social, economic, environmental, and political challenges of our time are global in nature. They cannot be resolved by one person, one country, or one business. They require unprecedented appreciation of differences and collaboration. In short, they call for Appreciative Leadership.

Diana Whitney, PhD, is president of the Corporation for Positive Change. She is a founder of the Taos Institute, a fellow of the World Business Academy, and a distinguished consulting faculty member with Saybrook University. She is a coauthor or editor of sixteen books, including the best-selling *The Power of Appreciative Inquiry* and the award-winning *Appreciative Leadership: Focus on What Works to Drive Winning Performance and Build a Thriving Organization.* She is a visionary thought leader whose clients include the University of Virginia Health System, Sisters of Good Shepherd, the Canadian School of Public Service, British Airways, and the United Religions Initiative. For more information, go to http://www.positivechange.org.

Amanda Trosten-Bloom is a principal with the Corporation for Positive Change. She is the coauthor of leading Appreciative Inquiry books, including *The Power of Appreciative Inquiry, Appreciative Team Building, The Encyclopedia of Positive Questions,* and *Appreciative Leadership.* Her award-winning work in the high-tech, service, manufacturing, and municipal sectors has been prominently featured in numerous books and articles. Her clients include Hewlett-Packard; Hunter Douglas Window Fashions Division; NASA; the cities of Longmont, Denver, and Boulder, Colorado; and the Unitarian Universalist Association of Congregations (UUA). For more information, go to http://www .positivechange.org.

| 5 |

Dancing on a Slippery Floor

Transforming Systems, Transforming Leadership

Kathleen Allen

Diana Whitney and Amanda Trosten-Bloom introduced us to the psychological shift in progress from focusing on problems to discovering and reinforcing the capacities people and organizations possess, so that we can have the confidence to implement desired future visions. In this essay, new ways of thinking, pioneered in the physical and biological sciences, illustrate how we as contemporary leaders can reframe our responses to twenty-first-century challenges. Building on the work of Margaret Wheatley (1992) and others, Kathleen Allen summarizes major themes in the advances from Newtonian to quantum physics and from an industrial to a biological paradigm. She then applies these lessons to leadership in ways that work with, rather than fight against, natural processes, showing how you can build your capacity for experiencing greater ease and less resistance to the challenges of leading in today's world.

How do we know when our thinking needs to be transformed? One way is when the beliefs and assumptions we have no longer provide a way to explain what is going on in our life and organizations. Another way is when our actions that flow from our beliefs require more energy and resources to achieve the same or fewer results (Lynch & Kordis, 1988).

There is a cost to holding on to old thought patterns and behaviors. We tend to narrow our thinking and collect only data that reinforce our point of view, which constricts our life and the meaning we make of it. I have found that I can transform my thinking by studying different disciplines and taking concepts from them to apply to my field of leadership. Discovering how different fields look at things enriches and challenges my own paradigms and underlying assumptions and raises my practice and my effectiveness when I work with organizations.

I have been fascinated by biomimicry (Benyus, 2002), which is the study of how nature can be used as a mentor, model, and measure for designing sustainable systems. Nature's underlying design creates infinite possibilities found in the following nine principles:

- Nature runs on sunlight.
- Nature uses only the energy it needs.
- Nature fits form to function.
- Nature recycles everything.
- Nature rewards cooperation.
- Nature banks on diversity.
- Nature demands local expertise.
- Nature curbs excesses from within.
- Nature taps the power of limits by maximizing the benefits of the constraints of the ecosystem like temperature ranges, soil fertility, rainfall, and so on.

These principles lead me to see organizations and their cultures, processes, structures, and leadership differently. For example, sunlight is a constant and abundant energy source that plants transform into a life-giving energy. Do we have an equivalent to a constant-renewal energy source in our organizations?

The principle of nature using only the energy it needs drives me to look for wasted energy in organizations. I have discovered that any system designed to control something uses more energy than it needs. And there is always a different design process that can achieve higher results with less energy (time, money, staff, or attention).

Over the last twenty-five years, I have used the new sciences and the shift to their underlying systems theories as a source for seeing differently, transforming my thinking, and enriching my practice to meet the extraordinary challenges of the twenty-first century.

From Newtonian to Quantum Physics

The shift from Newtonian to quantum physics is fundamental to the worldview shift from separation to connectedness. Newton saw the universe as a giant machine. The machine metaphor has influenced the structure of our organizations and our thinking about leadership. The machine needs a power source to run it, hence our framework of leaders as sources of motivation and vision and the great man theory of leadership. The shifts from Newtonian to quantum physics include the following:

- *Closed to open systems:* Newton's physics assumed a closed system, while quantum physics sees the world as a highly connected and open system (Capra, 1975, 1992, 1996).
- *Parts to whole:* Newton's mechanistic metaphor brought a focus on the parts instead of the whole. The phrase that people are "cogs in an organization" is a familiar extension of this logic. The quantum world is filled with connections and can be understood only from the perspective of the whole. Deming (1986) and the total quality movement, with its appreciation of overall process and stakeholders, is an example of a shift from the focus on the individual (part) to the system.
- *Focus on the individual to focus on the field:* The Newtonian focus on parts is reflected in much of the leadership literature, where the unit of analysis is the individual leader. The quantum world brings the focus to the whole reflected in field theory, which holds that invisible fields, like gravity or a magnetic field, exert significant influence on the behavior of all the parts of the system (Capra, 1996; Wheatley, 1992; Zohar, 1997). Organizational culture has the properties of an invisible field and influences how individuals behave at work. This helps shift thinking about leadership and change from "how do I influence the individual?" to a much more powerful question of "how do I influence the culture of an organization?"

- *Opposition splits to opposition necessary for wholeness*: One of
  the strangest discoveries of modern physics is the wave/particle
  duality (Wheatley, 1992; Zohar 1997), which moved us from a
  world of either/or to a world of both/and. It challenges us to think
  in terms of both potentialities and paradox within our organizations (Handy, 1994; Wacker & Taylor, 2000). The idea that opposition is necessary for wholeness and sustainable solutions has
  helped me significantly to see tensions as promising and resistance as something to pay attention to. Often, resistance can
  actually catalyze change in an organization. However, if we spend
  our energy shutting it down or avoiding it, we lose the power
  embedded in resistance to leverage sustainable change.

From Industrial to Biological Paradigm

The 2008 *Futurists* magazine introduced the new biological paradigm
as the framework for the twenty-first century and juxtaposed it with
the twentieth-century industrial framework (Brown, 2008). A biological paradigm looks to nature and the study of life and living systems to
think about how to produce things and structure and lead our organizations (Benyus, 2002). Some key shifts include the following:

- *Perfectibility to functionality/fit*: Living systems are constantly
  evolving and adapting. The criterion for effectiveness is a focus on
  functionality and fit with the environment, allowing an organism
  to mutate to survive. It lets go of the search for perfection that an
  industrial mental model pursues.
- *Universally applied best practice/universally applied to emergent
  practice designed to fit a unique context*: The industrial paradigm
  looked for a "one size fits all" framework. The concept of best
  practices assumes that once a best practice is identified, it can work
  in any context. The biological paradigm understands that in living
  systems, context matters. What works in one ecological region
  doesn't work in another without significant additional resources.

- *Mass production to mass customization:* Mass production was a strategy used in an industrial paradigm to scale the quantity and profits of production. The science of biomimicry (Benyus, 2002) looks to nature to understand how to design products that respond to the uniqueness embedded in all living systems. YouTube and Facebook are examples of mass customization. They both create a cooperative platform that allows diverse individuals to create their own pages or videos that reflect their uniqueness. Like nature, they reward cooperation and bank on diversity to sustain interest in these mediums.
- *Stable structures to adaptability, flexibility, and agility:* An industrial mental model is based in a hierarchical organizational structure that ensures stability and works for stable environments. However, nature is constantly adapting and evolving and is designed with interdependence and connectivity. Organizations that are designed to leverage networks can be more flexible and agile, which is required to keep pace with today's external environment. Wikipedia is an interesting example of something that is designed from a biological paradigm. It is open sourced and allows multiple people to shape the content. The goal of Wikipedia is one of functionality, not perfection. Its design reflects a living system instead of the stability of a Webster's dictionary.

From Mechanistic Bureaucratic System to Complex Adaptive System

The next shift is from mechanistic bureaucratic systems to complex adaptive systems (CAS), which are an outgrowth of chaos and complexity theory in science (Glieck, 1987; Hazy, Goldstein, & Lichtenstein, 2007; Olson & Eoyang, 2001). Some shifts include the following:

- *Static rigid structure to coevolving system:* A mechanistic framework requires a defined boundary. All the relationships are embedded in the design and do not change unless intentionally redesigned. The saying "change starts at the top" reflects the assumption that change is directed, not cocreated. In a CAS, there are many variables, each one influencing the others (Clark, 1985).

- *From control dynamics to unconstrained dynamics:* A CAS assumes the world is filled with open systems (Jennings & Dooley, 2007; Schwandt & Szabla, 2007) that influence other systems (Stacey, 1992). In a mechanistic bureaucratic system, the goal is to control the dynamics of the system. Its hierarchical organizational structure splits labor and management, and management is the place where control, resources, and knowledge are held. A hierarchical organizational structure assumes that cause and effect exist, are known, and can be used to generate leadership and action. In a CAS, the number of variables in play are numerous and expanding all the time. Cause and effect do not exist. It begs the question of what leadership looks like in a world that doesn't operate with linear cause and effect. Expecting the unexpected is a norm that emerges out of the interactions in the system and is more than a sum of its parts. This opens the way to see multiple agents of leadership initiating action and influencing in an intentional way.

- *From equilibrium seeking to adaptive striving:* CAS are living systems and, by their nature, are adaptive. They amplify feedback loops to help the system continually adapt to fit with the external environment. The interconnectedness of our global economy makes it impossible not to be affected by natural disasters like the earthquake and tsunami in Japan in 2011. Every affected company, like Toyota or Apple, and all of their supply lines, customers, and shareholders have been impacted by its ripple effects.

- *Linear causality to mutually shaping causality:* CAS are open to their larger environment and subject to an always-expanding number of variables. Think of a large, beautiful, and complex spiderweb. The web is filled with connections and anything that affects one section will ripple across the web and affect other areas. On a much larger scale, our world is filled with open systems (or webs) that keep interacting with and mutually shaping each other. The mechanistic bureaucratic framework created assembly lines to construct products. Assembly line logic is a perfect example of linear causality, and while linear causality can be created in a closed system, our world isn't closed. Our political dialogue often reflects simple causality that doesn't acknowledge the mutually shaping nature of complex adaptive systems. The "drill baby drill" slogan of the 2008 election season would be one example.

One of the new competencies needed for the twenty-first century is to see the integration and connections between multiple systems. The effective leader is one who can create a culture that sees the multiple systems that are in play and pays attention to how they influence each other. Where we used to see leadership as creating a critical mass of support, resources, or power to accomplish results, the current goal is to foster critical connections (Wheatley & Frieze, 2009). This creates a shift in the primary leadership question from "who can make this work?" to "what interactions (connections) will make this work?"

The unrestrained dynamics of open systems makes controlling all variables an outdated myth and an exercise in futility. Effective strategies for influencing change and achieving results require a shift in thinking (Allen & Cherrey, 2000; Olson & Eoyang, 2001), such as asking: "what can I unleash?" rather than "what do I need to control?" (see Table 5.1). For example, a domestic violence agency's usual approach was to see its clients as victims and the staff's role as meeting the clients' needs for safety. But then its leaders looked at everyone in the organization, clients and staff, as part of a whole system and asked what resource was being underutilized or ignored. They noticed the interactions among the women in the shelter and discovered that women were helping each other in their own healing and journey. This led to a more intentional change that was designed around the question, "how do we unleash the energy and talents of the women in the shelter to help in their recovery?"

Table 5.1 New Questions for Twenty-First-Century Leadership

Principles and Assumptions Based on Industrial, Mechanistic Bureaucratic Systems and Newtonian Physics	Principles and Assumptions Based on a Biological Paradigm, Complex Adaptive Systems, and Quantum Physics
Leadership question: What do I need to control? • Strategy: Control energy and talent. • Flows from the assumption that things are predictable and controllable.	*Leadership question: What can I unleash?* • Strategy: Unleash energy and talent. • Flows from the assumption that things are unpredictable and dynamic and that there are renewable and sustainable energy sources that are currently untapped in the organization.
Leadership questions: Who can make this work? What are the boundaries of the closed system? • Strategy: Reinforce the boundaries of the system. Find the person in authority who can make change happen. • Flows from the assumption that things are independent and separated; i.e., a closed system where variables can be known and controlled.	*Leadership questions: What interactions will make this work? What is the largest possibility in this situation?* • Strategy: Connect and integrate the organization and its external environment. Work with the flow of the system to design sustainable change. • Flows from the assumption that things are interconnected and holographic.
Leadership question: How do I avoid resistance? • Strategy: Resistance is eliminated, overcome, or shut down. • Flows from the assumption that opposition splits and conflict or tension hinder productivity.	*Leadership question: How do I welcome resistance?* • Strategy: Resistance is incorporated and welcomed as diversity of perspectives or opinions that enhances quality of decision making. • Flows from the assumption that opposition is necessary for understanding and achieving wholeness.
Leadership question: How do I influence individual actions? • Strategy: Build organizational structures and processes that control individual behavior and keep the organization in a stable and predictable state.	*Leadership question: How do I influence the field (or culture)?* • Strategy: Keep the organization in motion. Foster a culture that is constantly evolving, learning, and experimenting.

(continued)

Table 5.1 (*continued*)

• Flows from the assumption that things are simple and static. A body at rest tends to stay at rest.	• Flows from the assumption that things are complex, mutually shaping, and dynamic. An organization needs to adapt to thrive and a body in motion tends to stay in motion.
Leadership question: How can I create change? • Strategy: Drive change through the system. Allocate resources and attention to ensure the change stays in place. • Flows from the assumption that things are solid and static and require energy to shift the status quo and to keep the new status quo in place. Also flows from the assumption that we don't need to conserve resources or create sustainable change.	*Leadership question: How can I transform energy? How do I use the energy of the larger systems to help me design sustainable change?* • Strategy: Design change in a way that is sustainable and once in place does not require additional resources. • Flows from the assumption that things are made up mostly of space and are constantly dynamic. And every organization has an excess of energy that is not currently tapped or that is wasted on processes or structures that don't help the organization achieve its highest potential.

Dancing on a Slippery Floor: A Metaphor for Leading in the Twenty-First Century

Leading effectively today is not only about the questions we ask. It is also about our emotional stance toward the challenges we face. About twenty years ago I was walking down a newly waxed floor at the UCLA campus, where I witnessed a tableau that helped me know how the way I think about things affects how I experience them. Ahead of me were a mother and daughter. The mother was in high heels and walking tentatively down the hallway, holding onto the wall in fear of falling. The daughter, on the other hand, didn't see danger—she saw fun. She backed up and started running toward the end of the hallway. When she got up speed, she slid the rest of the way. Where the mother saw danger, her daughter saw opportunity.

In 2009 the nonprofit sector hunkered down to ride out the recession. The primary strategy was to conserve, cut, and try to stay alive. Like the woman walking down the highly waxed hallway, most non-profits were afraid of falling. So they held on tight to their organizational thinking and structures.

A few leaders chose a different path. One was a new president of a settlement house in St. Paul. He saw opportunity instead of fear and decided to use the tensions and difficulties to trigger the evolution of the agency. Despite needing to reduce the staff by one-third, he unleashed talent and energy at all levels of the organization and invested in the organizational culture. He also attracted new talent to the fund development department, which cultivated individual donors to help fill the financial gap left by the changing economy. He hired me to help with the culture work to shift the organization from a top-down, leader-led, bureaucratic, low-risk, highly centralized, controlled organization to a horizontal, leader-full outfit that engaged many members to help redesign the organization, its processes, and even its strategic plan. Work teams cocreated new processes in finance, HR, grants management, facilities, and so on. He didn't lead or attend these work team meetings; instead, he created a container for them to occur and provided simple attractors to the groups. The function of these attractors was to simplify, increase transparency, engage and involve different people with different ideas (instead of the usual suspects), involve others in decisions that affected them, and move toward implementation. He modeled experimentation and made it known that informed experimentation and innovation were needed to help the organization thrive.

A culture of innovation quickly emerged. The organization became known for emergent practice, and funders were attracted to the innovations and impact they were having. A 2011 culture audit showed a staff that was excited and engaged in working in a mission-focused organization that was doing things that mattered in their community. Like the little girl, this organization decided to start running so it could get a good slide on the slippery floor.

Leading in the twenty-first century is like dancing (or sliding) on a slippery floor. If you try to stay in control, your energy will be focused on not falling. But if you relax and use the wax on the floor to facilitate your dance moves, it will be a lot more fun and effective.

Kathleen Allen, PhD, is president of Allen & Associates, which specializes in leadership coaching and organizational change work. She has written and presented widely on topics related to leadership, human development, and organizational development. Dr. Allen has coauthored *Systemic Leadership: Enriching the Meaning of Our Work*, written many articles, and contributed to a variety of monographs and books over the years. She is a contributing author of *Leadership Reconsidered: Engaging Higher Education in Social Change* (2000). She is a skilled facilitator who helps organizations achieve long-term sustainable change. For more information, go to http://www.kathleenallen.net.

| 6 |

On Mattering

Lessons from Ancient Wisdom, Literature,
and the New Sciences

Barbara Mossberg

The new sciences, especially chaos and complexity theories, show us that everything affects everything else, which undermines the notion that any one country, any one kind of people, or any one set of ideas is central while others are at best tangential. This realization also can free you up from any remaining fear that only certain leaders—at the top of countries, global corporations, or international agencies—have power and the rest of us are nobodies without the means to make a difference. In the final essay in this section, Barbara Mossberg demonstrates how ancient wisdom, literature, and modern science combine to affirm that we all do matter—and hence how important it is that each of us steps forward to make a difference. Her essay is, thus, a call to you to assume responsibility for your own part in making the difference needed today. In the process, she also urges you to take the time to understand complexity, beginning with your own.

> To believe . . . that what is true for you in your private heart is true for all men,—that is genius. Speak your latent conviction, and it shall be the universal sense. . . . A man should learn to detect and watch that gleam of light which flashes across his mind from within. . . . Yet he dismisses without notice his thought, because it is his.
> —Ralph Waldo Emerson

> I'm Nobody—who are You?
> Are you—Nobody—too?
> —Emily Dickinson

Who are you? The struggle for identity and belonging is our human work. We may not know who we are, but we long to be present in our

75

world, accountable and responsible. We need a self-knowledge that locates us within our community. But what if Emily Dickinson speaks universally—that in society's eyes we feel we are nobodies?

Society itself is at stake in the encouragement—and recovery—of what Ralph Waldo Emerson calls the "genius" within each of us. To feel unimportant is to be alienated from public life. In the catastrophe of social invisibility, we lose each other; we waste human capital. Our civic life depends upon a reading of our capacities and our hunger to serve, to be heroes, to matter vitally. Recognizing who we are, invoking meaningful engagement with our world: this is leadership's transforming role.

Observing that we devalue our own thoughts, Emerson coaches the spirit to rise up from a conviction of inferiority or irrelevance or misuse. Speak your truth, Emerson says. The encouragement of our particular "genius" is transformative: in so doing we discover as well as heed our truth. And like Emerson's invocation of our genius, leadership's vision serves as a magic mirror, revealing the power of individuals and communities to become fully realized through self-knowledge.

The lens of literary and cultural analysis provides a way for leaders to nourish the desire to be so much more than how we are perceived. Transformational leadership "reads" our identity's letter and spirit with hope; it opens a way to conceive of our larger possibilities for being in our world. The possibility of viewing oneself and our external world in ways that transcend the chaotic surface is transformational leadership's gift. To be considered essential for what we can give others nourishes meaningful engagement with our world. In such reading, no one is a "nobody," obscured in insignificance; we can imagine ourselves into who we really are, and in our change, change this world.

Transformative Leadership Is Rocket Science

Leadership is rocket science. I offer that equation in playful seriousness, linking one field of genius, poetry, to another, physics. When we say "rocket science," we often mean knowledge out of our sphere (literally). What unfathomable equations can make a rocket lift off into space against the laws of gravity? Poetry makes its own unfathomable equations (that is to say, metaphor) to make something equally improbable happen: the heart's lifting, the spirit rousing into the realm of stars, the mind thrusting in neural heat. Both poetry and rocket science blast one away in transformative velocity to another level. It is from this vantage point, the rocket ship or poem, from which one acquires a perspective of how we belong to each other and the earth. To see earth from space is to see a spherical perfection, a harmony that reveals the flow of things that from this height appear as one: water, cloud, land. As astronauts have observed (and in the process, become poets, like Story Musgrave), from this vantage, divisions disappear, the "whole" appears; and the whole is beautiful.

Drama, story, and science record a holistic vision of interdependence vital to community. As Mary Zimmerman (2003) in *The Arabian Nights* says: "It is a precondition of war that we view other people as fundamentally different from ourselves. It is a precondition of literature that we view other people as fundamentally the same." Revelation of the whole is a corrective vision. Victor Hugo (1996, p. 735) writes in *Les Miserables*: "Civil war? What does that mean? Is there any foreign war? Isn't every war fought between men, between brothers?" And Einstein (1950) said:

> A human being is part of the whole called by us "universe," a part limited in time and space. We experience ourselves, our thoughts and feelings as something separate from the rest. A kind of optical delusion of consciousness. This delusion is a kind of prison for us, restricting us to our personal desires and to affection for a few persons nearest to us. Our task must be to free ourselves from the prison by widening our circle of compassion to embrace all living creatures and the whole of nature in its beauty. . . . We shall require a substantially new manner of thinking if humanity is to survive.

The words "compassion" and "embrace" are integral to conception of "the whole." From perspectives of the whole, it's obvious how all things are interconnected and essential. No one is Nobody. Brought to us by rocket science and poetry, this ecological and spiritual vision frames leadership's opportunity and challenge. Responsive to and responsible for "the whole," leaders face communities experiencing themselves as fraught with seemingly impossible incompatibilities. Diversity seems an obstacle to coherence. Organizational categories separate and divide even as they blur, collide, realign, and overlap in shifting alliances. The organization may seem illegible as a coherent text, but if it can't be read, what hope is there for its leadership?

Chaos Theory: Reclamation of a Fragmented and Fraught Spiritual Landscape

This is where theory comes into play, for chaos theory and literacy theories conceive the whole as not broken but defined by diverse, changing, complex elements. Metaphoric and literal altitude enable equations of the fractured and the whole, a vision of how each element is essential to the integrity of the system.

Chaos theory revelations of the dynamics of the whole illuminate interdependence: any element anywhere can affect the system; a gesture can influence far-reaching changes. The energy of an initial action generates turbulence: even mandated changes destabilize. Yet in due course, turbulence "self-organizes." And when a leader upholds a vision of the whole that does not whitewash conflict and turbulence but recognizes dynamic connections and flow, people's understanding of what seems hopeless or fearful can change.

The Butterfly Effect: A Transformational Understanding of Leadership and Power

Expressed as the theory's famous anthem, "the butterfly flapping its wings in Brazil causes a cataclysmic storm system in Texas," chaos theory provides an alternative view of power not determined by size or position. The most demoralized Nobody speaking one's truth can change a community and its future. Intrinsic to the redemptive way leaders can visualize and interpret coherence of the whole is the notion of "fractals" in complex system behavior. "Irregular" and diverse viewpoints and ways of knowing that appear irreconcilable coexist simultaneously; the behavior of each part expresses a truth about the whole.

For me as a new president of a historic college (the whole) with conflicting constituencies and contested mandates (the pieces) (Mossberg, 2001a, 2001b, 2006), the lens of chaos theory revealed an institution whose needs and capacities were intelligible. I was responsible for bringing together and moving forward diverse elements of a community in transition (each part equally important). Reason and imagination seemed applicable to a vision of the whole behaving according to natural laws. Dynamical systems theory is a corrective to a traditional understanding of power and opens new ways of understanding leadership in an interdependent organization. My thinking was transformed; I recognized that my own leadership responsibilities to help preserve the institution's history and character of innovation while adapting to new mandates was one of many changes perturbing the system. Knowing how initial turbulence self-organizes over time gave a long-term perspective that liberated community creativity.

The "chaos" of diverse ideas on how to proceed as a whole was a crisis of institutional identity undergoing necessary growth. As an interpretive literacy tool, chaos theory helped me "read" and know that, as Mark Twain (2010, p. 288) said of the music of Richard Wagner, "it's better than it sounds." Success for the organization could be understood not in terms of change outcomes per se, but rather in terms of promoting the expression of community "genius" —what is productive for nourishing human aspirations. Transformational leadership can help both individuals and communities in mutually supportive work that fosters identities of significance. To visualize a butterfly when one sees a cocoon is to read with optimism and hope stages of emergence in our journey from physical matter to socially matter-*ing*.

Chaos theory's special gift to leadership is trust in the whole dynamic system of community. Based on "hard science" and documented history, the theory supports faith in each fractal as an inseparable part, illuminating, and not undermining, the efficacy and integrity of the whole. In this way, chaos theory supports trust for the discordant, the eccentric, the slow and the hyper, the different. It supports trust in the system when things are turbulent, for the leader of a chaotic system knows that things will self-organize: they have to. It's not just a good idea. It's the law.

Chaos Theory as Transformational Literacy

Seen with trust, a community experiences its fractious, fractured identities in more positive ways. Each person is a fractal, a butterfly, a strange attractor, with the capacity to matter. To imagine oneself as representative of others, the genius on which Emerson says community depends, is the empowering work of transformational leadership. Transformational leadership invokes respect of the self—both humble and heroic—in relation with others. Ancient stories chanted struggles of identity. In Homer's *Odyssey*, a man leading a team confronts multiple monsters that obstruct and demoralize their journey home from the war. Trapped by the cannibal Cyclops eating his teammates two by two, Odysseus saves himself and his crew by creatively calling himself Nobody. Of course, this is clever, because when the Cyclops calls for help and is asked who is doing him wrong, he yells, "Nobody!" Nobody comes, and Odysseus and his crew escape.

This story offers a window into the role of leaders whose community may comprise people who are so-called nobodies in the world—or suspect that is how they are perceived. Identity is tragic or triumphant. If someone feels indispensable to community, community is nobly served. From the times of *The Odyssey* to today's *Wizard of Oz*, we see transformational leadership practice, a recognition promoting essential community needs—bravery, problem solving, compassion, loyalty, and love. The identity generating these qualities is often a struggle with "monstrous" forces making one feel inadequate or insignificant. In the nineteenth century, the poet Tennyson reprised the character of Odysseus as an old man, who longs to "shine in use." He exhorts his companions to never give up the effort to "seek a newer world" (Tennyson, 1990, p. 166).

In fact, the necessity to see ourselves "shining in use," inextricably connected to a larger whole, is identified as cultural wisdom. In one of the earliest Greek dramas, the Sphinx is the gatekeeper to the city of

Thebes; it does not allow anyone to enter the city who cannot pass its citizenship test. If this were a *Jeopardy!* episode, the question would be "man," and the answer would be, "What walks on four feet in the morning, two feet at noon, and three feet in the afternoon?" The test is a poem, an equation, a metaphor, of the human being as complex, chaotic, diverse, changing—and continuously coherent. As unrelated as our growth processes seem, they express the same being. But, as the story goes, people cannot recognize this description of the dynamic whole of human identity. They not only are denied community; they are killed.

Ancient Wisdom Requires Leaders to See What We Mean

A vision of ourselves, diverse but one, ever evolving into new forms as we live out our common destiny, is critical: to live with, or live at all, we need this vision of how our complex individuality shows itself differently at different times—and how all these "selves" relate and contribute to the whole. Our community depends upon an ability to envision our shared fates. Our ability to be empathetic, sympathetic, and compassionate, our motivation to be generous and fair, derive from a fractal knowledge of how our various realities each speak to the whole of human experience. Thus, it is not only community at stake in the self-knowledge required by the Sphinx. It is life itself.

In Sophocles's (1996) drama, the fateful riddle is finally interpreted by Oedipus. Oedipus enters Thebes and is crowned king; literacy makes him leader of the community. But his knowledge of "man" is limited. He does not know who he is—how connected to others. Unbeknownst to him, a man he has killed is his father; a woman he marries is his mother. The whole community suffers for his crimes. In his leadership role to save the community, Oedipus must identify who jeopardizes the community: himself. He must learn not simply that he has killed the wrong man and married the wrong woman, but that everyone matters: metaphorically, everyone is related. Self-knowledge is rooted in mutual belonging. This portrait of leadership is a call to "read" our experience in this world in transformational ways based on an understanding of what we each mean to each other.

Some might object that the Sphinx is a literary fiction. But that's part of the point. Historically, education in the liberal arts has been considered essential to leadership because such studies take us out of ourselves to imaginatively experience the diversity of the complex world around us. Engaging with literature, for example, we identify with men and women, young and old, cultures and personalities and values different than our own; we are Willy Loman and Blanche Dubois and Huck Finn and Holden Caulfield and the Invisible Man and Henderson the Rain King and Ishmael and Nikki Giovanni "ego tripping," we are kings and queens and fallen women, we are elephants and lions and pigs (as in Dr. Seuss's *Horton Hears a Who*; Robert Kraus's *Leo the Late Bloomer*; E. B. White's *Charlotte's Web*). Each becomes part of how we see and value and understand our world and ourselves. We are like Tennyson's Ulysses, "part of all that I have met," and thus, we become more global, and (who knows?) perhaps more compassionate citizens—the wisdom behind the Sphinx story.

Combining insights from chaos theory, psychology, and the humanities reveals an inspiring understanding of what we each mean to our community. Leadership "reads" a community and how its individuals belong. In encouraging people to speak their truth, leadership casts everyone in a role of dignity and worth. Chaos theory and other emergent sciences support a conviction of our connection with each other and the world by which we need to go forward. Literature is a model of such imaginative engagement that invokes self-knowledge. Identity narratives, scientific revelations of how the world works, and human psychology are fractals of the same human story of longing and belonging: the ambition and power of the human spirit to matter to someone and something beyond oneself.

... And It *Is* Wizardry

Revelations of interdependence come from the perspective of time and space. Revelation's root is *revelare*, "to lift, to raise." Our ability to perceive ourselves as connected to each other and our world depends upon a leadership vision that "beams us up." This transformational literacy is artfully expressed in *The Wonderful Wizard of Oz* (Baum, 1987), where characters are convinced they do not have what it takes to be human, to be literally present in their community. They need a "wizard" to recognize their abilities to get the courage, empathy, and intelligence called for.

Literature and physics, history and math provide the same wizardry for the Nobody within: a vision of ourselves that allows for expansion beyond ourselves into the realms of knowing and being in the universe that release us into a greater understanding of our capacity to be . . . greater. This literacy is the wizardry of transformational leadership, theories supporting an essential view of the world that is—given time— as orderly, as creative, as resilient as a poem or equation expressing a complex whole: the genius of "I" and "us" together all at once.

Barbara Mossberg, PhD, is president emerita of Goddard College, a prize-winning international author, an affiliate faculty member of Union Institute and University's interdisciplinary doctoral program in Ethical and Creative Leadership, director of integrated studies at California State University Monterey Bay, and a contributor to Pacifica Graduate Institute's MA program in Engaged Humanities and the Creative Life. She has integrated science and humanities for leaders as senior fellow for the American Council on Education, U.S. Scholar in Residence for the U.S. State Department, Mellon Fellow at the Aspen Institute, Senior Fulbright Distinguished Lecturer, core faculty of the Lilly Conference on College and University Teaching, and others. She is poet in residence for Pacific Grove, California, and hosts a weekly hour-long radio show on poetry.

PART TWO

BEING THE CHANGE: INNER WORK FOR TRANSFORMING LEADERS

Setting the Context for Part Two

Deepening and Expanding Inner Capacities for Becoming the Change

Our success as leaders begins with how we think, as described in the introduction to Part One; but by itself, changing the content and structure of our thinking is not enough. Leadership success today depends equally on developing our inner capacities in ways that fundamentally change who we are. As Mahatma Gandhi (1913/1958) said:

> We but mirror the world. All the tendencies present in the outer world are to be found in the world of our body. If we could change ourselves, the tendencies in the world would also change. As a man changes his own nature, so does the attitude of the world change towards him. This is the divine mystery supreme. A wonderful thing it is and the source of our happiness. We need not wait to see what others do. (p. 241)

Inherent in Gandhi's words, and reinforcing Mossberg's injunctions in Part One, is the belief that what we embody has weight beyond what we say, do, or even think. And certainly, most of us today look beyond mere leadership strategies and even inspiring words to assess the quality of the person leading.

As the organization of this book attests, transforming leaders need to align transformational thinking and inner psychological development, and act in ways that reflect these perspectives. It is sad when people try out the latest leadership strategy without having done their inner work, and then fall on their faces because they lack the presence to inspire cooperation. It is a great shame when those who have responded to a call, clarified their values, and are passionate about an informing vision become frustrated, even demoralized, when they cannot convince others to change. It is a horrible loss when leaders become excited about a promising organizational strategy but get poor results because their personal development is inadequate for them to fully implement the kinds of ideas they are so fervent about. The transforming leader must bring thinking and being together—which is a tall order.

Listening to leaders who have made a real difference, it is clear to me that most understand how to be connected to their hearts, souls, and spirits, not just their minds, and to reflect their inner richness in their outer leadership practice. This capacity is explored in a very influential book titled *Presence: An Exploration of Profound Change in People, Organizations, and Society* (Senge, Scharmer, Jaworski, & Flowers, 2004). In it, a number of distinguished scholars and experts associated with the Society for Organizational Learning—Peter Senge, C. Otto Scharmer, Joseph Jaworski, and Betty Sue Flowers—describe "presencing" as the active quality that a leader who embodies a needed change of consciousness is able to bring to any situation.

My depth psychology background gives me some useful psychological language concerning presencing, specifically what it means to connect with the deeper parts of myself and in so doing better connect with other people and the world. Depth psychology tells me that as long as I am living from the perspective of the ego alone, I inevitably will remain stuck in us/them thinking, essentially alienated and self-involved. Also, I will, unconsciously, protect my ego's positive view of myself by either projecting negativity onto others or collapsing into self-doubt every time I make a mistake. To be transformational, we must connect with a deeper part of ourselves that feels an underlying commonality with other people and the natural world. Jung called this deeper part "the Self" and saw it as connected to the "collective unconscious" to which we all have access.

Many psychological and spiritual traditions help us deepen and bond in this way, though they articulate it differently. Most religions emphasize the desirability of connecting with a better part of ourselves and offer a process for becoming peaceful, loving, and wise, linked to the divine within and without. Those with a secular orientation, as well as those supported by a religious or spiritual faith, often also know how it feels to tap into a peaceful part of ourselves, to sense a profound connection with nature and/or those we love, to experience the joy of moments of flow when all seems easy—and how, when we are in this place, we are kinder, more compassionate, and more authentic. And contemporary neuroscience provides us with information on how our brains and bodies work when we are seized with panic, when we are calm and centered, when we think in a shallow way, or when we tap into some deeper wisdom and way of living. Indeed, neuroscience and new thinking about intelligence break down the separation between mind, body, and emotions, recognizing that cognition involves all of these—and more.

Being the change requires a different and higher-order mode of thinking than intelligence as measured by an IQ test or logic alone. Indeed, it involves self-knowledge, emotional intelligence, intuition, and many other integrative ways of knowing.

Harvard Professor Robert Kegan has written extensively about cognitive complexity. His ideas provide a conceptual bridge that links the emerging thinking included in Part One with the essays on inner work in Part Two, as both are aspects of cognition. They also prefigure how the inner work in this section prepares us to lead groups, which is the subject of Part Three. Before we can become more effective leaders, we must both find our deeper selves and get out of our own way enough to truly empathize with and understand the gifts and perceptions of others that differ from our own.

Kegan (1994) demonstrates that the cognitive intelligence required today demands an ever-increasing awareness of our inner lives, our limitations, and our reliance on others who hold important pieces of the puzzle related to understanding the issues and potential before us. In his groundbreaking book *In Over Our Heads: The Mental Challenges of Modern Life*, he warns that most people lack the cognitive complexity needed today to thrive as individuals, much less to lead others. He identifies five orders of complexity related to the quality of our relationship to our inner and outer worlds, and concludes that the majority of us are stuck at what he calls an Order Three level of cognitive development: we recognize the validity of others' views but feel stressed by difference and want to know who is right, or have difficulty making decisions when various parties want different things.

This, however, at least beats Order Two consciousness, which Kegan says is characteristic of the self-involvement of adolescents. Even people who are smart according to the prevailing standards in their fields can lack the complexity to see (or care about) their part in the big picture or to factor into their decisions concern for others outside their immediate circles. We might think, for example, of those Wall Street executives who, following their bailout by U.S. taxpayers during the global financial crisis of 2008, were so oblivious or uncaring about their part in precipitating the collapse that they celebrated with lavish events and huge bonuses. Such real-life examples reinforce Kegan's argument that Order Two consciousness is dysfunctional when it persists beyond adolescence into adulthood.

Success as a person, much less a leader in the twenty-first century, Kegan argues, requires at least an Order Four level of cognitive development. As he describes the attributes that characterize this level, we can see connections with capacities fostered in this volume:

- A facility for self-authorship, self-regulation, and individuation
- An aptitude to see relations between abstractions and to understand the perspectives of various people and social systems
- An ability to feel in relationship to others, as a separate self to separate selves, which allows us to deal with difference respectfully, understand multiple perspectives, and still be able to make decisions about what we should do.

The essays in Part Two help us to develop these capacities, which together give rise to the relational stance in transformational group practices outlined in Part Three and the ability to act on the ideas described in Part One of this book.

Many of the essays in *The Transforming Leader* reflect not only Order Four but also Order Five cognitive capacities, which flesh out the quality of consciousness Kegan considers the emerging level needed today. What do Order Five capacities look like? At this level, you have the ability to transform your own self, achieve an awareness of inner multiplicity, and be involved in an individuation process that is experienced in connection with others. You are at ease with paradox and complexity and can appreciate people who hold truths different from yours because you are aware that their truths provide essential complements in productive tension with your own.

You also realize that some people act out anachronistic and even harmful habits of thinking that are part of the cultural consciousness. You understand that you need to deal with people who reflect these low levels of cognition, without denial, by setting appropriate boundaries to stop their negative behaviors and ameliorate their impact on the world. With Order Five consciousness, however, you know you are in an interdependent reality with the perpetrators and that people can and do change, and that not enabling counterproductive behaviors may motivate that change.

A Jungian idea also is helpful here. Such people's actions make visible some part of the cultural shadow that we can find in ourselves even if we do not act on it. Thus, a constructive task is to identify the underlying needs or desires that energize that shadowy motivation. Doing so can allow you to discover more positive ways to meet such needs, further your goals, and support the greater good. (For example, some people will cheat or lie to get what they want. But, even short of this, any of us may sometimes inadvertently do less obvious but still harmful things. We can value our underlying desires while still seeking more mature and responsible ways of fulfilling them.)

Respecting others and their perspectives is aided by the Order Five understanding that your own truth is a product of your socialization, culture, and unique experiences, and hence not absolute—and so it is with others as well. Thus, you can recognize how larger cultural systems give rise to the individual experiences within them. At the same time, individuals within those systems are affecting the whole, creating a continuous dialectical reshaping of experience for everyone involved.

By now it should be clear that the higher orders of complexity Kegan describes require a linking of big-picture intuition, rational analysis, emotional clarity, and the sense of connection with others that occurs when consciousness shifts from being defined only by the ego and the conscious rational mind to a more complete way of being. Indeed, in a more recent book, *Immunity to Change: How to Overcome It and Unlock the Potential in Yourself and Your Organization*, coauthored with Lisa Lahey, the research director of the Change Leadership Group at Harvard, Kegan emphasizes how the connection between the conscious and the unconscious minds can increase our ability to adjust quickly in the face of rapidly changing conditions or to meet our desired goals (Kegan & Lahey, 2009).

In analyzing the relationship between the conscious and unconscious minds, Kegan and Lahey shed light on the mystery of why so many of us, as individuals, groups, and organizations, commit to goals we think we want to achieve and then make little or no progress toward them. Their explanation is that the unconscious mind has made an equally reasonable commitment that is in direct conflict with what we think we want. Using an example with which almost anyone can identify, Kegan contrasts the conscious mind's commitment to healthy eating and getting exercise with the unconscious commitment to living a full and pleasurable life. Similarly, leaders might make a conscious commitment to lead more collaboratively, while they unconsciously commit to guard against limiting their ability to get the right thing done if others don't agree.

Kegan and Lahey (2009) argue that if your conscious mind believes you should push harder to achieve its goals by will alone, you will repress the wisdom of the unconscious, and the results will be counterproductive. The unconscious will continue to sabotage the conscious goal. Surfacing the tension between our conscious and unconscious minds can generate a respectful inner dialogue, leading to a sense of how both commitments can be integrated in action. Belief in that vision can be reinforced by small experiments that test out what happens when you act on the new vision in ways that reassure both the conscious and unconscious minds that this new mode is viable.

The essays in Part Two provide various languages and strategies, from different traditions and fields, to show you how to grow your cognitive complexity as you link up your conscious and unconscious minds, and how to enhance your ability to utilize a wider range of inner resources that can help you embody the change you wish to promote in yourself and the world. After reading this section, you may find it valuable to apply these ideas to particular situations you face. Should you wish to do so, you can go to Appendix A and complete the exercises there before going on to Part Three.

| 7 |

The New Basics

Inner Work for Adaptive Challenges

Katherine Tyler Scott

Katherine Tyler Scott's essay describes why it is that leaders need to do their inner work to be able to meet the challenges they face today. Many of the participants in the Fetzer dialogues credited an internal call in the face of a compelling need in the world as their motivation to lead. Many also described a feeling of certainty that a particular setting or issue was theirs to take on. This awareness drove them to develop inner qualities that incrementally allowed them to meet the next challenge (and the next and the next) that arose on their leadership journeys. The forms of such spurs to growth are many, but Scott focuses primarily on the necessity of facing one's fears and repressed qualities to be able to surface conflict and manage change.

> A well-developed self in a leader—what I call self-differentiation—is not only critical to effective leadership; it is precisely the leadership characteristic that is most likely to promote the kind of community that preserves the self of its members.
> —Edwin Friedman

In the work of transformation, who the leader is, is as important as what the leader does. If we desire to be leaders of transformation, we must focus much more on developing the discipline of inner work connecting our cognitive functions with the unconscious and introducing individuals and organizations to a much larger and richer internal world. While leaders and leadership educators need not have clinical social work, psychology, or psychiatry degrees, a competent understanding of adult psychological development within a larger sociological context is an advantage.

Inner Work

When we engage leaders in an exploration of the deeper parts of the self, we are laying a foundation that enables them to bridge the outer and inner aspects of life, and we are helping them to see themselves and others in ways that make more of themselves and more of others. The inner work of leadership leads to increased consciousness and healthy ego development.

Jung likened the ego to "a cork bobbing along in an ocean"—the ocean being the unconscious. This image conveys the enormity of the unconscious in comparison to the ego, but what the ego lacks in size it makes up for in consciousness. While the conscious and unconscious are indistinguishable in the beginning of our lives, the journey of individuation and ego development is simultaneous. The ego serves as the mediating force between our conscious and unconscious selves.

The task of becoming a person, of becoming self-differentiated, involves the ego's ability to go to the center of the unconscious and work with both the divine and the demonized aspects of one's self. The work of reclaiming these aspects of the self, which have been denied and repressed, and finding ways to constructively engage and integrate them into our conscious lives is the inner work needed for transformational leadership.

As Robert Johnson (1986) writes in *Inner Work*,

> The purpose of learning to work with the unconscious is not just to resolve our conflicts or deal with our neuroses. We find there a deep source of renewal, growth, strength, and wisdom. We connect with the source of our evolving character; we cooperate with the process whereby we bring the total self together; we learn to tap that rich lode of energy and intelligence that waits within (p. 9).

As one executive described the journey:

> The process of inner work helps me to consider how I handle myself during the big setbacks, because that is what defines a leader. I find that I have to be straight and honest with myself because unless I

am straight with myself, I can't be straight with others. This is the deep trust factor that emerged from the inner work. It all starts with the internal awareness, and then moves to the external awareness. When your values are aligned, and you deliver on what you say you are going to do, people begin to trust you. . . . This work eventually links you to your sense of spirituality; it deepens your perspective on what you're really all about—what makes you tick. That deep sense of inner awareness is what helps me in becoming a more effective leader every day. [participant in The Inner Work of Leader workshop, (2009)].

Leaders who don't engage in inner work are more prone to incongruent behavior and disconnects between what they believe and what they do, between what they intend and what actually happens. We have observed this dynamic in public leaders involved in scandalous situations that destroy their careers and reputations. Accounts generally describe their behavior as "uncharacteristic" or "out of character," implying they were not themselves. But what emerged is what had been previously disowned and denied.

In the field of health care, the disconnect between intent and impact is termed *iatrogenic*—the intention is to heal but the impact is to do harm. Leaders are likely to be iatrogenic when they act from a place of unawareness and unconsciousness. An example follows.

George was the gregarious, outgoing, well-liked CEO of a large institution, who hated conflict and would do almost anything to avoid it. He frequently used his great wit to quell any sign of discontent or emerging disagreement. George was so competent at repressing his own anger, he could convincingly say, "I never get angry." He consciously believed this, but his inability to recognize and claim his own anger made it difficult for anyone else in the organization to express it openly, so his shadow became theirs as well, and his behavior became a cultural norm.

The avoidance and repression of anger made his executive team unable to consciously develop the skills needed to resolve intragroup conflicts. Although he could see that this was a problem, George could not make the connection between his behavior and the culture that had been created. Engaging in inner work would have enabled him to gain insight into the relationship between his avoidance of conflict and the team's inability to address or solve problems in which there was a conflict or the possibility of it. When George left the company to take another position, what lay unresolved and smoldering between staff erupted. Without having had the experience of openly working through conflict, the organization went through a period of crippling chaos, confusion, and incivility.

The ego's engagement of the shadow is essential to transformation, for it is a vital part of the psyche. Denial of its existence only serves to strengthen its power and the possibility of destructive and damaging behavior. John Sanford (1994), Jungian analyst and Episcopal priest writes about the perils of ignoring or repressing the shadow; "the shadow is never more dangerous than when the conscious personality has lost touch with it." (p. 55). He continues; "We are more likely to be overcome by the Shadow when we do not recognize it." (p. 64).

Leaders of transformation understand that just as individuals have both public and private realms of their being, organizations have visible and invisible aspects of their culture. Experiences over time have shaped their responses to certain circumstances and created a pattern of what is acceptable and unacceptable, what will ensure sustainability and what is threatening to the organization's survival. What the organization learns becomes internalized in the culture—norms, values, expectations, beliefs, behaviors, and assumptions—some of which are unconscious and unquestioned. The behaviors and decisions of an organization and its leaders and followers are influenced by all of these factors.

As with individuals, organizations seek approval and want to publicly project an ideal image. Those aspects of their culture that don't fit this image are repressed and become part of the organization's shadow. Some behavioral indications of the existence of shadow in organizations are overly polite behavior in meetings in which nothing of substance gets identified or discussed, overreaction to an issue, extreme defensiveness, information overload with no time to really deal with it, meetings in which no one in the group speaks up or shares an opinion that differs from anyone else, and so on. Many organizations spend millions of dollars annually helping their employees learn to deal with the symptoms of shadow rather than dealing directly and constructively with the source of the symptoms.

Leaders of transformation understand that the suppression of shadow is time and energy consuming and reduces the creativity and productivity in an organization. Making the shadow within an organization conscious and integrating it quickens the pace of change and transformation.

Leading Change from the Inside Out

An organization can be transformed when the leadership has the capacity to claim both the visible and invisible aspects of its culture. Understanding how change occurs and its impact on individuals and organizations is central to the work of transformation.

When individuals and organizations encounter change, there are predictable emotional states and responses. The traditional norms and behaviors that have served as defenses in keeping the shadow at bay are challenged, which means that feelings and behaviors that usually are invisible become visible. The Three-Stage Model of Change is an integration of the research on change, systems theory, and grief work, and describes what happens in this process.

When change is introduced, individuals and organizations experience an ending, the gap, and a new beginning (Figure 7.1).

In the Ending, or the first phase of change, about 75 percent of people are in denial and resistance. Many feel highly anxious and fearful, and may act to keep the status quo in place. About 10 percent acknowledge the change but aren't clear about what it means or how they will adapt. The remaining 15 percent embrace the change and move to implement it.

In the second phase, the Gap, about half of those affected by the change have transitioned into a phase of mixed anxiety, confusion, bewilderment, grief, a beginning of letting go, and embracing the new

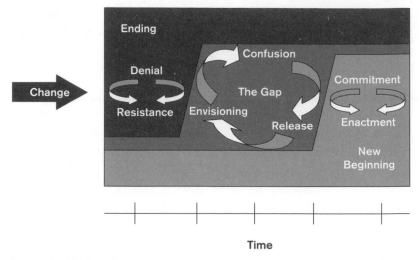

Time

Figure 7.1 Ki ThoughtBridge's Three-Stage Model of Change (copyrighted); influenced by *Hero of a Thousand Faces* by Joseph Campbell. Princeton, NJ: Princeton University Press. Revised in 1972. Adapted from William Bridge's and John Kotter's work. William Bridge's presentation to the TLD Leadership Education Forum, April 16, 1999, Indianapolis, IN.

beginning. Individuals and organizations experience considerable stress during this time. Attempts to alleviate the anxiety and confusion can be regressive unless there is frequent, consistent, and clear communication by the leader of the change about process and progress. Those who have already embraced the change remain constant in their commitment, but even under the best of circumstances about 25 percent of those in the change process remain in a stage of denial and resistance.

During this time, ways of speaking and acting that may have been taboo in the past may now be encouraged. Yet, emotionally, people still have fear about speaking the unspeakable or trying what was perceived as undoable. For example, in the previously described organization, even after George left, some remained fearful of expressing anger, and others felt like they expressed it so destructively that it was dangerous to acknowledge it. The lack of skill and low confidence contributed to the persistent reticence to discover the shadow within.

The leader of transformation has the task of easing people into the work on the shadow so that they can be freed from their fears and liberated to claim the gifts the shadow has in store as well. When equipped with the right tools and skills, people can learn how to deal with conflict with grace and ease.

In the New Beginning, the third and last phase, 75 percent of the people are on board. The release and envisioning that began toward the end of the Gap continue, gaining momentum and shifting the energy and focus toward creative visioning and implementation. Those involved begin to openly invent ways to bring about the change. It is now clear that people who are dispensing with old rules and trying new ways are being rewarded, not punished. The emotionality in the organization changes from anger, fear, anxiety, and ambiguity to anticipation, openness to learning, excitement, and a sense of efficacy in accomplishing the change. There is still a small percentage of those who have not moved from denial and resistance and who are still caught in the Gap. Whether they can move from being stuck or not is a key question that leaders of transformation need to answer when deciding how to invest and maximize resources and on whom to focus attention and support.

Managing the intensity of emotions and the vast range of behaviors found in each of the three phases of change requires conscious, self-differentiated leadership. If leaders lack the ability to recognize and manage their own emotions, it is unlikely they will be able to manage others' emotional responses to change. Those who have done such work have the advantage of being able to empathize with what others are going through and can normalize feelings by talking about them and how and when they are appropriate. In addition, they can express how a part of them also misses how things used to be, making it acceptable for some not to be fully on board with the new changes. If what has been in shadow is now out in the open, the wise leader also understands that its expression at first may not be pretty—but in time the new behaviors will become integrated into people's ways of being and acting with one another.

The Arthritis Foundation provides a positive example of what can happen when emotionally intelligent leaders who have grappled consciously with change in their own lives lead organizational change. Originally structured as a federation with a national headquarters and a network of fifty local affiliates, separate corporate entities, bound together through a charter process, the foundation recognized that it needed to be structured in ways similar to other respected not-for-profit organizations.

Maintaining a strong local presence and the capacity to raise funds and deliver programs was critical to success, and bringing staff and volunteers along in the process was very important. So the board convened a design team of approximately 100 respected leaders, representing every chapter across the country, to help define and design the new governance structure. These leaders became the "change team" with whom we worked to lead this large-scale change.

As with any major change initiative, there were multiple, often critical, negotiations to reach a new consensus regarding structure. The Arthritis Foundation's leadership did not panic when conflict emerged because they had the tools to manage it and achieve constructive outcomes. Arthritis Foundation chief operating officer Roberta Byrum's investment in her own inner work enabled her to see that the design team and her staff needed a different set of skills and tools to navigate the transition. She reached out to equip her team with (1) an understanding of the process of organizational change and transition, and (2) a set of adaptive skills, tools, and processes to equip them to get through the Gap, a stage best described as "a time of no longer and a time of not yet" (a phrase inspired by Hannah Arendt [2006]).

Roberta Byrum says, "This work has had a lasting impact on our organization. As we moved forward with the restructuring, those who served on Design Teams had integrated the tools and processes introduced to them." (2010).

Leaders, such as those of the Arthritis Foundation, who are in touch with their own phases of change and are aware of the impact of such changes on their own psyches and those of others in the organization can implement transformational structural change in ways that also build the change management capacities of the organization. In the process, they develop the organizational abilities needed to thrive in today's fast-changing world.

Wise leaders know that the process of transformation takes time, but that people and organizations can and will change. The ability to know and understand change and transformation, to persist and persevere with empathy and strength through difficult and challenging phases, is the mark of leaders who have done their own deep inner work in which the whole self has been engaged, and in doing so can become catalysts for transformational change.

Katherine Tyler Scott is the managing principal of Ki ThoughtBridge, a company specializing in an integrated model of leadership development, the management of change, resolution of conflict, and negotiation training. She is the founder and former president of Trustee Leadership Development, Inc. Katherine is a nationally recognized speaker and consultant and the author of *Creating Caring and Capable Boards: Reclaiming the Passion for Active Trusteeship* (Jossey-Bass, 2000); *The Inner Work of the Leader: Discovering the Leader Within* (1999); and *Transforming Leadership* (Church, 2010); and contributing author to *Spirit at Work* (Jossey-Bass, 1994). She serves on the board of the International Leadership Association and is a contributor to the *Washington Post*'s On Leadership blog.

| 8 |

Integral Leadership

Opening Space by Leading through the Heart

Jonathan Reams

While Scott uses practical examples of change management to show why it is so important to do our inner work, the next essay in this section, by Jonathan Reams, provides research findings from integral psychology and neuroscience that can help you recognize, name, and utilize the toolbox of inner resources we all have that can support your efforts to become a more transforming leader. Reams shows how an enhanced understanding of the function of the soul in its psychological meaning, the importance of intuition, and the neuroscience of the heart fosters a quality of consciousness that others can sense in you. It also can help you become open to more expansive options and increased opportunities.

Today's world calls for a new consciousness from leaders—this is clear enough. However, the contours of this new consciousness are less clear. It is well known that we cannot solve our problems from within the same level of consciousness that created them (as noted by people such as Albert Einstein, Gregory Bateson, and Chris Argyris). But what does this really mean when as leaders we are called to go beyond the cliché and make it a reality? We have been living in the full blossoming of rational thought, and in reaching its limits have created the kinds of crises we see all around us. To lead today requires us to transcend (while including) the rational, mental structure of consciousness and lead from an integral consciousness. From it, we can get a perspective on the hypercomplexity of issues by relating to the heart of them. Indian sage

Sri Aurobindo (2000), consciousness researcher Claire Graves (1974), philosopher of science Ervin Laszlo (2007), leadership and consciousness researcher William Torbert (& Associates, 2004), and integral theorist Ken Wilber (1996, 2000), among others, have all contributed to our understanding of integral consciousness. For example, Swiss mystic and transdisciplinary consciousness researcher Jean Gebser (1985) described five structures of consciousness that have emerged over human history: *archaic, magic, mythical, mental,* and *integral.*

This integral consciousness enables us to relate to our thinking rather than come from it. Research over the last thirty years has revealed that how we relate to the contents of our consciousness can mature well beyond what we have taken for granted (see, e.g., Kegan, 1994; Torbert & Associates, 2004; Wilber, 2000). This maturing process enables a connective knowing of the heart that is not merely a static process of coming to grasp objective facts, but a dynamic relationship between the knower and known (see Palmer, 1993, 1997). The question then arises: What is the source of this knowing?

Spiritual Beings Having Human Experiences

The source of this integral consciousness that integrates mind, emotions, and body is soul. The consciousness of soul is implicitly different from and goes beyond the consciousness of the mind. But during the Renaissance, the development of the mental structure of consciousness internalized a belief in the material world as the ground of reality. Thus, materialist science, for the most part, disregarded concepts like soul and spirit. In this view, human beings are composed of complex enough arrangements of physical matter to be able to produce consciousness and spiritual experiences. For example, the majority of neuroscience research on spiritual or religious phenomena has attempted to explain such experiences as an evolutionary genetic predisposition, or symptoms of brain malfunctions.

However, neuroscience also can be approached from a nonmaterialist perspective. A good example of this is Beauregard and Paquette's (2006, 2008) research. In line with this view, Deikman (1996) equates the essence of our Being or the "I" with pure awareness. Klemp (2002) talks about the creative nature of soul. Such nonmaterialist views enable us to transform our core beliefs about the essence of who we are. They open up space for viewing ourselves as spiritual beings, souls, having human experiences. Thus, we can define soul as a *creative unit of pure awareness* (for information on the spiritual practice that has shaped my view in this area, see http://Eckankar.org).

Presencing as Soul's Presence

As leaders, we often look to the past to get a sense of how the future might unfold. Scharmer (2007) recognized the limits of this approach and pointed to *presencing* as "the blending of *sensing* and *presence*, [and it] means to connect with the Source of the highest future possibility and bring it into the now" (p. 163). In developing his definition of presencing, Scharmer draws on Ray's (2004) notion of Self and Work, the capitalizations indicating our highest sense of being and purpose in this world. Reflecting on this, I am drawn to ideas coming from the works of Plato (1992), Hillman (1996), and Newton (1994, 2000). They all discuss purpose in conjunction with the importance of character—what we do with what we have in this life (a cornerstone of leadership).

An early articulation of the transcendent sources of purpose is outlined in Plato's (1992) *Republic*. This cornerstone of Western philosophy closes with the myth of Er, in which Plato describes the journey of souls in the afterlife. The end of this journey is a meeting with a daimon, or guardian angel, who guides the soul in the process of choosing lessons to learn when coming back into this world. Hillman (1996) draws on this myth to make it clear that we are not blank slates when we are born, but come into this world with a sense of character and calling. Newton (1994, 2000) goes further by drawing on numerous case studies of hypnotherapy regression to outline the details of this process. As leaders, we are expected to provide a sense of purpose that can motivate others. Being able to draw on a profound sense of purpose can be a source of inspiration and meaning for ourselves and others. The ability to do this is linked to character, the sources and seeds of which we bring into this human life as soul.

Central to being true to our character and calling is integrity. Palmer's (1993) conception of truth as troth shows that truth is not a noun, fact, or objective thing, but a verb, or relationship. Troth (as in betrothed) becomes a living pledge wherein we learn how to live in integrity. Having integrity links the transcendent character of soul with our human character. The process by which we come to know this is emergent. Bohm (1992) says that "who we are is unknown, but constantly revealing itself" (p. 167). Scharmer describes presencing as our capacity to perceive the future that is trying to emerge. This concept of "emerging" in relation to our "highest future possibility" can be viewed as aligning, or bringing into integrity, our human consciousness with the consciousness of soul. Scharmer calls this having an "open will."

Thus, presencing can be seen as a process of suspending the reactive tendencies and limitations of the human will in order to be open to the call of soul. It implies acting in integrity with soul's purpose for our human experience. The alignment of purpose and action is a balancing act that requires intention and choice. As leaders, we must maintain a quality of presence as we direct our attention from the inward opening of our will, to the call of soul, to the outward movement into action.

How can we translate this call of soul into action? Through learning how to make good choices. Leaders help shape the boundaries of what is real and not real. We give life to what we choose to give attention to. With this comes the responsibility to be conscious of how we choose to direct our attention. Frankl (1992) is known for saying that no matter what our external circumstances, we can always choose our attitude. Pattakos (2004), Isen and Klein (1999), and Owen (2000) build on this notion to show how we choose to believe myths or stories about our lives and the world around us and become trapped into living out these stories. To get beyond these traps, we have to move from being "subject to" them to making them objects of reflection (Kegan, 1994). An integral consciousness can support such a transformation in how we perceive our choices. But what is at the heart of this consciousness? Asked another way, what is the role of the heart in this consciousness?

Presencing and the Knowing of the Heart

Scharmer (2007) also describes presencing as "the phenomenon of see-ing and thinking with the heart" (p. 160). We commonly associate the heart with both soul and emotion. It stands in as a way to talk about what is not only intellectual. Goleman's work on emotional intelligence has highlighted the importance of seeing and thinking with the heart (Goleman, 1995; Goleman, Boyatzis, & McKee, 2002). To understand what this might mean for leadership beyond a metaphor for emotional intelligence, intuition, or nonrational thinking, I draw on research from the field of neurocardiology.

The discovery of a "little brain" of about 40,000 neurons in the heart has led to research on its nature, functioning, and potential. Drawing on a systems view of our body's physiology, McCraty, Atkinson, Toma-sino, and Bradley (2009) note that the heart does far more than pump blood—it conducts a flow of information throughout the body. In this role of the heart they found four distinct psychophysiological modes: mental focus, psychophysiological incoherence, relaxation, and psycho-physiological coherence. The coherent state is shown to have a signifi-cantly positive effect on functioning in numerous areas of health and well-being.

The authors establish a direct link between coherence and emotional well-being (which is also an aspect of the quality of soul's presence). In addition, they show evidence for positive effects on cognitive function-ing resulting from coherent psychophysiological states. From their re-search it becomes clear that the coherent state is a desirable one to be able to access, and has significant implications for leadership (Goleman et al., 2002).

Yet the actual role and impact of the heart goes well beyond these psychophysiological phenomena, venturing into the energetic realm of holographic electromagnetic fields. The patterns of information that have the most influence on the body will be those with the strongest field, and "the heart generates by far the most powerful and most exten-sive rhythmic electromagnetic field produced in the body" (McCraty et al., 2009, p. 55). McCraty et al.'s research shows that the heart has sixty times greater electrical voltage amplitude and 5,000 times stronger magnetic field than those produced by the brain. This electromagnetic field "can be measured several feet away from the body with sensitive magnetometers," thus providing "a plausible mechanism for how we can 'feel' or sense another person's presence and even their emotional state, independent of body language and other signals" (p. 55). From this it appears that our heart states will not only have a significant impact on the body and brain but also generate a field that can be detected by other people.

Thus, if we talk about our quality of character as leaders creating an aura or field around us, we are referring to a measurable electromagnetic phenomenon. I want to phrase this as the space that leaders create. This is a foundational element of a view of leadership as opening space. Yet this research goes beyond explaining how we can sense the space or field of another person. Perception of future events also is within the realm of explanation.

Central to Scharmer's concept of presencing is the notion of sensing and connecting with our highest future possibility. The quantum physics principle of nonlocality (that there is a domain of reality beyond time and space) can give us a way to understand intuition as future perception (Bell, 1964; Bohm, 1980). McCraty, Atkinson, and Bradley (2004) describe a rigorous experimental study that, along with other research (Bradley, 2007), indicates that sensing the future is possible. We as leaders are called upon constantly to make choices based on limited information. Cultivating access to *pre-sensing* what wants to emerge from the future can give us an edge by offering us access to new realms of information. Thus, presencing as "thinking with the heart" is much more than an abstraction or metaphor. It also is describing a specific activity of the heart that can be cultivated.

The phenomenon of thinking with the heart implies something qualitatively different than thinking with the mind. A simple reframing of this concept to a "knowing of the heart" can help us link it to the HeartMath research findings (McCraty et al., 2009). The scope of this research shows that this knowing of the heart can transcend the thinking of the mind. Kriger and Seng (2005) note that in relation to Islamic understandings of leadership, the "heart, as a psycho-spiritual organ of perception, not the intellect of brain, is believed to be the faculty of knowledge" (p. 779). In this reframing, we also can make a link between the consciousness of soul and the knowing of the heart. We could say that while the mind thinks, soul knows.

Leadership as Opening Space

By reframing our core beliefs about who we are (spiritual beings having human experiences) and cultivating an integral consciousness, we can begin to lead in new ways. As leaders, we create space through the quality of our presence, consciousness, and actions. This can go either way. We can create spaces that Owen (2000) characterizes as "soul pollution" (p. 1), constricting the spiritual, mental, emotional, and physical area we and others have to work in. We also have what Carey (1992) calls a "fundamental option for self-transcendence" that opens these spaces (p. 217).

A few years ago, I attended a "dialogue" between two leaders in the field of new paradigm thinking. Friends who knew very little about these speakers came along as well. We listened as the speakers took turns offering their thoughts on the topic of the evening and each other's remarks. After the event, my friends commented on how much they were put off by the first speaker, feeling as if he had been pontificating, talking down to them, and almost demanding that his views be accepted, not only by the audience but, by implication, by all those who thought differently on the subject. They then commented on how with the second speaker, they felt invited into an inquiry and encouraged to think for themselves, and had a sense of a heartfelt connection.

Such differences are not always so easy to spot. I was hired to facilitate preparations for two agencies facing accreditation reviews. On the surface, meeting the first executive director (ED) was not so much different than meeting the second. However, as the work unfolded, the differences in attitude between the two became apparent. The first felt the accreditation process was a hoop to be jumped through, after which the organization could go back to the comfort of business as usual. The second saw the process as an opportunity for growth and revitalization of the agency. Both ultimately were successful in gaining accreditation, but the impact of the processes on their organizations was markedly different. For the first ED's agency, it was indeed back to business as usual, with everyone relieved that the extra work had passed and they could get back to "normal." They simply added some paperwork to the surface of how they went about their tasks, but nothing fundamental changed.

For the second ED's agency, accreditation was a transformative process that was followed up by a staff-driven strategic planning process to articulate a new vision for evolving how they did their work. Conflicts and tensions left by the ED who preceded the current one were healed by the integration of the preparations for the accreditation review with a very authentic inquiry into how things had come to be as they were. The process allowed everyone in the agency to reframe their work in ways that enabled growth. I believe many of us can relate to such spaces being closed or opened.

A full illustration of integral leadership is well beyond the scope of this chapter. What I have aimed to do is illustrate the kinds of leadership that can emerge from moving toward an integral consciousness. Integral leadership's capacity to open a transformational space offers a way to understand what is called for to meet the challenges of today's world.

Jonathan Reams has a PhD in leadership studies from Gonzaga University and is an associate professor at the Norwegian University of Science and Technology, where he teaches leadership development, organizational transformation, coaching, and counseling. He also is editor in chief of *Integral Review*, http://integral-review.org. He is coeditor of *Integral Education: New Directions in Higher Learning* for SUNY Press. He presents at international conferences on topics such as leadership, consciousness, transformative learning, spirituality, and science and religion dialogue. Jonathan also conducts consulting and leadership training for a diverse range of clients in the United States, Canada, and Europe. For more information, see http://www.Jonathan Reams.com.

| 9 |

Mindful Leadership

Discovering Wisdom beyond Certainty

Susan Szpakowski

Scott explored why leaders need to be the change and Reams showed us that we have the inner equipment to do so. The four essays that follow provide various takes on how consciously living into your journey can develop advanced leadership capacities. The next essay, by Susan Szpakowski, augments Reams's work by exploring how we can recognize and harness the impulses of ego that become triggered in situations of uncertainty. Szpakowski shares practical principles and strategies for relaxing ego's struggle, releasing intelligence and creativity, and creating the conditions for transformation in ourselves and in others. She illustrates how these strategies can enable you to see options more accurately, make better decisions, and lead with more grace.

Everywhere we hear the drumbeat of change. Organizations and communities must become more innovative, resilient, adaptive. As leaders we are increasingly called to reinvent our strategies, companies, even entire social systems, while inspiring others to do the same.

We are also called to reinvent ourselves—to let go of familiar habits, stretch in new ways, rise to meet accelerating challenges. But even the most adventurous and risk loving among us have our limits. Too much uncertainty and our survival mechanism kicks in, and we are at the mercy of fight-or-flight impulses.

Both change and resistance to change are facts of life. Any living system is constantly balancing these two imperatives. As we lead through situations of high complexity and heightened uncertainty, how do we manage the deep-seated resistance, fear, and impulse toward retrenchment that inevitably follow?

Default

It is not as if we can dismiss this resistance lightly. It seems that our brains are programmed to continually create as much certainty as possible. In his book *Your Brain at Work*, David Rock (2009) cites evidence from neuroscience that this impulse exists even at the level of perception:

> You don't just hear; you hear and predict what should come next. You don't just see; you predict what you should be seeing moment to moment. . . . The brain likes to know what is going on by recognizing patterns in the world. It likes to feel certain. Like an addiction to anything, when the craving for certainty is met, there is a sensation of reward. . . . When you can't predict the outcome of a situation, an alert goes to the brain to pay more attention. An overall *away* response occurs. (pp. 121–122)

Thus the tendency to move toward certainty, or to fabricate it when it isn't there, is one of the brain's primary impulses.

Anyone who has studied Buddhism will recognize parallels between these conclusions and the traditional Buddhist understanding of how the mind works. In both cases, insights into our default responses can offer much-needed guidance for today's leaders. For these leaders must learn how to linger in a state of not-knowing, facing the anxiety that arises, rather than holding onto comforting certainties that are ultimately blinding and deceptive.

Ego's Craft

Much of my own understanding of Buddhism comes from my years studying with the Tibetan teacher Chögyam Trungpa, who arrived in North America in 1970 as a young but already accomplished meditation master intensely committed to making a genuine link between Western culture and the wisdom tradition he had inherited. He shed his monastic robes and became immersed in the language, idiom, and questing minds of his new Western students. As a teacher he was delightful—inquisitive, magnetic, wise, playful. This was my first and most powerful encounter with a leader operating from a place beyond ego.

According to the Western Buddhist definition, ego is the process of fabricating certainty. A sophisticated, moment-to-moment process freezes, judges, anticipates, and assumes what is going on, driven by an unconscious anxiety that something is missing, something needs to be secured. But reality can't be secured; ego's mission can never be accomplished. Thus, ego's process is the source of misunderstandings from the most trivial to the most profound and is at the root of a pervasive sense of dissatisfaction.

While this process is ongoing, any indication of threat sends it into high gear, producing elaborate self-justifications, fantasies, and fears. Trying to suppress, rationalize, or override ego's process just adds to the struggle. According to Buddhism, the primary antidote is to relax the momentum by establishing a different kind of ground, one that is not ego-based, through the practice of mindfulness.

While many leaders practice formal mindfulness meditation as an ongoing support for their work, not everyone is motivated to adopt such a practice. However, anyone can apply the foundational principles of meditation to their everyday leadership.

Grounding

One of Trungpa's early teachings was on the Four Foundations of Mindfulness, a traditional Buddhist instruction on how to meditate. Trungpa (1991) described the first foundation, *mindfulness of body*, as "connected with the need for a sense of being, a sense of groundedness" (p. 28). Bringing one's attention to the physical sensations of the body creates a simple, dependable reference point that sidesteps ego's tendency to create false ground by churning out reactive thoughts and emotions, which deplete focus and energy. In sitting meditation, the posture of straight back, relaxed front shapes one's mind in a way that is stable, open, and available.

> The psychosomatic body is sitting, so your thoughts have a flat bottom. Mindfulness of body is connected with the earth. It is an openness that has a base, a foundation. A quality of expansive awareness develops through mindfulness of body—a sense of being settled and of therefore being able to afford to open out. (Trungpa, 1991, p. 31)

Mindfulness of body can be practiced in any context, at any time of the day. At our desks, we can set a time to take a break, sit straight, and let the mind rest, anchored by a general sense of body awareness. When we find ourselves distracted, we simply return to the experience of body. We can also cue ourselves to come back to mindfulness with a physical gesture or activity we do regularly, such as answering the phone or walking across the office. The activity itself—the sensation of one's hand on the receiver or feet on the floor—becomes a reminder to tune in to the body.

A regular physical activity such as running, sports, dance, yoga, aikido, or taking a lunchtime walk also helps us stay grounded and increases the likelihood that we will come back to mindfulness of body many times during the day.

All these ways of paying attention to the body can help provide a base that increases our chances of being able to "open out" our attention and be expansive and accommodating without being overwhelmed or triggered by anxiety.

Recognizing and Releasing

The second foundation, *mindfulness of life*, addresses the survival impulse even more explicitly. Mindfulness of life involves recognizing and releasing the tightness, struggle, and distraction that characterize obsessive thinking. When we find ourselves preoccupied, we let go and come back to the body, the outbreath, the present moment. Trungpa describes this process as "touch and go." Rather than dismissing, suppressing, or judging, we simply "touch" the thought, as well as the energy and impulse behind it, and then we "go," let go, into the next moment. We don't feed the momentum with more attention and energy.

> Touch that presence of life being lived, then go. You do not have to ignore it. "Go" does not mean that you have to turn your back on the experience and shut yourself off from it; it means just to be in it without further analysis and without further reinforcement. (Trungpa, 1991, p. 36)

When touch and go is an ongoing practice, we become intimately familiar with the particular ways we try to manage uncertainty, because we have "touched" them with mindfulness many times. This familiarity makes recognition easier.

Other frameworks can serve the same purpose. In *Your Brain at Work*, David Rock (2009) reflects:

> I noticed a surprising pattern while putting this book together. I saw that there are five domains of social experience that your brain treats the same as survival issues. These domains form a model, which I call the SCARF model, which stands for Status, Certainty, Autonomy, Relatedness, and Fairness. The model describes the interpersonal primary rewards or threats that are important to the brain. Getting to know these five elements strengthens your director. It's a way of developing language for experiences that may be otherwise unconscious, so that you can catch these experiences occurring in real time. (pp. 195–196)

Rock defines the "director" as the aspect of attention that is self-aware, that notices an impulse and can choose to let it go in the moment of recognition. He explicitly links this function to mindfulness. Rock's five domains also resonate with Buddhist descriptions of the ego's concerns: to be recognized, to be certain, to be in control, to gain approval, and to be reassured that one is getting a fair deal. When any of these is challenged or denied, ego goes into hyperdrive, reinforcing its defenses out of fear of losing ground.

Shortly after reading Rock's book and contemplating his categories, I had an excellent opportunity to apply the touch-and-go practice of mindfulness of life. I was about to board an airplane with my son when I received an email that literally stopped me cold. Someone I had invited into a new project had become offended. He referred to a conversation he'd had with a mutual friend but didn't provide details. He mentioned withdrawing funding support for another unrelated project. I quickly responded, expressing genuine confusion and suggesting we talk. Then I got on the plane.

During the flight the anxiety triggered by the email kept breaking through conversations with my son. The initial shock was now producing wave after wave of speculation. If this person turned against me, the repercussions would be far-reaching. The project, which I knew was ambitious and risky, would backfire. I would fail, be humiliated, shunned. Why did I always go out on a limb like this? Why didn't I know better? Why had I trusted this person in the first place? How could he do this? As each line of thinking rose to a crescendo, I would suddenly recognize the pattern and apply the label—Oh, right. Status. Relatedness. Fairness. And I could see the underlying fears begin to freeze into a solidified position: righteousness, self-doubt, closing the door on the other. With each recognition, I would touch these thoughts and emotions with mindfulness, recognize them, then go—return to the simplicity of sitting in the seat, in the present, on the plane, with my son.

Over the following days, efforts to reassure myself that this message was simply a mistake, soon to be cleared up, became less convincing during the notable silence that ensued. I even woke up one morning dreaming that I was telling my colleagues I had failed them. Touch and go was not a quick fix but something that I needed to keep applying while the impulse continued to play itself out.

Obviously the email had hit a nerve, or multiple nerves, connected to my survival imperative. Recognizing this helped prevent me from solidifying a conclusion, an emotional stance, complete with elaborate

justifications, which would be difficult to undo and which would probably only exacerbate the problem. I was able to avoid feeding my deep-
seated insecurities. By the time I returned from my trip, I was able to
have the needed conversation from a place that was grounded and sympathetic both to myself and to the perspectives of the other person. I
was ready to voice my concerns while keeping the door open. I could
hear the other person recognize his own sense of threatened certainty,
triggered by unrelated events, which had led to the misunderstanding.
The crisis was over, and we were ready to move forward.

Mindfulness of life is a very personal practice. Every time we are able
to catch ourselves being triggered, we have a glimpse of our own survival pattern as well as the possibility of responding a different way. We
are able to choose. And every time we choose a more generous, considered response, that neural pathway, that mental habit, that relationship
with the other, is strengthened and our leadership grows a little larger
and a little stronger.

Willing to Be Here

The third foundation is *mindfulness of effort*. Preconceptions about
meditation in action often conjure images of someone moving slowly,
deliberately, dutifully through their day. In this case, mindfulness is
much less somber and self-conscious than that. It is more like an attitude
or an atmosphere. In the midst of whatever we are doing, we "come back"
because we have made an intention to be mindful and because mindfulness is a natural aspect of mind, always available. Trungpa (1991) describes it this way:

> There is just suddenly a general sense that something is happening
> here and now, and we are brought back. Abruptly, immediately,
> without a name, without the application of any kind of concept, we
> have a quick glimpse of changing the tone. That is the core of the
> mindfulness-of-effort practice. (pp. 38–39)

There is effort involved, but it may not be the kind we are used to. It is
more like tuning in. We are willing to be mindful. We understand the

value of mindfulness and we have an intention to keep coming back. Like transformational leadership itself, we neither control so tightly that we squeeze the life out of ourselves and others, nor do we abandon ourselves and our projects to whatever habitual impulse comes our way. Both extremes become reminders to return to a middle path: alert and relaxed; not too tight, not too loose.

Mindfulness of effort involves intentionally creating conditions— a culture of awareness—rather than simply driving down a linear path toward a goal. It also involves courage, because even though our preoccupations and struggles are distracting and get us into trouble, at least they are familiar. Applying mindfulness of effort takes away our security blanket. We have to be willing to let go of ego's false ground.

Simplicity

Trungpa (1991) describes the fourth foundation, *mindfulness of mind*, as "intelligent alertness," "aroused intelligence," and "being with your mind." This foundation highlights the precise simplicity of mindfulness. Fundamentally, we can only be in one place at a time. We are either present to what is happening or we miss it. This realization comes with a healthy dose of humility:

> We think we are great, broadly significant, and that we cover a whole large area. We see ourselves as having a history and a future, and here we are in our big-deal present. But if we look at ourselves clearly in this very moment, we see we are just grains of sand—just little people concerned only with this little dot which is called *nowness*. We can only operate on one dot at a time, and mindfulness of mind approaches our experience in that way. (Trungpa, 1991, p. 53)

Even mindfulness can be another way of fragmenting our attention. We split ourselves into watcher and doer. In reality, there is always just one thing going on, a "one-shot deal." Multitasking is therefore a sleight of hand, an illusion:

> It is easy to imagine that two things are happening at once, because
> our journey back and forth between the two may be very speedy.
> But even then we are doing only one thing at a time. We are
> jumping back and forth, rather than being in two places at once,
> which is impossible. (Trungpa, 1991, p. 46)

From a practical point of view, maintaining the illusion of being in
more than one place at once drains mental energy and is counterproductive. Switching back to a neuroscience lens, research tells us that
rapidly shifting back and forth between cognitive tasks results in plum-
meting capacity and rising levels of error. The only way to maintain
performance is to transfer all tasks but one to parts of the brain that can
function on autopilot. So, for example, we can drive a car while working on a solution to a problem. But even this can be a poor use of mental
energy. We arrive at our destination slightly spaced out, because our
prefrontal cortex, which is an intensive energy consumer, is already tired,
and because body and mind (or different parts of our brain) are out
of sync.

Our body-mind system is our personal leadership instrument, capable of sensing, attending, knowing, learning, and acting with sensitivity
and accuracy. This instrument functions at its best when it is not hi-
jacked by the impulses of ego. As leaders, we are more resilient, compassionate, and intelligent when we are grounded in mindfulness of
body; when we touch and go in response to habitual tendencies and reactive impulses; when we maintain an alert, relaxed self-awareness; and
when we tune in to the simplicity and potency of nowness.

Mindfulness and Transformation

Mindfulness is an age-old practice that can be used in support of a
spiritual path, a leadership path, or simply a path of becoming more
fully human. Mindfulness relates directly with the ongoing, universal
fear of uncertainty, which, if left unchecked, distorts perception, freezes
intelligence and learning, and leads to spiraling interpretation, emotion, and reaction. As leaders, we can observe all these tendencies in

ourselves, and we can readily see how these tendencies become amplified in our organizations and societies. In these times of great change, the need for alternative ways to manage uncertainty is critical.

Most, if not all, practices and methodologies of transformational leadership contain elements that we can recognize in the four foundations of mindfulness. As leaders, we intuitively know that we need to establish enough ground, enough trust and continuity, for people to be able to explore and embrace change, and to step into a shared reality that is larger and more dynamic than the territoriality and impulses of ego. We need ways of uncoupling the seemingly solid links between the momentum of the past and the possibility of the present, and between assumption and reality, so that true innovation is possible. And we need structures, traditions, and rituals that sustain and continually refresh our efforts, without becoming overly rigid and burdensome. And finally, a culture of nowness arises when we are present in a simple way, whether in a circle check-in or while silently holding an open question in a planning retreat. Nowness is the incubator of transformation—of meaning, insight, courage, commitment, and synchronicity.

Perhaps what is less evident in either the mindfulness or neuroscience literature is the great bank of wisdom and compassion that becomes available when ego's impulses have been harnessed. This is the potential I have experienced most vividly in my encounters with great Buddhist teachers such as Chögyam Trungpa. Simply through their presence, these teachers provide a contrast to ego's small strugglings and a glimpse of a more enlightened way of being.

Although Trungpa died in 1987, his vision of a secular enlightened society sustained through personal and collective practices continues to inform a multitude of initiatives in the arts, business, health, and education. In every case, the premise is the same: when we harness the impulses of ego, we free up creativity and intelligence. Our institutions and communities become more alive and resilient. We are able to fully inhabit a world that is already transformational. We find ourselves present for that one-shot, straight-up reality from which there is no escape.

Susan Szpakowski is executive director of the Authentic Leadership in Action (ALIA) Institute, which convenes thought leaders and offers programming in the field of transformational leadership and systems change. ALIA programs include both formal mindfulness and meditation-in-action. Susan also is author of ALIA's *Little Book of Practice* and editor of *Speaking of Silence: Christians and Buddhists in Dialogue*. For more information, see http://www.aliainstitute.org.

| 10 |

Leadership as a Spiritual Practice

Vocation and Journey

Matthew Fox

The practice of cultivating awareness of the observing self that Szpakowski describes is necessary to fully realize the lessons from the next essay. In this piece, Matthew Fox explores the importance of seeing leadership as a sacred vocation and honoring archetypal paths on the leadership journey, each of which furthers comfort with essential elements of the process of transformation. These paths foster normal human journeys of personal development that help us have a positive, hopeful attitude, so important to promoting needed change; the ability to let go as the shifting sands of changing times require us to relinquish even things to which we are profoundly attached; the flexibility and creativity to promote continual innovation; and the capacity to inspire visions of a more just world that can lead to both group and whole-system transformation. Recognizing and naming these paths can normalize the growth needed in transformational times, thus decreasing people's resistance to change as they also develop essential leadership capacities. Other sections in this volume flesh out these paths. Indeed, the whole of Part One encourages what Fox calls Via Positiva, and the whole of Part Three, Via Transformativa. The essays in Part Two that follow illustrate in more detail Via Negativa and Via Creativa.

The failures of leadership are everywhere to be seen in the globe today. Whether one speaks of the failure of Wall Street tycoons and AWOL government regulators, the failure of the Catholic hierarchy (including the Vatican) in the pedophile priest scandals, the failure of legislators to free themselves of narrow ideologies and marriages to cynical power brokers, or the failure of Greek banks to operate wisely, we seem to be living through a deluge of the shadow side of leadership just as, with the Gulf oil disaster, we lived through months of gushing oil twenty-four hours a day, seven days per week. The darkness of this excessive yang energy (isn't oil all about powering our industries and transportation, thus yang and fire energy?) has damaged our yin resource (the Gulf waters, their teeming hatcheries and living systems of countless species).

Perhaps one underlying reason for all these failures is that we have secularized, that is to say desacralized, the very meaning of leadership. In my book *The Reinvention of Work*, I submit that all work worthy of the name, that is to say all work that brings joy, healing, justice, or celebration to others, is sacred work. When we do our work (as opposed to just our jobs), we are midwives of grace (Fox, 2004).

When I speak of the sacredness of work, I am speaking in a universal or archetypal language and drawing on the spiritual teachings of East and West, North and South (Fox, 2004). All healthy societies celebrate the sacredness of work. They often do this through emphasizing work as vocation, as a sacred calling (*vocare* is the Latin word for "call").

Call and Response

Leadership is one's own response to a call and it always includes the call and response of others. No one is called alone. It is a call from the ancestors and those not yet born, to be thoughtful, just, caring, courageous, imaginative, creative—that is, alive. The answer we give to the invitation to be a leader is everything. Work and leadership are our radical response to life itself; therefore, as I argue in my book on the nature of prayer, work is our very prayer (Fox, 2004). It is because we are giving the best of ourselves that we invest so much time preparing for (we call that education), recovering from (we usually call that weekends and holidays), and struggling at (our forty- to sixty-hour work weeks) our work.

Leadership and Vocation

The late poet, essayist, and teacher Bill Everson (also known as Brother Antoninus for his years as a Dominican friar) taught a course on the archetype of vocation at the University of Santa Cruz that for years was one of the most popular on campus. Thanks to interviews conducted by a former student, Steven Herrmann, we have access to his deep thoughts. Everson noted, "The human race cannot go forward unless vocations arise to constellate the collective energies into true realization. It is the race that creates the vocation. All an individual can do is answer the call" (quoted in Herrmann, 2009, p. 40).

The Call comes from some deep place. We might call it Destiny, or the Collective, or the Future, or God, or the Source. We are merely the responders. A leader is essentially humble. As Moses said to God, "Don't send me; I stutter." Humility is key to leadership because the Responder knows he or she is not the Caller.

Everson also teaches that vocations are both personal and collective in nature, pointing to the conscious and unconscious motivations inhering in the life span of the unique individual. The Call bridges at least two worlds, that of the conscious and that of the unconscious. This is what makes it deep. This is what makes it worth heeding. This also is what makes it daring. All leadership (as opposed to bureaucratic top-of-the-ladder hegemony) is an adventure, an exploration of the deep.

Everson defines vocation as a "disposition," a "calling," which holds the key to a person's identity. The vocational summons may come from a book, an outer situation, a relationship, or the laying on of hands by a master figure. I have a habit of asking scientists when they first knew they wanted to be a scientist. Invariably I hear stories such as, "I fell in love with the stars when I was five years old" or "I fell in love with a worm when I was six years old." Their vocations are seeded in childhood and they are about falling in love. One feels called; one feels the need to respond; one feels joyful.

Everson sees rites of passage, particularly the vision quest as practiced among indigenous peoples, as an important and effective recognition of this process. Unfortunately, today's rites of passage that we witness among gangs and in prisons where young people congregate have no invitation to vocation; they are leaderless (and elderless) rites of passage. They are the shadow side of the vocational archetype.

A powerful sign that one is responding to the call of one's vocation is synchronicity (or meaningful coincidences). Vocation is too sacred to occur just in linear time. Nor is it about chance alone. Nor is leadership primarily about career. It cannot be, for vocation and career are not synonymous. Says Everson:

> I distinguish between vocation and career. Vocation is the disposition, where your faculties are ordered. It has to do with your sense of identity; career is the impact of your vocation on your life, and on the world around you. A person may have a supreme vocation and no career at all. For some people, their careers don't occur until after they are dead. Gerard Manley Hopkins is an example of that. Emily Dickinson is another. Neither one published in their own lifetime; yet their work is as good as any. Neither Gerard nor Emily struggled with career; they ignored it; Emily more than Gerard. (quoted in Herrmann, 2009, p. 52)

In reflecting with William Everson on the archetype of vocation, we can summarize our findings in this way: a true vocation is always a call from the Sacred (a secular culture destroys vocation and crushes the young because it has no authentic rites of passage calling them into their vocation). Leaders are called to humility because they know that they did not invent their position of power but are called to employ it for the common good. The call is a deep call, bridging the worlds of the conscious and the unconscious but also of the deep personal identity and the needs of the entire species. This call evokes joy and it evokes pain. It brings about breakthrough or conversion. Thus, it includes violence or wildness, requiring surrender and courage, maturity, magnanimity, and generous individuation. It also requires sacrifice and solitude and leaving the masses at times.

Leadership is not ego driven; it is about service and helping one's coworkers as well as those yet to be born. It calls on the strength and wisdom of the ancestors as it operates as a cyclical, not a linear, process. It requires spiritual practices, including vision quests and rites of passage and deep grieving. Leadership is itself a school, a deep way of learning the most important lessons of life, including wisdom that always means embracing the feminine aspects of life and balancing the yin and yang, the feminine and the masculine. It announces and proclaims therefore the Sacred Marriage of the two in practice as well as theory (Fox, 2008, pp. 221–276).

The Four Paths of Creation Spirituality and Leadership

Having a sense of a vocation as a leader, however, is just the beginning. Leadership itself is both a spiritual practice and a journey. In my case, I had a call to the priesthood that then required me to be in a variety of leadership positions, both within and outside of the church. But first, some context for those who do not know my work.

In my scholarly work, I have demonstrated, first, that before the notion of original sin was introduced, the focus was on original blessing, so that Christianity was a positive, life-affirming, creation-affirming spiritual path—and it still is for many of us whose spirituality focuses on the blessings of creation and the grace of God. I then researched the lives of major Christian mystics. From this work I identified four major spiritual paths, which I later came to realize were actually archetypal mythical paths that also exist within other faiths. These four paths have come to provide the basis for living into a life-affirming, creation-affirming (that is, nature and human nature) spirituality.

Over what has been both a glorious and in some cases challenging journey as a leader, I've come to realize that for those for whom leadership is a spiritual vocation, these four paths also provide leadership journeys that assist us in deepening into our spiritual natures and also in being faithful to those natures in becoming forces for revealing the potential for heaven on earth. This understanding has provided me with humility in heady moments of success and comfort in times of pain and suffering.

The first of the paths of creation spirituality is the Via Positiva, the way of delight, awe, wonder, and joy (Fox, 2000). As a leader, what makes us happy? What calls us from joy to joy? How do we assist others in their journey to wonder, awe, and joy? How is our work affecting that result? Thomas Aquinas taught that "joy is the human's noblest act." Are we and our work and our leadership style engaged in humankind's noblest act? Does our leadership reflect the truth of joy as a bottom line? If not, why not? Aquinas also taught that people are changed more by delight than by argument. Is our leadership that kind of leadership? What joy do we derive from our role as leaders? Can we nourish joy more deeply? Give it more time and space?

Ultimately, leadership is a joy because it is a tremendous opportunity to serve, to bring truth and compassion into the world. Aquinas says the proper objects of the heart are truth and justice. Our work, our service, is to bring truth and justice into others' hearts. What vocation is more joyful than that?

The second path on our spiritual journeys is named the Via Negativa. This is the path of darkness and silence, of letting go and letting be, of grief and bottoming out. As Everson insisted, pain is a necessary part of the archetype of vocation. Pain carries us deep. Grief does that too if we allow it to. Grief can open us up, stir things up, and bring the best out of us. If we fail to grieve, we become bottled up and our creativity cannot flow properly.

Because the Via Negativa is also about silence, it is about letting go of all input and all projections. It is what we do when we meditate, however we choose to do so. It is calming the reptilian brain—the part of us that operates on an action/reaction response. A crocodile is win/lose. A leader who cannot calm his or her reptilian brain and help others to do the same is no leader at all but a carrier of an action/reaction virus that can kill us all and is killing the planet at this time—such as the response to 9/11 being an invasion of Iraq. A leader must find practices for letting go and letting be, for finding stillness and courting solitude. Reptiles respond to solitude. Thus, meditation practices calm the reptilian brain since they teach solitude.

This is how one develops one's mammal brain, from which we derive the powerful force so underutilized that we call compassion. By being in touch with one's own pain, one can share solidarity with others in pain—but only if one has learned to let go and let be. An emptying occurs in the Via Negativa. A deep power of listening emerges—a listening that encompasses both heart and head. Listening to one's deeper self, but also to others and to the needs of the times. Such deep listening is required of authentic leadership.

The third path on the spiritual journey is the Via Creativa. This is the path of imagination and creativity. Creativity flows ever so easily and organically from the first two paths: Those "ruptures" (Everson's word) that awe and love trigger (Via Positiva) and that silence and pain trigger (Via Negativa) give way to new birth. We are made for creativity. This is, after all, what distinguishes us as a species. Anthropologists define our species as distinct from our near relatives as bipeds that make things. We are makers. Authors. Creators. That is where the word "authority" comes from: our powers of authorship or creativity.

Only a leader who is creative and respectful of creativity—a hunter-gatherer of creativity, so to speak—can truly lead. This is especially true today, when so much in the world is new and requires new solutions. New networks. New alliances. New ideas. New directions for energy needs and for global interaction. New work. New healing. Newly understood connections with our ancestors and past efforts to live fully and peacefully on the earth.

Part of creativity is honoring the child, the *puer* or *puella* in oneself, being able to see the world newly, with freshness. There is no creativity without fantasy and play, as Jung observed. Playfulness, youthfulness are essential modes for survival and surely for leadership today. To honor and welcome the child within. To heal the child within. To unleash the child within. Work "without a why," Meister Eckhart advised. Then and only then do we enter the world of regeneration and renewal.

The fourth path on the spiritual journey is the Via Transformativa, the way of transformation and the way of compassion, celebrating, healing, and justice. Every leader worthy of the title strives for compassion. To teach it, to live it, to bring it alive. Compassion is, after all, the way of the mammal—both the Hebraic word and the Arabic word for compassion come from the word for "womb." The mammals, the womb people, bring compassion to the planet in a special way. There is a reason why all deep spiritual leaders—Buddha and Isaiah, Jesus and Muhammad, Black Elk and Martin Luther King Jr., Dorothy Day and Mother Teresa—call us to compassion. We can do away with all religion, but not with compassion. The Dalai Lama confesses that compassion is his religion. Jesus said: "Be you compassionate like your Creator in heaven is compassionate." (Luke 6.36). In Islam, "The Compassionate One" is by far the most-used name for Allah in the Koran. Compassion is the "secret name for God" in Judaism.

Compassion is about solidarity, "passion-with." It is about our shared joy and our shared sorrow. It is all about our interdependence. Living it out, it manifests as celebration (our shared joy) and as healing (our shared pain). All true leaders work on their powers of compassion, and their decision making derives from that place deep inside themselves. Authentic leadership today is more about "dancing Sara's circle" than about "climbing Jacob's ladder." Ladder climbing is rarely joyful; it is elitist and vertical; it separates one from earth and others. Circle dancing, on the other hand, is eye-to-eye, curved, embracing of others, close to the earth, and joy-filled, playful.

Which path of leadership is compassionate? Which is elitist? Which do we strive for? (Fox, 1999). Eckhart warns that "compassion begins at home with one's own body and one's own soul." (p. 105). Leaders must be compassionate toward themselves and must find time and space for their own inner life and physical well-being. A leader is not a superman or superwoman. A leader needs coworkers, co-helpers, colleagues. Friendships. Mentors.

Knowing that leadership itself carries one through the four paths of creation spirituality is to know that the call and work of leadership is itself a spiritual practice, a yoga, a discipline for one's inner work and one's outer work, for oneself and for the collective, a work that taps into conscious and unconscious, personal and communal. To be a leader is to journey through these four paths on a regular basis. The challenges of leadership, whether positive or negative, break us open and we are reminded of Eckhart's promise, "the outward work can never be small if the inward work is great, and the outward work can never be great or good if the inward is small or of little worth. The inward work always includes in itself all size, all breadth and all length" (Fox, 2004, p. 58). Psyche and cosmos marry. The personal journey becomes the community's journey and all are part of the cosmic journey.

What a noble journey we are on. What a noble calling. What generosity is called for. What an opportunity. To inspire others to the greatness of their work, both inner and outer. And to show the way by entering into the journey ourselves. To listen and answer the call for our own vocation. Such a vocation tastes like milk and honey. It ushers us into the Promised Land. We are grateful. The leader in us is grateful. Perhaps it is in this context that Meister Eckhart exclaims, "if the only prayer you say in your whole life is 'Thank You,' that would suffice" (Fox, 2011, p. 52). Gratitude reigns. This is evidence that our work is sacred, not profane. Spiritual, not secular. Meaningful, not meaningless.

Matthew Fox, PhD, is author of twenty-nine books on spirituality and culture that have won many awards. They include *Original Blessing, The Reinvention of Work, Creativity, The Hidden Spirituality of Men, Christian Mystics,* and *The Pope's War.* He created a highly successful educational model thirty years ago and founded and was president of the University of Creation Spirituality, which he ran for nine rich years. He has since applied that proven pedagogy to inner-city high school students with promising programs in Oakland and Chicago. He is the recipient of the Abbey Peace and Conscience Award and shares that honor with others such as Rosa Parks, Mother Teresa, and the Dalai Lama.

| 11 |

Transmuting Suffering

A Leadership and Advising Perspective

Arthur Colman and Éliane Ubalijoro

Fox's idea of Via Negativa is reflected in learning from experiences that require us to let go of things we believe define who we are or that we think are necessary for our happiness. This path helps us develop the capacity to grieve and still function, which is needed if you are to confront nonstop change—or even the horrendous loss, victimization, or scapegoating leaders sometimes face. Having skilled and empathetic confidants and advisors can help us to heal and find the positive learning from whatever we experience, as well as from our own less than noble impulses. This daunting task of facing your own shadow, and the shadow in the world, is the subject of the next essay, by Arthur Colman and Éliane Ubalijoro.

Transformative leadership, especially in the context of collective trauma and suffering, is fraught with difficulty, inevitably blending positive intent with negative power issues. Leaders in these situations need the largest possible perspective to inform their goals and actions. A partnership with a trusted advisor whose ego is less involved and whose vision is therefore more capacious is of inestimable value.

The advisor-advisee relationship takes many forms. Our interest is in the leader-advisor relationship in which the focus of leadership is on healing and transforming past and present trauma in a collective. Our premise is that leaders and their advisors need to move toward a wider consciousness, which requires new strategies to match the changing problems and opportunities of the twenty-first century.

We emphasize a process that encompasses an amalgam of insight, reflection, support, and personal and collective development, all through a perspective of love and healing. It is a mode of interactive work emphasizing reflection and insight focused on the analysand's personal development and includes the analyst's own feelings and experience. It is carried out in a carefully bounded relationship, which usually precludes direct help or instruction.

The Developmental Roots of Leaders

Suffering, vulnerability, and fear have profound effects in shaping leadership styles and directions. In the movie *Invictus* (Eastwood & Peckham, 2009), we witness the reenactment of a dialogue between Nelson Mandela and Francois Pienaar, two leaders of vastly different age and experience, one leading a nation out of apartheid and the other leading a rugby team that hosted the 1995 Rugby World Cup. Here is their conversation:

> *NM.* Tell me Francois, what is your philosophy on leadership? How do you inspire your team to do their best?
>
> *FP.* By example. I've always thought to lead by example, sir.
>
> *NM.* Well that is right, that is exactly right, but how to get them to be better than they think they can be? That is very difficult I find.
>
> *FP.* Inspiration perhaps.
>
> *NM.* How do we inspire ourselves to greatness when nothing less will do? How do we inspire everyone around us? I sometimes think it is by using the work of others. On Robben Island, when things got very bad, I found inspiration in a poem.
>
> *FP.* A poem?
>
> *NM.* A Victorian poem, just words but they helped me to stand when all I wanted to do was to lie down. But you didn't come to hear an old man talk about things that make no sense.
>
> *FP.* No please, Mr. President, it makes complete sense to me. On the day of a big match, say a test, in the bus on the way to the stadium, nobody talks.
>
> *NM.* Ah yes, they are all preparing.

FP. Right.

FP. But when I think we're ready, I have the bus driver put [on] a song, something I've chosen, one we all know, and we listen to the words together and it helps.

NM. I remember when I was invited to the Olympics in Barcelona. Everyone in the stadium greeted me with a song. At the time the future, our future seemed very bleak, but to hear that song and the voices of people all over our planet made me proud to be South African. It inspired me to come home and do better. It allowed me to expect more of myself.

FP. May I ask what was the song, sir?

NM. Well, it was "Nkosi sikelel' iAfrika."

FP. A very inspiring song.

NM. We need inspiration, Francois. Because in order to build our nation, we must all exceed our own expectations. (Eastwood & Peckham, 2009)

Their mutual goal is to open the inner space of their countrymen and women through a more open consciousness and knowledge of their interconnectedness, a fundamental principle of African Ubuntu philosophy, to move away from a consciousness of polarity toward unification and toward a common goal that transcends apartheid, a "third thing" (Montero & Colman, 2000). The third thing transcends ego, crossing to a stage (which Jung [1963] describes as the third conjunction) in which individuation culminates in living one's truth in and through the world (Colman, 1997).

The men confront the obstacles from the world of depth and unconsciousness by practicing vision making together. Poetry, song, and sports take the dialogue beyond egos to a place of higher purpose and create images and feelings that unite all South Africans, a nation heretofore symbolizing oppression and subjugation, and create a glimpse of what a healed and integrated whole society could look like.

Overcoming painful experience is often an entryway into leadership. We come to trust leaders like Mandela, Roosevelt, or Gandhi who have known profound physical and social pain as well as fear. Leaders with profound personal experience of trauma must evolve through a "counterphobic stage" in which fear and pain are first denied, then "mastered." But a "counterphobic leader," however well adapted, carries the history of victimization, which may include a substrate of anger and the need for revenge, which may emerge in times of stress. Advising such leaders requires reflective techniques that focus on helping individuals gain a great deal of self-knowledge. The fruits of this hard-won self-knowledge can then be brought into the collective. The advisor can help the leader identify the roles projected onto him or her and help amplify those that are best suited in collective interactions to achieve change.

Advising as a form of healing taps into the core energy akin to biological rites of passage, mirroring in the social collective our species's evolutionary needs. As Eric Kacou, a strategist who works with leaders from postconflict nations, suggests, at organizational, societal, and national levels, preconditions for change formulated by his colleague Michael Fairbanks are needed: moral purpose, tension, receptivity to change, and new insight. Kacou (2009) stated, "When . . . these conditions are not met, wrong choices are made, and meaningful change is unlikely. Furthermore, prosperity-inducing change remains elusive, and leaders alienate themselves from their industries and political base" (p. 249) and, most important, from themselves. The touchstone for transformation is always at the individual/collective interface.

The Archetype of the Scapegoat in Working with Leaders

Prometheus, an ancient Titan god, stole fire from Zeus and gave it to humans. Enraged, Zeus created Pandora to bring misfortune to mankind and punished Prometheus by having him bound to a rock while a great eagle ate his liver. When leaders are involved in transforming a system (bringing fire to humans would certainly qualify), it is rare for them or their followers to emerge unscathed, as with Nelson Mandela, spending much of his early life in prison for challenging the oppressive system of apartheid. As in this situation, the mythic figure of the scapegoat is frequently in play, illustrated by the torture of Prometheus as well as the fate of humans facing the dark mischief released from Pandora's box. The story of Prometheus and his powerful gift is also that of Joan of Arc, Jesus, Gandhi, Martin Luther King Jr., and many less deified transformational leaders maligned and venerated for their work.

The experience of being scapegoated taps into a primal human fear of being exiled from the group, which in many times in human history could result in death. Indeed, if the scapegoat is not exiled, he or she is likely to be sacrificed—if not literally killed—fired from a job, or dismissed from a position or suddenly persona non grata. At the very least we experience being mirrored by those around us in negative ways, threatening our basic sense of goodness and worth. Surviving this requires tapping into some deeper core identity and value. In finding an inner treasure of strength and resilience, we may also find the font of our inner creative imagination that can serve us ever after.

Leaders whose ideas and policies have significant impact are myth makers filled with our projections for a better life, who, like Prometheus, bring fire: a new technology, ethos, and esprit to us. But they also bring fear, for change carries with it instability and the risk of failure inherent in implementing new and innovative models.

In the alchemical classification of the four elements—fire, water, earth, and air—fire is the great transformer. Bringing fire to a system metaphorically describes one of the key functions and defining characteristics of transformational leadership. Unlike a "catalytic" leader, who provides an essentially unreactive surface on which a chemical reaction takes place but in which he or she is unchanged by the reaction, the Promethean "fire bringer" leader ignites and alters the reaction while being transformed by it. Advising such a leader requires knowledge of the leader's role and fate in the process of transformation, the archetype of the scapegoat.

Leaders of complex systems, where change and development are needed and the archetype of the scapegoat therefore looms, may benefit more from deep reflection and challenge rather than support and positive feedback. This is especially true for those who know their own competence, have already achieved a great deal, and want to learn more about themselves in relation to their organizations and work career.

The advisor must ask the leader to evaluate change and risk. Do they want to understand more, to develop further, and to leap beyond the known inner and outer worlds? Are they satisfied with the status quo and their current level of functioning and success, or do they want their leadership efforts to touch and change the world?

To find a psychic center, the leader and the advisor need to stand together at the crossroads of an enterprise, intent on bringing the inner and outer worlds of the leader's mandate together. What is required is a reborn connection with the collective, an attitude that embraces that which is difficult to say and difficult to hear, and therefore includes the risk of becoming a scapegoat by bringing the Promethean fire close enough to feel its heat. We see more than enough evidence around us that truth doing is a dangerous path to take, often leading to personal isolation and collective chaos. But there is also pervasive proof of the life-numbing risk of not living one's truth. It is present in depressed faces, physical illness, dead relationships, and unrealized potential and creativity.

If we identify scapegoating as the collective analogy to ignoring the shadow in the individual, then bringing the scapegoating process to the surface is a powerful way to heal society. We need to recognize what we have scapegoated and repressed in ourselves and bring it to the light of day before we can effectively become a healing force for those who have been oppressed. This requires facing the depths of our own pain, suffering, and victimhood so that we can also face that of others, while adding a balm of curiosity, compassion, and passion. Without that, the practice of leadership becomes a cruel and sterile experiment rather than a place to rekindle spirit for enlightened leadership.

It is the advisor's role to create a safe and sacred space that diminishes the desire for flight and helps the leader without invoking a relationship that fosters dependence. The advisor must be able to hold the largest point of view separating herself from the leader's personal goals and conscious desires. This impersonal perspective helps leaders guard against the inevitable psychic bombardment of expectation and dependency, and the development of psychic inflation that leads toward the scapegoat/messiah complex.

Music, art, dreams, travel, fantasies, vision, and relationships facilitate intersections with large non-ego and collective forces that define individuation in the world. When playing, singing, or listening with transformational intent to Brahms's *German Requiem* or Mozart's Mass in C, for example, some of us will enter sacred space and the "death and rebirth archetype" and emerge transformed. When we interact with this third thing with that intent, when we join with it, shape it, play it, and sing it, we can enter the realm of ecstatic transformation. It is a place of passion, where pain can be transcended.

Going from the personal task of embracing one's own light and shadow to becoming a vessel for whatever the universe wants to accomplish through us requires deep work and the presence of another. Here the advisor's role is critical, for the personal and collective risks are considerable. As advisors to leaders, we must ask ourselves: Can we stay in deep awareness watching our own light and shadow dance? Can we inspire leaders and followers who look to us to do the same for them?

Perspectives of Love and Healing in an Era of Global Interdependence

In an era of globalization, when a crisis in one part of the world reverberates in so many places, overcoming trauma through compassionate understanding is central to effective leadership. When healing enters the realm of transformation, the transcendent catalyst of the third thing is needed to engender deep change of personality and profound shifts in life goals and ways of being with oneself and in the world. The process of leaders and advisors investing in themselves and their dialogue to strengthen this "muscle" and decrease their isolation is essential for positive growth.

Leaders learning about their inner self and owning their personal truth goes hand in hand with turning these self-reflections toward their organizations and communities. It goes beyond team building to untouched depths inside the group that are usually guarded but can be opened up by going through crisis with a guide that keeps the free space safe. Advisors feel the need to help and inevitably, the temptation to participate. The advisor needs to find an ethical center from a different perspective and build on a variety of techniques (e.g., attending to countertransference, strict ethical boundaries with the outside world) as the process makes demands on the relationship.

This stage involves "the integration of the unique and distinct elements of the individual with the collective so that both are served." Beyond the loneliness of being a leader and the desire to be of service to a greater collective even when we feel alienated from it, a space needs to be bridged. The leader's knowledge of this is critical. When the deepest and most grounded spiritual vision is married to a practical and pragmatic drive to transform all existing political, economic, and social institutions, a holy force—the power of wisdom and love in action—is born. Andrew Harvey (2008) calls this Sacred Activism.

In this phase the advisor's work is critical. It must include more than techniques designed to help leaders with their fears and shadows. It must include helping with their vision as it connects to the larger society. The role extends beyond the boundaries of coaching/consulting or therapy into a deep analysis of the world of reflection and action. It is not simply about inner or outer development; it is about the interface of the individual and collective. Then what is learned between leader and advisor is taken out into the world and lived.

Journeying to the Heart of Change in Society and in Leadership

The rejected parts of ourselves, our shadows, are eventually projected onto our leaders. It is easier to give these negative parts to the leader than hold them ourselves. We also project onto leaders parts of ourselves that seem too grand and wonderful to fit into our view of ourselves or that we repress because we know that people who seem to be too powerful or wise can evoke envy and resentment and thus be dangerous. Often the best among us are actually killed, from Christ to Gandhi or Martin Luther King Jr. It is no wonder, then, that we want others to act as saviors, saving us from taking on the danger of experiencing the scapegoat's fate.

Leaders who understand this dynamic use our guilt and relief at their acceptance of these projections (as the villain who enacts the shameful things we want or the savior who frees us from difficulty) to advance their cause. It increases their charisma and influence for good and bad. But few leaders are sufficiently developed to hold these projections and still be of service to the hearts and healing of the collective. Here the trusted and trustable advisor is a critical catalyst and firewall to the challenges of leadership.

The advisor is also critical to helping move the leader to be able to admit mistakes without bringing on fear, debilitating remorse, or paranoid censure of others. Such acceptance is necessary to allow solutions to emerge without blame or entitlement. When leaders function at this level, they touch the sacred in depth work. But entering the sacred attracts both light and dark forces, and differentiating and integrating these polarities is difficult even for the most experienced leaders. That is why the enlightened leader must not be alone as he cultivates this inner reflection and integration.

In the broken world we live in, leaders are called to be the aperture through which the light shines. The phenomenal existentialist Gabriel Marcel guides us to see the world as a mystery instead of problems we need to solve. He states: "a mystery is something in which I am myself involved, and it can therefore only be thought of as a sphere where the distinction between what is in me and what is before me loses its meaning and initial validity" (Marcel, 1935/1949, p. 117). With this attitude, intent, and perspective, we open our hearts to a new kind of leadership where our personal development serves societal transformation. Only then will we give leaders the complex set of assets needed to face the daunting tasks of the twenty-first century.

Arthur Colman is a Harvard-educated physician, psychiatrist, and author; currently a Jungian analyst in Sausalito, California; and professor of psychiatry at UCSF School of Medicine. His books, which include *Earth Father/Sky Father: The Changing Concept of Fathering* (Prentice Hall, 1981), *Up from Scapegoating: Awakening Consciousness in Groups* (Chiron, 1995), and *Group Relations Reader* (A. K. Rice Institute), have sold more than half a million copies worldwide and have been translated into many languages, including German, Spanish, French, Portuguese, and Chinese. He has consulted on issues of scapegoating, revenge, and reconciliation in South Africa, Israel, Brazil, Mexico, Canada, and the United States.

Éliane Ubalijoro is an adjunct professor of practice for public and private sector partnerships at McGill University's Institute for the Study of International Development (ISID). Dr. Ubalijoro currently is designing ISID's Executive Leadership Initiative, an upcoming program to help equip executives in international development with tools that support inner and outer sustainable transformation toward global prosperity. Dr. Ubalijoro is the founder and executive director of C.L.E.A.R. International Development Inc., a consulting group harnessing global networks for sustainable systems development. She is a member of the Presidential Advisory Council for Rwandan President Paul Kagame.

| 12 |

Shapeshifter Leadership

Responding Creatively to the Challenges of a Complex World

Carol Burbank

By not mincing words about what often is required of leaders seeking to make a major difference in the world, Ubalijoro and Colman provide a balance to the positive thrust of the essays in Part One. If you have experienced Via Negativa and learned from it, you have confronted what is best and worst in yourself and in the world, and you are neither in denial nor overly fearful that you are incapable of facing whatever comes. Moreover, you know who you are in your wholeness, as you have ventured into your unconscious as well as your conscious mind. This means you do not have to hold onto roles and static ideas limiting who you are, or what you can do or be, thus gaining the flexibility to respond to what is required of you by new challenges. When you accomplish this, you are ready for Via Creativa. The final essay in this section, by Carol Burbank, provides examples of game-changing innovation and describes how, through integrating the qualities of the shapeshifter archetype, you can demonstrate a capacity for creativity and innovation.

As a species, as nations, as communities and individuals, we are moving into the twenty-first century ungrounded by the loose and chaotic world of developing technologies, shifting global influence, waning and waxing tides of capitalism and reform, and startling transformations in the environment and resources of our planet. We are at a turning point of survival and discovery, collectively confronting a moment when the old models of identity are up for grabs, and new models are still forming.

Innovation is required, as well as the ability to be flexible, to fill many roles without taking any one role so seriously that we get locked into its rules and limitations. Today's creative leaders must work hard, and work with a twist. In addition to facing anomalies or unexpected problems with enthusiasm and tough-skinned robustness (Gardner, 2006), leaders need to move freely into many positions within and outside a problem as they reframe and challenge rigid limitations to the solutions.

A good example of the innovative leader is Steve Jobs's work at Apple Computer. He structured his organization more like a think tank than a conventional office, rewarding and branding innovation and exploration in its workforce and its products. Beck and Cowan (1996) describe this as the "wild duck pond," the "play pen," or "the wizard's treehouse" (pp. 191–192) model of organizational culture, activating individualism and boundary crossing to the extreme. Such an organization reframes questions and problems so that what needs adapting, strengthening, and discarding becomes clear. Innovation becomes a norm, not a tactic for problem solving. The products Apple creates reflect this culture; they do not merely repackage old models or correct problems in whatever version preceded the newest application. They reimagine the interface between computers and people, shifting the ways we connect and anticipating new networks of people, not machines.

Another example of out-of-the-box innovation, this time reframing conventional wisdom about good economics, is offered by 2006 Nobel Prize winner and economist Muhammed Yunus (2010), pioneer of a new kind of banking known as microlending. His Grameen Bank grants small loans to poor people who would never be considered by traditional banks. Ninety-six percent of them are women (individuals and groups) who receive an average of $200 per loan, usually to develop a small business idea. Although Yunus is not the only lender focusing on microloans, the Nobel recognition identifies him as a leader in this innovative and world-changing practice, both economically practical for the bank and empowering for its clients, who have an opportunity to become leaders in their own communities. With a default rate of less than 2 percent, and records of business concepts spreading virally beyond the local innovation funded, microloans are proven leadership tools. Yunus broke all the "commonsense" rules of late capitalist economics to build this success:

> If the banks lent to the rich, I lent to the poor. If banks lent to men, I lent to women. If banks required collateral, my loans were collateral free. If banks required a lot of paperwork, my loans were illiterate friendly. If you had to go to the bank, my bank went to the village. (Lovgren, 2006, Preventing War section, para. 2)

A powerful voice in the development of community-based, innovative economic practices he calls "social business," Yunus (2010) offers a business model that values creativity and usefulness over profit and dividends, and persuasively reimagines the source and result of business success as joy.

There are many other innovators who surprise and expand our consciousness and community, whose work and organizations transform not only the world's commercial and social structure but also our expectations for the future. Leaders who ask "what if?" and "why not?" are the most valuable leaders in times of crisis and transition. These leaders are the ones we need most on our problem-solving teams, and yet they are also the ones we find most difficult. They not only see the "truth" differently than we do, but require us to be different, despite our "commonsense" habits, assumptions, and expectations. Sometimes that shift from habit to alertness feels painful, but it is required for survival.

How do we define this kind of leadership? Why is it so often difficult to understand or tolerate this level of creativity and innovation? How can we successfully include radical innovators on our teams and teach ourselves to find creative innovation in our own leadership? I believe the answer to all three of these questions is in the archetypal role-play of the shapeshifter, a kind of trickster-leader, with three core qualities: an ability to perceive the global cultural challenge with a broader vision for change that often looks like disrespect or foolishness; a creative mobility that often is expressed as amusement at habitual limitations and hierarchies; and the flexibility to take on many roles and therefore see many sides of a question, often misinterpreted as inauthenticity or "flip-flopping."

In archetypal terms, the shapeshifter is able to move effectively in many worlds and see farther than most, an almost shamanic figure. The word "shaman" may seem strange in a business context, but the role is about mastery of many worlds for the higher good of a community or organization. The shamanic trickster is a master in the dance of change, mature and flexible, a positive if sometimes irreverent force on any team. The archetype of the trickster, in its less developed, shadow manifestation (greedy thief, sexual predator), obviously is not the pattern I am advocating here. Cruel and invasive greed, as represented by the voracious Coyote, is unfortunately familiar from recent financial scandals. Because of the easily confused terms, I refer to the higher aspect of the trickster, the shapeshifter.

Activating the higher values of the trickster's playfulness, flexibility, and appetite for change, the shapeshifter leader acts out of curiosity, not greed, and therefore finds solutions that benefit the common good rather than his own shortsighted agenda. A higher-level shaman/shapeshifter such as Helen Keller's teacher Annie Sullivan demonstrates the liberating power of breaking the patterns that limit our perceptions. Sullivan changed the way Keller lived and learned, from an enraged and caged wild thing to an articulate and learned human being, ultimately giving her the tools to become an influential educator and public intellectual. Sullivan's greatest gift to Keller (and the world) was her curiosity: What if she did it differently? What if she tricked Helen into learning? So tricked into learning, Keller became a force to be reckoned with, a shaman leader in her own right.

Such curiosity is the key to long-term solutions to our complex global problems, when we sometimes seem as frustrated and inarticulate as Keller. Keller became curious about the world and its powers, and listened not only to the men and women she encountered, but also to her dreams, in which she could see and hear. Of her dreams, Keller (1903) later wrote: "Perhaps they are the ghosts of thoughts that once inhabited the mind of an ancestor. At other times the things I have learned and the things I have been taught, drop away, as the lizard sheds its skin" (Kindle ed., 5006–5008). The shapeshifter leader offers his wider (and sometimes wilder) vision to open up new possibilities in complex times.

Physicists today acknowledge that "complexity is the nature of things" (Tippett, 2010, p. 25). Since complexity is the playground of change, the shapeshifter leader can be of great service as we seek to find our way. Now is the time to open up our leadership habits and values to include an appreciation of the possibilities in chaos and embrace the shape-shifter leader as an essential member of our internal life and our external leadership teams.

> Even if we are not aware of any inner need for transformation, our outer world is changing so dramatically that we will not be able to remain as we have been. Today our workplaces are in transition. We are "reinventing" government. Most of the organizations we work for are in the process either of metamorphosis or dying. . . . Transitional moments are dangerous, disorienting, and full of opportunities for magic. (Pearson & Seivert, 1995, pp. 5–6)

Psychologist Carl Jung (1976) wrote: "The upheaval of our world and the upheaval of our consciousness are one and the same. Everything has become relative, and therefore doubtful" (p. 471). In the face of transformation experienced as upheaval, most of us long for clear solutions and organizations that foster a sense of stability and familiarity. We want to be empowered, but often we yearn to be protected. In *The Political Mind*, George Lakoff (2009) argues that this paradox is more than psychological—it is our political and social experience, expressed in oppositions and primary metaphors that become comfortable even on the neural or cellular level. These patterns translate into concepts of morality, economics, identity, community, and values.

For example, the metaphor "survival of the fittest" justifies a range of behaviors in Western business practices. Yunus's model of joy, not competition, is radical because it challenges that metaphor and requires a social entrepreneur to develop intimate community connection rather than disconnect into the individualist, stereotypic "rat race." Lakoff's work demonstrates the need for the courage to challenge these apparent certainties and metaphors embedded in our communities, organizations, and laws, in order to find solutions that help us work together.

If we cannot step outside the metaphors that unconsciously frame our daily human practices in old paradigms, then we may not be able to survive the upheavals we face today. The shapeshifter leader's gift is to make these narratives conscious and their application visible, challenging the polarized and contradictory simplicities that block our understanding of the world's complexity.

> Leadership is about change, moving people in new directions, realizing a new vision, or simply doing things differently or better. Change, in turn, involves deeply rooted values. These are the ideas and commitments—about oneself, about others, and about one's work—that people cling to based on faith and conviction. It is in large measure because of these values that significant change is almost always accompanied by emotional turmoil. (Denhardt & Denhardt, 2006, p. 8)

There is a passionate yearning for more authentic leaders who can guide and empower followers through this turmoil—leaders who are willing to examine their own lives and internal values, acknowledge their failures, and create a vision that moves followers to meaningful solutions, consistently modeling core values like service, integrity, and compassion. (Avolio & Gardner, 2005; Avolio, Gardner, Walumbwa, Luthans, & May, 2004; Endrissat, Muller, & Kaudela-Baum, 2007; Gardner, 2006; Gardner, Avolio, Luthans, May, & Walumbwa, 2005; Gardner, Fischer, & Hunt, 2009; George, 2003, 2007; Kouzes & Posner, 1995). Yet authenticity must not be limited by our yearning for guidance and stability. Shapeshifter authenticity acknowledges the multiplicity and flexibility of the identities we carry. A rigid stance grounded in consistency rather than creative flow offers a false security that limits innovation.

In the face of global warming, reduced natural resources, and nationalist conflict, we, as leaders, must embrace our shapeshifting abilities to innovate. We need to pay attention to the diversity of roles available within ourselves and in our organizations. These can guide us into an integrated implementation of the "great public values" James McGregor

Burns (2003) calls for. To reach a full expression of those values, we must acknowledge the physical and psychological power of narratives, "brain structures that we can live out, recognize in others, and imagine" (Lakoff, 2009, p. 93). Then we can tap into the diverse archetypal resources we all carry, with varying skills and awareness, activating the holographic and dynamic process of becoming fully human, and therefore able to be present to the challenges of our century.

The final key to understanding the power of the shapeshifter is understanding the concept of liminality. *Liminality* is the space between certainties, often understood in anthropology as the doorway between childhood and adulthood or a ritual space that carries us from one identity or role into another. It is not a comfortable space for most people, because it contains within it the uncertainties of initiation and the necessity of transformation. In a liminal space and time we have the opportunity to let go of who we were, but we are not yet who we might become. We move through the unknown facing freedom and anxiety in equal measure.

The part of us that can hold both freedom and anxiety without shutting down is energized by the shapeshifter archetype. Lewis Hyde (1998) notes that the shapeshifter, in mythology and in the ordinary world, thrives in "relationship to other powers, to people and institutions and traditions that can manage the odd double attitude of both insisting that their boundaries be respected and recognizing that in the long run their liveliness depends on having these boundaries regularly disturbed" (p. 12). Everyone has this capacity to some degree, but some people are natural, mature shapeshifters. I believe they are a neglected resource in our organizations and communities.

In practical terms, tapping this resource means inviting the shapeshifter into our organizations, making a place for change within so there can be positive change in relationship to new global conditions. Consider:

• How many times have we let ourselves be pleasantly surprised by the so-called dark horse team member, who reframes a question to transform a debate, who demonstrates a skill no one would

have expected, who creates a program that solves six problems,
several of which we had given up on solving?

- How many organizations make space for the risk-taking voice, the
  shamanic visionary who makes everyone laugh at the simplicity
  of a solution, once limiting assumptions have been lifted away to
  support clear innovation?
- How many of us have left organizations because our innovative
  visions, our ability to play many roles, has been punished rather
  than welcomed, and then seen the company we left stagnate or
  struggle?

It is time for organizations to create a place for the shapeshifter, the
master of change, who shakes things up for the highest good of the
community, activating the best of everyone while shifting the stories,
patterns, and expectations that keep us in our boxes.

The advantage of teaming up with the shapeshifter is that our boundaries are, with or without them, already being disturbed by the in-
between conditions of contemporary life. We are changing, whether we
want to or not. The shapeshifter, innately comfortable with that lively
disturbance, is a natural if irreverent guide. "Clown and creator, gift
giver and thief . . . [the shapeshifter] mocks and disrupts convention,
order and preconception, full of irreverent vitality and creativity, [em-
bodying] the life-giving power of the human imagination, . . . [and
marking him] as a world maker" (Combs & Holland, 2001, pp. 87–88).
In a chaotic time, with our identities being unmade and remade daily,
we need this model of flexibility to support our own imaginative world
making.

In his conscious, highest manifestation, a shapeshifter leader uses his
or her cleverness to solve not only problems no one perceived, but also
those no one thought solvable. Alexander Fleming observed the antibi-
otic potential of mold and opened the door to bring penicillin into scientific testing and production. Odwalla's juice engineers, spurred by an
outbreak of *E. coli* in its nutritious, unpasteurized apple juice, created a
process called flash pasteurization that preserves nutrients while puri-
fying food, saving the company and contributing a new standard in

the organic food market. With the shapeshifter leader, the old cliché becomes true again: challenges really are opportunities.

Many business, education, and political leaders acknowledge the need for shapeshifter flexibility. Max De Pree (1995), CEO of Herman Miller, Inc., notes that leaders today need to embrace the improvisational idea of "leadership jazz," collaborations that build on musical playfulness and "combine the unpredictability of the future with the gifts of individuals" (De Pree, 1995, p. 453). McFarland, Senn, and Childress's (1995) research into the "Changing Game" of leadership defines twenty-first-century leadership as "mastery over change, which goes beyond merely reacting to change as it comes up, but rather predicting and redirecting change before it comes up" (p. 459). They argue that we are living in an increasingly holistic era, and need to develop a diversity of skills, perspectives, and approaches within ourselves and our organizations, and ask "Am I a leader in a big enough game?" (McFarland et al., 1995, p. 463). Shapeshifter leaders understand the word "game" as a metaphor that invites play and invention. Howard Gardner (2006) calls this flexibility

> the creating mind . . . which breaks new ground, . . . puts forth new ideas, poses unfamiliar questions, conjures up fresh ways of thinking, arrives at unexpected answers. . . . By virtue of its anchoring in territory that is not yet rule-governed, the creating mind seeks to remain at least one step ahead. (p. 47)

Shapeshifter leadership celebrates the why not, invents a way as it goes, breaks the rules that need breaking, and integrates innovation into a new framework that expands old ways of knowing and being. This improvisational force empowers roles and relationships that strengthen our ability to innovate. In order to prevent a poverty of options, we need to consciously embrace archetypes that help us build a holistic leadership practice. The shapeshifter archetype is one of the most valuable we have to support this development and give joy to our dance with change.

Better to dance with the highest manifestation of the shapeshifter than to stumble forward, blinded by our habits and assumptions. Shapeshifter leaders mirror and master the complex conditions we face in the world, taking their authenticity from a process of being that is rooted not in a stable story of self but in a process of becoming, nurturing our evolution as a species. They show us a natural way to navigate change—by claiming the power of making the world from a position of flexibility and strength. With the help of the shapeshifter, we can learn to innovate, playfully, so we can face the serious task before us. We might just thrive.

Carol Burbank, PhD, is president of Storyweaving Coaching and Consulting, building holistic and creative leadership development programs and supporting organizational change. She teaches interdisciplinary and blended learning at Pacifica Graduate Institute, in the Engaged Humanities MA program. She has served as faculty for Union Institute and University's interdisciplinary PhD program (Leadership Area) and the University of Northern Virginia's International MBA program in mainland China, and was a senior fellow in the James MacGregor Burns Academy of Leadership at the University of Maryland, College Park. She has published in *Business Leadership Review,* International Leadership Association publications, *Women and Performance, Indigenous Issues and Culture,* the *Philadelphia Inquirer,* and other newspapers. For more information, see http://www.storyweaving. com/creativeleadershipconsulting.html.

PART THREE

THE ART OF WORKING WITH AND TRANSFORMING GROUPS

Setting the Context for Part Three

Shifting Perspectives on Inner/Outer Connectivity

The very nature of leadership demands the capacity to influence individuals, groups, and organizations to achieve transformational ends. Part Three explores how the thinking described in Part One and ways of being described in Part Two result in transforming how, and how well, we exercise such leadership. Indeed, leadership becomes easier when we change our stance toward those we lead and let go of the idea of the leader as directing the action from above and causing people to act, as if they are without volition.

The transforming vision of the twenty-first century calls us to understand that we are part of the complex adaptive systems that we are trying to transform. Moreover, because we and the world are forever in a state of flux, we can let go of the heroic illusion that we need to exert incredible effort to compel other people and social systems to change. Indeed, the requisite effort may be more like diverting the course of a ball rolling down a hill than struggling to push a huge boulder up it—or even to get the boulder moving at all.

Furthermore, when we have learned to commit fully to our own callings and vocations, as the essays in Part Two encourage, our entire

151

relationship to the outer world shifts, moving us beyond an us-versus-the-world point of view to recognizing a mysterious connection between the state of our consciousness and what happens. Drawing on the work of Jung, Peter Senge (1996) explains, "when we are in a state of commitment and surrender, we begin to experience what is sometimes called 'synchronicity'" (p. 88). This surrender is to the natural processes of life and to the unfolding of our true nature, vocation, and calling. In Senge's view, when you stop fighting your genuine relationship to the whole and trust its emergent unfolding, meaningful coincidences (i.e., synchronous events) happen.

I have personally experienced the reality of this notion of synchronicity. One example during the course of my own leadership journey particularly grabbed my attention. Over the winter break two years ago, I was journaling about my values, listening for what inner guidance might arise. I found myself writing about how I wanted to support depth psychological perspectives in the world. But I did not share this new commitment with anyone or make an effort to act on it. Shortly afterward, I received a call from a search firm asking if I was interested in being interviewed for the position of executive vice president and provost at Pacifica—a graduate school whose mission is to support depth psychology and mythology scholarship and education. The recognition of the match between my inner desire and a surprising outer opportunity eventually led to my accepting the job. It also enabled me to avoid what, unbeknownst to me, would turn out to be a less supportive situation at the University of Maryland for others who remained where I had been.

I have found that recognizing and acknowledging synchronous occurrences, rather than dismissing them as just luck, can shift one's perspective from how difficult it is to live in such a complex world to being aware of some of the mysterious and helpful connections that link us to each other, thus making everything seem easier. And you can be assured that, as Senge points out, the fact that synchronicity seems to work in mysterious ways does not mean it is esoteric or mystical. Scientists do not really know how gravity works, either, but they do not discount its reality.

Reflecting on synchronous occurrences, Joseph Jaworski (1996), a former attorney who worked with Shell Oil, among other clients, and more recently as CEO of the American Leadership Forum, concludes that an interesting tension exists between our sense of personal autonomy and being "caught up in vital forces that are larger than ourselves, so that while we may be protagonists of our own lives, we are important participants in a larger drama" (p. 88).

The conscious mind can help to transform our relationship with others, but it is the unconscious mind that is our greatest ally in living in dynamic interaction between the inner and outer worlds. Too many people view the unconscious negatively rather than as a powerful ally. Sigmund Freud, for example, is known for identifying our pathologies as arising from the unconscious. Yet the unconscious mind tracks much more data than the conscious mind can handle and makes emotionally resonant decisions for us all the time, often with great wisdom. As New York Times columnist David Brooks (2011) observes in *The Social Animal*,

> We are living in the middle of a revolution in consciousness. Over the past few years, geneticists, neuroscientists, psychologists, sociologists, economists, anthropologists, and others have made great strides in understanding the building blocks of human flourishing. And a core finding of their work is that we are not primarily the products of our conscious thinking. We are primarily the products of thinking that happens below the level of awareness. (p. 9)

Brooks (2011) goes on to say that the unconscious is not only the largest part of the mind; it is also the "seedbed of accomplishment." Indeed, he continues, "mental processes that are inaccessible to consciousness organize our thinking, shape our judgments, form our characters, and provide us with the skills we need in order to thrive" (pp. 9–10). Given the unprecedented fast pace of modern life as well as information overload, the ability of the unconscious to take in great amounts of information and process it quickly is a great asset to any leader whose conscious and unconscious minds are in dialogue.

The essays in this section suggest ways of leading for those who not only want to be the change but also are able to trust in a positive relationship with the outer world, including their relationship with the people and systems that they lead. This trust allows them to learn from others as well as promote their own vision and values.

Harvesting the Wisdom of Groups and Promoting Group Effectiveness

Such leaders do not just sell others on their vision; they share their vision as they also harvest the vision of others, within and outside of their group. Anyone who has done work with the Myers-Briggs Type Indicator™ or other typology systems, or who has seriously studied cultural differences, recognizes that no one of us and no group has all the answers. What we are able to see and understand depends on our type, our socialization (including the imprint of our cultures), and our individual experiences. We inevitably will see only a part of the reality in front of us (as in the famous Sufi parable of the blind men describing an elephant, each one holding a different part of its body). The complexity of modern life requires that we piece together various parts of the puzzle in order to gain an adequate perspective.

However, you can put those pieces together only if people are speaking their authentic truths. Unfortunately, many people match what they say to what they believe their leaders and other group members are open to hearing, saving their true and often more accurate reflections for quiet sharing in hallways and behind closed doors. Others simply posture, saying what they think will get them ahead.

We all pick up verbal and nonverbal cues, consciously and unconsciously, as to what the leader wants to hear or what it takes to fit into a group. This means that if we as leaders want to get the real information, we need to show enthusiasm for hearing divergent voices and surfacing conflict. What is tricky is how sensitive most people are to nonverbal communication. For example, I may say honestly that I want to hear divergent views, but if I look disquieted at hearing something new, or if someone heatedly shares their disagreement with my opinion and my eyes show I'm feeling defensive, they pick it up.

Brooks (2011) explains how it is that we track social cues and accommodate so unconsciously:

> If the conscious mind is like a general atop a platform, who sees the world from a distance and analyzes things linearly and linguistically, the unconscious mind is like a million little scouts. The scouts careen across the landscape, sending back a constant flow of signals and generating instant responses. They maintain no distance from the environment around them, but are immersed in it. They scurry about, interpreting other minds, landscapes, and ideas. (p. 11)

This would be complicated enough, but most of the time these "scouts" are not reporting to the general. Indeed, they make decisions on grounds that may be very different from the general's. Brooks (2011) explains that our unconscious minds are emotionally quite intelligent, and in response to stimuli they shape "our interpretation of the world" and serve as guides for us "as we chart our courses. If the general thinks in data and speaks in prose, the scouts crystallize with emotion, and their work is best expressed in stories, poetry, music, image, prayer, and myth" (p. 12).

In this respect, different parts of us are called forth by different environments. When we go to church, synagogue, or mosque, our more pious (or religiously oppositional) self shows up quite unconsciously. If we go to a party or a bar or the beach, our gregarious, fun-loving part shows up—or if it does not, we may have trouble enjoying our time there. We take a class and our intellectual, studious sides emerge, and so on. Our behavior shifts when our spouse is there, our boss comes into the room, our oldest best friend shows up, or we suddenly feel watched (or private and alone). All this can happen on automatic pilot because those unconscious scouts are doing their job. In *The Tipping Point* and in *Blink*, Malcolm Gladwell (2000, 2005) identified the public policy implications of this phenomenon, recounting how not allowing people to jump turnstiles or write on the walls of the trains decreased crime overall in the New York City subways.

In the introduction, I shared insights from my students at the University of Maryland and the Fetzer Institute dialogue participants. The students were in a graduate program in public policy that emphasized critical thinking and pragmatic practice. The classes were held in typical business conference-style rooms on campus and in a downtown Washington, DC office building. Might this have influenced their tendency to argue from reason and demonstrate critical thinking in their remarks, sounding very much like corporate managers, government bureaucrats, or policy wonks, albeit very smart ones?

The Fetzer participants were invited to share their knowledge of transformational leadership by a foundation whose mission is to promote love and forgiveness in the world. They sat in a circle in a beautiful building made of natural materials with large windows connecting us to a lovely natural landscape, every session beginning with poetry and music. Might this have enhanced their readiness to share such deep and soulful insights?

Setting the stage for what we want to unfold is essential to leadership. We do this by creating visual and verbal cues appropriate to the kind of responses we want to draw from group members. However, we need to remember that these cues skew the information we get, so we also must look for divergent thinking in other settings.

Dialogue is an important complement to discussion and debate, committed as it is to extracting the wisdom of the entire group. Our ability to engage in genuine dialogue with one another at an unconscious as well as a conscious level augments our ease in working together to achieve results. During the Fetzer dialogues, Deborah Meehan, the founder and head of the Leadership Learning Community, astounded us by a simple exercise that brought home the power of a deeper level of group cohesion, even in accomplishing a simple task. Twenty of us stood in a circle out in the fresh air at twilight. She gave us the task of counting to twenty, in any order, but with only one person speaking at a time—or we were to start over. We all looked earnestly at one another, trying hard and repeatedly failing. Then she had us do some deep breathing, consciously connect with one another, close our eyes, and try again. Inward panic ensued, at least in me, but, to my amazement, we succeeded easily on the first attempt. And the sense of group communion arising out of this exercise nourished a powerful sharing in the next session, where participants disclosed very revealing (and confidential) stories about their own leadership experience.

Because it is not yet common in the corporate or political worlds to reveal insights from the unconscious, such as dreams or somatic feelings, leaders often operate as if they had one hand tied behind them, functioning explicitly from only one part of the mind. Moreover, when the messages we consciously and unconsciously send out discourage members of the group from communicating anything beyond what their conscious minds know or can rationally defend, we should not be surprised to receive reductive groupthink rather than the collective wisdom of the enterprise.

For these reasons, transformational leaders access their own unconscious knowledge and help others to become aware of what external influences on them are evoking, align energies and connections within the group, and encourage group members to share the wisdom they have, whatever its source: rational analysis, fact finding, intuition, hunches, dreams, and listening to a still small inner voice within them (or the voice of conscience).

The essays in Part Three provide a series of lessons about utilizing the inner work we continue to do in interaction with groups we lead and of which we are a part. By doing this work, we can bring out the transformational capacities not only in ourselves but also in our organizations, communities, and the larger world. The bridging sections highlight capacities that support our overall ability to transform groups.

Depth Entrepreneurship

Creating an Organization Out of Dream Space

Stephen Aizenstat

The first essay in this section, by Stephen Aizenstat, describes the process he followed in founding and developing Pacifica Graduate Institute, employing both inner intuitive guidance and sound management practices. At Pacifica we now host Pacifica in Depth dialogues with the faculty and staff where we discuss a range of topics, including dreams we believe to be about the school as well as the impact of archetypes we see as being active in the institution. Discussing dreams and archetypes provides a means to enter into a conversation about what the soul of Pacifica wants from us (as well as some exploration of its shadow). Aizenstat's essay models how you can utilize the fruits of your inner work in creating transformational organizations.

Organizational leadership and dream work seem like contradictory practices. But are they? In practice, I have found that success in entrepreneurial leadership requires the capacity to access intelligence from both the rational and dreaming mind. Imagination, intuition, and the resources of the unconscious bring as much to entrepreneurial achievement as does the skill set of a well-earned MBA. Developing a business model animated by the "capital" of both dream and coin inspires devotion to mission and profit.

Thirty-five years ago I cofounded an educational institution and business rooted in these dual ideas. Pacifica Graduate Institute began with a vision and just enough capital to provide instruction to one cohort of counseling psychology students. Today we operate on two ample campuses offering advanced degrees in psychology, mythological studies, and the humanities. Our continuing success speaks to the value of listening to the multiple voices of good management practice and psyche alive within the corporate body. I believe that in the marketplace of the twenty-first century, enlightened leadership can gain from our experience. "Depth entrepreneurship" has as its originating intention a more broadly conceived bottom line: an end game that values the synergy of profit, dream, and informed intuition. None other than the corporate soul, an expression of the world soul, is making this request.

The Corporate Space Is the Dream Space—or Is It?

It is common practice in founding an enterprise to start with a dream. When we develop a business plan, pitch a start-up, or raise capital for virtually any new corporation (profit or not-for-profit), we begin with a dream. Of course, along the way there are countless market studies, financial models, product tests, and the like. Yet the central idea, the essential impulse, the "juice" that inspires the inception and implementation of an organization originates in the imagination.

Virtually all entrepreneurial enterprises begin with a dream, and often a dreamer. The core idea, the new concept, bubbles up from the deep psyche, from the dream space, not from the intricate calculations of the analysts. How curious that the generative force that begins it all, the intelligence of the dreaming psyche, is so quickly left behind, virtually abandoned, like unwanted leftovers, ready for disposal. Oh, what a loss. When the dream dies, so too does the extraordinary intelligence that incubated the idea. The corporate space is robbed of its inheritance, split off from its origination.

Keeping the dream space alive in corporate space opens the doors to untold resources. With dream consciousness comes access to intuition, innovation, curiosity, and a kind of animation that enlivens a company, and, yes, it also feeds the bottom line. Imagine for a moment the excitement that fills the room when a "new idea" emerges. "We could connect people through the Internet, a kind of social networking, a Face Book."

For weeks, months, perhaps even years, the creativity of the dreaming powers the entrepreneurial initiative, forever adding new dimensions, complexity, and out-of-the-box possibilities. Taken a step further, some might say that in dreamtime consciousness, a connection exists with the dreaming of others inside and outside the company, further informing and shaping the business. From product lines to distribution networks, the business model responds to the energetic vivacity of the originating dream and the corporate space continues as a dream space.

When the dream space is cultivated, imagination is ignited. Employees are encouraged to offer new perspectives, imagine into business options, and contribute their voices (even their dream images) to the ongoing evolution of the corporate enterprise. An imaginative attitude is sustained in the organization, and the intelligence flowing from the fountain of inspiration continues to be valued and heard. With this vast potential, one wonders, how hard would it be to open an hour or two a week where the wisdom of dreams could be heard? The answer is a simple one: very hard.

In the manic rush to bring more efficient management systems into the workplace, little room is left for dream space. The science of doing business often replaces the art of conducting business. And when the generative intention fades, the potential for stagnation, low morale, and loss of competitive edge become real problems. Keeping the dream alive is vital to a healthy and prosperous business. Like a magnet with its own energy field, when the deeper psyche of corporate space is enlivened, the abundance that comes with generativity activates. It is what every successful entrepreneur knows in the gut. When the business of doing business in the corporate space complements the ongoing spirit of the dream space, a company or school thrives and has the viability to meet the challenges of an ever-changing marketplace. Keeping the dream alive can be encouraged by paying attention to the dreams we have at night and what they might be telling us. We who are in positions of leadership often have dreams of the workplace. On other occasions the dream may come from an employee other than the leader. If only we made time to listen, to hear their guidance, act upon their urgings, heed their warnings.

Recently I was dealing with a foundational academic program at the institute that was suffering very hard times. This created angst institute-wide. One night this dream came forward: I witnessed a bull that had become lost in the streets of a city, floundering about without direction, and becoming weakened and emaciated, its bones beginning to stick through its decomposing flesh, its eyes bulging as hunger threatened its life. Then the bull made a sudden turn and charged in another direction, back into the high mountains, away from the city, and to a meadow. There it looked more at home, and began to eat the natural grasses it had fed on as a calf. Then the dream came to an end. I woke up and reflected on this image as I prepared for my workday and a meeting about that particular troubled program.

Knowing something about the way of dreams, I appreciate that their language is metaphoric, and that they often pick up situations in awake-life circumstances and make comments on them from the deeper places of psychic life. When dreams speak, I have learned to listen. They pull together events from the day, personal tendencies, messages from the collective, and even knowledge rooted in something named the world soul. In addition, dreams respond to the pull of the future, offering hints of what is to come. Then in the "poetry" of the dream they combine all of this information and present a response in images. I sometimes like to imagine dreams as theatrical productions, complete with settings, characters, feelings, and actions. Almost always there is a "dramatic moment." In this dream, the bull was suffering starvation in the cityscape, not a usual place for a bull to be roaming about. This typically potent, strong-bodied animal was disoriented, starving, and near death, with bones showing through his flaccid hide. Then, the dramatic moment: the bull turned and broke away from the confines of the civilized, constructed world. Suddenly, he galloped. He made his way back to his native grasslands. He had returned to his place of birth, to his origins.

Knowing that dreams are about the dreamer as well as situations he or she is facing, I first looked at the way I might need to go back to the meadow of my youth, renewing myself through eating the grass that first motivated me in this endeavor. I then felt a deeply resonant connection between the dream and what was happening in that beleaguered program.

This perspective from the dreamtime proved to be very helpful later that afternoon at a meeting regarding the "disorientation" of the program that was experiencing difficulties. It became clear to me that the program we had for years felt most "bullish" about (dreams love to speak in puns) was being so overregulated that it was losing touch with its origins, its homeland—a loss of body and soul. This program, because of newly adopted (one-size-fits-all) national assessment standards, had found itself in the urban world of "city," split off from the "natural" world of its animating impulse, its mission, its dream. What was so in the dream seemed so for the program as well. In entrepreneurial terms, if we wanted to return to success, to recover the "bull market," then we had best find ways to combine the technology of modern practices required by the city with the animating spirit of the program's early days still living in the grasslands of its wilderness place. The next step was to share the dream with the group to see the degree to which they resonated with it, and what form a return to a fecund meadow might take in their eyes.

Informed Intuition: It's Not Rocket Science; It's Not Esoteric

Informed intuition means trusting an intelligence that lives beyond the rational mind that is accessible to all of us. It is a broader way of knowing, informed by subtleties, multisensory experiences, and historical memory. Intuition and dreams are sourced from actual events, interactions throughout the day, and literally thousands of bits of information drawn from more subtle sensory perceptions (both contemporary and historical). Intuition relies on information outside the familiar, the habitual, outside of common sense or the logical.

The leader using informed intuition as a guide more often than not finds herself on the "road less traveled," guided along the way by a deeper navigational system. Time and energy get invested in meanderings outside the demands of obligatory business practices and static organizational compliance requirements. The door is open for intuition to walk through and have its place at the table. And with intuition come its dear companions: curiosity, fascination, and emotional intelligence—all contributors to keeping a business vital, fresh, and renewed. The entrepreneurial spirit, some may even say the "entrepreneurial genetic predisposition," of the leader experiences a homecoming of sorts. She feels refueled, nourished, fed by a reconnection to a way of knowing that is integral to her core. With renewed vigor and heightened sensibility, responsiveness to the marketplace strengthens; ways to develop new product lines reveal themselves; and the psychic energy (morale and motivation) within the company percolates. The corporate space intersects with the dream space when leadership includes an active working relationship with informed intuition and the processes of the deep psyche.

In the Field of Dreams, When the Depth Entrepreneur Builds It, They Will Come

When experiencing corporate space as dream space, the depth entrepreneur conducts business on a very different playing field. The essentials of the game are the same for the most part (ensuring revenue over expense, overseeing organizational advancement, hiring the best and the brightest, making the hard calls, watching the marketplace, and so on), but the rules of engagement are quite different. To run a business or organization as if it were a dream requires a new way of seeing and another way of listening. In essence, the entire enterprise, from top to bottom, from beginning to end, is imagined in the paradigm of a dream. This does not mean we sacrifice practicality, business expertise, or down-to-earth operations. Quite the contrary, when one directs the business from the perspective of dream consciousness, there is a sharpening of focus, more attention to detail, heightened awareness of new opportunities, an elevated sensitivity to market conditions. Our lens of perception gains focus; we see differently.

The depth entrepreneur cultivates a mode of perception keen on noticing the occurrences of acausal phenomena. Please note that acute perception differs from delusional paranoia, though on occasion we are hard pressed to make the distinction. Seriously, paranoia, when not a pathology, may simply be a hint asking the leader to pay closer attention to what is active outside the existing range of awareness. The depth entrepreneur keeps an eye on the emergence of synchronicities, complementarities, and those events that occur that seem out of the ordinary or even dreamlike. From a depth perspective, when these phenomena occur, something else becomes available. We are not in Kansas anymore. Perception shifts, seeing into these events as portals to another way of knowing.

Put practically, when a synchronicity occurs, one might ask, "What is it about the fate, the destiny of the organization, that is being affirmed?" When complementarities present themselves (events or situations occurring simultaneously), as in dreamtime consciousness, the question being opened is, "What is being underscored, affirmed, or asking for more resources?" Seeing into the depth dimensions brings attention to these other ways of accessing information, and offers leadership an opportunity. When the "synergy" happens, in the form of something either synchronistic or complementary, an opening occurs in the fabric of the organization. The timing is right for decisive action. At these moments of intersection between the realms of ordinary and extraordinary, there exists a readiness for going deeper into what is working or making a change in direction toward something more generative.

In addition to seeing with a different set of eyes, deep listening also brings its rewards to a leadership of depth. That which lives in the back places, in the margins, like the employee who "acts out," is listened to as one would attend to a figure from a dream. Time is taken to truly hear into his particular slant on the operations of the business. The employee is not suppressed, marginalized, or even terminated. Rather, the opposite occurs. Viewed from a dreamlike perspective, consideration is brought to what is being spoken on the lines and between the lines. Though time consuming, hearing into the uncomfortable often reveals a perspective not otherwise taken into account. Put simply, when "nightmare" situations present themselves in dream, more often than not there exists an opportunity for a breakthrough, not a breakdown. As in dream, so too in business, the questions become, "What is speaking through this figure? What aspect of the corporate soul is being expressed and seeking attention?" Rather than being silenced or condemned, the behavior of an acting-out employee is, within reason, attended to, given place, and valued for the perspective offered. The intolerable, the repugnant, and the least desired often provide constructive information that supports success in business.

The Bottom Line: A Visit to the Depths

Attention to the bottom line starts with a question, not with crunching numbers. When we founded Pacifica Graduate Institute we asked: "What is the world wanting or needing from another educational institution?" As we listened to the call of the marketplace, we heard something more. Beneath the competitors, the customer base, the existing market conditions, the voice of the *anima mundi*, the soul of the world, was telling of its needs. The more deeply we listened, the more we felt the pull to the bottom. Like Alice falling through the rabbit hole, we kept going down. It became clear that the direction was vertical, deeper, under, and behind the familiar. Down we went until we landed on the ground of conviction that lives "at the heart" of what was being asked of us. This verticality happened to manifest in a business structure for a school of depth psychology. Yet the process is relevant to any type of organization. The first move is always down.

The depth entrepreneur lands on the ground of conviction that distinguishes his company from all others. Its unique vision is found by walking about on the bottomlands of imagination. There, the leader is grounded and infused with the DNA of the vision. He becomes confident, empowered, strengthened, on a cellular level, for the challenges and opportunities that lie ahead. To sustain vision and to compete in the corporate world, a mission-centered leader requires this kind of initiatory experience. Financial sustainability requires the courage to take risks, invest capital (often your own), innovate, improvise, and, above all, sustain the strength to persevere. Generating revenue over expenses also means focusing attention on best business practices, and gaining the confidence needed for flexibility and adaptability, while at the same time remaining true to the originating dream.

Depth entrepreneurship requires an ongoing connection to the energetic source (inner and under) that generates the means of production. When the leader is connected to the underground (underworld) sources of energy, the needed fuel becomes available to pull together a team, develop a business plan, raise capital, conduct market research, and make financial projections. When disconnected from this foundational resource, leaders often suffer the plight of so many who have come this way before: they simply run out of gas and burn out. It is best to begin the journey with a visit to the depths and continue to reconnect with that source on a regular basis. What lives in the deep psyche, the birthplace of the vision and mission, energizes the leader and the whole organization and enhances the bottom line.

Through the years, I have found one principle, above all others, that has ensured bottom-line success. It is first to ask a simple question before proceeding to decision making. "How does the 'soul' of the institution weigh in on business transactions?" Before and during financial analysis, I come back to the principle that the psyche of the place has an important role to play. When I have been in service to the depth of mission, not in control or exploitation of its resources, I have found the path to the most abundant source of profitability—the "win-win-win" of the triple bottom line. The mission prospers and is advanced; the institution and employees benefit; and I, as founder, also reap rewards. The key is to be in service to something larger than my or the institution's immediate short-term needs or desires, financial or otherwise. In depth psychology, this consideration is framed as moving from a more limited, ego-centered decision process toward a larger, Self-centered source of guidance.

For example, when a major business decision came up at Pacifica—the opportunity to purchase a new campus—I considered far more than the move-in infrastructure costs, the risk in high-interest financing secured by personal guarantees, and the possibility that this new campus might overextend our resources and exceed what we could reasonably handle. In making the final call, I returned to the guiding "principle" of listening to the soul of Pacifica. She spoke with clarity. "Secure the ground. Future generations will walk this campus and sit in these classrooms for decades to come." As it turned out, now, just five years later, after the purchase of a thirty-five-acre additional campus, we find ourselves again squeezed for office and classroom space. I put faith in the intelligent deep psyche of the institution, and, as is often the case, was guided in the right direction. As a depth entrepreneur, I have learned that to be in service to the whole is to serve the best interests of the multiple bottom lines—the mission, the shareholders, and the world. To serve the mission is good business. To align with the vision helps dream the dream forward, and supports what lives at bottom: abundance.

Stephen Aizenstat holds a PhD in clinical psychology and is the chancellor and founding president of Pacifica Graduate Institute. Aizenstat's book, *DreamTending*, describes applications of dreamwork in relation to health and healing, nightmares, the World's Dream, relationships, and the creative process. His other recent publications include *Imagination and Medicine: The Future of Healing in an Age of Neuroscience* (coeditor with Robert Bosnak); "Dream Tending and Tending the World," in *Ecotherapy: Healing with Nature in Mind*; and "Soul-Centered Education: An Interview with Stephen Aizenstat" (with Nancy Treadway Galindo) in *Reimagining Education: Essays on Reviving the Soul of Learning*.

Deep Dialogue

Harvesting Collective Wisdom

Alan Briskin

Most of us have had experiences in which our own knowledge was partial but was augmented by insights from others that made all the difference. James Surowiecki is one of many observers who make a compelling case that groups can outperform experts in coming up with answers, even when the issues in question are factual and data driven. In *The Wisdom of Crowds,* Surowiecki (2004) offers numerous examples of this phenomenon, from groups of uneducated rural people beating the professionals in guessing the weight of an ox, to the capacity for self-organizing cooperation, to coordinated behavior, as on the freeway. Once we understand the richness that comes from connecting to our unconscious and conscious wisdom and becoming more whole and clear as individuals, the question naturally arises: "How can we foster this level of authenticity and wisdom in a collective?" In the next essay in this section, Alan Briskin compellingly describes a dialogue process for harvesting group wisdom that answers this question. This process, and the disciplines it promotes, can inform your practice, promoting generative and productive group communication.

"I absolutely take no pride in what I'm going to share with you," stated the superintendent of schools to his school board. "There are things in here that go against my beliefs" (Tucker, 2010). He then outlined decimating cuts to summer school programs and teacher training, and the loss of hundreds of jobs in both staff and teaching positions.

Faced with the worldwide belief in the ever-growing scarcity of resources, echoes of this heartfelt confession are heard throughout public
education, health care, business, government, and a myriad of public
services. Is there an alternative future? For anyone seeking transformational change, this is the question that should hold our feet to the fire.

After years of research and published evidence of a growing number
of scholars and practitioners, we believe the field of collective wisdom
may hold the answer. *Collective wisdom* is an alternative belief system
about our world and its future. At its simplest, collective wisdom is
knowledge and insight gained through group and community interaction. At a deeper level, it is about our living connection to each other and
the interdependence we share in our neighborhoods, organizations,
and world community.

Challenging Our Basic Assumptions about
Leaders and Groups

In our research on group transformation (harvesting collective wisdom), we learned that there are principles and practices that invert and
reframe some of our most commonly held assumptions about leaders
and groups. We called these principles and practices *stances*, signify-
ing the intent or source behind the outer manifestation of behavior. A
stance is an attitude and bearing that involves mindfulness—an alertness to what is going on inside us and a simultaneous awareness of what
is happening around us. Rather than being caught in the downward
spiral of fragmentation that accompanies social crisis and group incoherence, these stances can open a portal to a different kind of knowing,
one that grasps our interconnectedness as a group, a nation, a species.
Transformation of this kind introduces us to deeper mysteries, but there
is nothing mysterious about the process itself. The stances include the
following:

- Deep listening
- Suspension of certainty
- Seeing whole systems and seeking diverse perspectives
- Respect for others and group discernment

- Welcoming all that is arising
- Trust in the transcendent

Stance 1: Deep Listening

Often leaders and group members share an assumption that what matters most is what we say and the certainty in how we say it. This has legitimacy to a degree, but the assumption breaks down when new ideas and new possibilities are needed. The first stance arises not from what we say, but from how we listen. We call this stance *deep listening*.

Deep listening comes from a desire to understand another's worldview and a willingness to feel what it might be like to be in someone else's shoes. Deep listening invites us to be curious about what is really going on inside the person, the group, or the larger collective. It is an act of truly being present with others.

We asked Paula Underwood, clan mother of the Turtle Clan, Iroquois nation, how one learns to listen deeply to another. She described a time in her childhood when, after learning to memorize the words spoken by her father's friend, her father asked her if she could hear his heart. The question stunned her. She went around for days with her ear to people's chests listening to their heartbeat. Soon after, her father said that if she wanted to truly understand what was being said in the newspaper, she must learn to read between the lines. Putting the two suggestions together, she arrived at a new understanding. She realized we each have the capacity to hear more than what is being said by the words alone. We can listen for the emotional context of the words. We can hear the frequencies of human meaning that echo deeply within the person and within the group. When you listen at that level, Underwood told us, you can hear what the Universe is saying (Briskin, Erickson, Ott, & Callanan, 2009). To listen deeply requires a discipline of being able to suspend our personal certainty long enough to allow new meaning to emerge.

Stance 2: Suspension of Certainty

To *suspend certainty* does not mean we must pretend to lack knowledge. Rather, it is a reflective inquiry consistent with deep listening, a willingness to be changed in the course of interaction with others. Like

the Zen parable of the master who continues pouring tea over the lip of
the cup to teach the student what it means to be truly empty, we cannot
learn new ways if we are filled up with the certainty of our own ideas,
assumptions, and mental models. Only as we learn to listen and suspend our certainty does it become possible for a new idea to enter the
collective mind.

Historically, there is a vivid example of the value of suspending certainty in the creation of the U.S. Constitution. When the representatives from the various states first debated, they could not agree on
whether they were modifying the existing Articles of Confederation or
creating a new constitution for the nation. They could not agree on the
extent of power for the central government or how representation
should be distributed. They could not agree on much at all. Shuttered
in a hall in Philadelphia, the heat rose figuratively and literally in the
room.

After a month or so, Benjamin Franklin, now in the last years of his
life, rose to speak to the group. He acknowledged their despair at ever
finding a way forward and suggested they were looking for democracy
in all the wrong places—backward in history and sideways to existing
governments in Europe. He encouraged them instead to pray together
each morning and to look forward to an emerging future. He asked
them to consider the aid of a "Father of Lights" who he referred to as a
Friend, the word used by the Quakers for a higher divine source found
within each person. The group rebuffed his suggestion to begin the day
with prayer but continued, against all odds, to carry on with their work.
Out of bitterness, partisanship, and fierce debate arose some measure
of listening and agreement—and miraculously a document that became
the founding structure for a nation based on democratic principles.

Then on the very last day of the convention, when it was necessary to
ensure that as many representatives as possible signed the draft document, Franklin addressed the convention again, although this time he
was too ill to speak for himself and his address was read by a fellow
representative from Pennsylvania. He argued that democracy is born
from our human capacity to suspend the certainty of our positions.
And even though he believed the current document before him was

flawed in significant ways, he noted he had learned in his life that his judgment could change over time.

Drawing upon his extraordinary wit, he argued that the Church in Rome was different than the Church of England only insofar as one believed it was infallible and the other that it was never in the wrong. And both were like the French woman who believed she was always in the right. Democracy depended, he insisted, on our capacity to suspend the inclination to be always in the right in order for something new to be born. That *something new* became the U.S. Constitution. This is the legacy of our democratic institutions and the lesson we must continually learn and relearn. Suspending our personal certainty is the source of our transformation. When we maintain this discipline, we create the spaciousness required to allow new ideas to be born and brought forward from the group itself.

Stance 3: Seeing Whole Systems and Seeking Diverse Perspectives

Leaders, understandably, often attempt to align group members with the organization's mission, seek ways to gain agreement, and then hold them accountable. The emphasis is on individuals, even if the venue is collective, such as group meetings or a company newsletter. The process is often sequential and linear, with the objectives typically developed before communication with the group occurs.

The stance of collective wisdom to see the whole system shifts the traditional orientation. The leader is cognizant first of the collective as a whole and works with individuals, subgroups, and teams to discover what lies in the best interest of the whole. Each perspective functions to reveal more of the whole and each individual is required to understand something more about the choices, challenges, and opportunities the whole system faces. Committing to this stance requires us to synthesize diverse information, whether through multiple personal conversations, data collection, or group methodologies that emphasize listening and discovery. What holds the multiplicity together is the strength of an underlying intent and the resiliency of relationships built over time.

As a clan mother, Paula Underwood sought to hear what was in people's hearts, even when no one was speaking. Consensus to Underwood was not 9,000 people agreeing together at a single moment in time, but a network of relationships that reinforced that each voice mattered, that people's concerns were heard, and that practical responses to human needs were addressed.

The starting place for our collective wisdom begins with hearing all the voices, especially voices that have been disenfranchised, and to reinforce positive emotions and goals for the group as a whole. Seeing whole systems means asking questions that may be initially uncomfortable and raising issues that may have a history of being systematically ignored or demeaned. No doubt this commitment to hearing all the voices requires courage and a discipline of respect and restraint. It is out of this regard that the group itself begins to mature into an organ of discernment.

Stance 4: Respect for Others and Group Discernment

Respect is often viewed as something one has to earn or a result of a mutually satisfying relationship. From a collective perspective, taking a stance of respect for others goes further. It places respect in the foreground of group interaction.

Sawubona is the isiZulu word for "I see you" and is one of the greetings of respect in South Africa. The other replies in response, "Yebo, sawubona," meaning "Yes, I see you." The significance of the interaction goes beyond formality, to the capacity we have to *see* each other, to recognize that there is a bond between us.

Respect has a way of deepening group interaction by creating safety and inclusion. We feel seen, heard, respected, and acknowledged. The gravitational force felt from being in respectful settings is palpable. Even before we are conscious of feeling safe, the part of the brain that senses threat sends out an "all clear" message, immediately diminishing the fight-or-flight response that is our biological reaction to danger. Blood can flow more freely to the brain rather than to the legs (in case we have to attack or run) and cortisol, which is the hormone generated under stress, is reduced. Our brains function with an increased capacity for tolerating ambiguity as well as complexity, and imagination and reason become further integrated; our hearts literally beat in a more coherent fashion.

Yet how can we demonstrate respect when we can barely tolerate someone on a personal level, or strongly disagree with a contrary position being taken? Respect takes on a whole new dimension when it includes respecting differences and coping with dissonance and diversity. Respect suddenly becomes more like a rigorous discipline, continually practiced and renewed, than simply a feel-good concept or lofty aspiration. Respect for others is where many people find their most severe limitations in groups. Yet respect is a necessary ingredient for group discernment, both qualities intimately linked together in cultivating collective wisdom.

Discernment is a particular form of group comprehension, the capacity to grasp what may seem initially obscure, to distinguish accurately among many shades of feelings, and to make meaning from disparate elements. Respect has a way of binding together the cognitive and affective resources of a group. Discernment offers a pathway to action.

Group discernment is a capacity within groups for the emergence of new thinking and new images of what is possible. With discernment, we are capable of being with differences, uncertainties, and doubts without reaching immediately for closure, agreement, or excess simplification. The poet John Keats saw this quality, which he termed *negative capability*, as the foundational skill of the artist. The pioneering scholar and practitioner of collective group process, Wilfred Bion (1965), understood negative capability as linked with discernment and central to personal and group transformation. Discernment requires faith that with patience clarity can be achieved. And with clarity, a new level of coherence emerges capable of managing far greater complexity. Bion associated this capacity with reverie, a transitional state between dreams and new beginnings. From this kind of group reverie comes new mental models of reality and new ways of acting in the world.

Stance 5: Welcoming All That Arises

Transformational leadership requires the ability to embrace the unexpected and sometimes disturbing aspects of group life. Welcoming all that is arising demands an interior calm accompanied by a skill for knowing when to intervene.

Two very different kinds of transformative moments illustrate this stance. The first took place in the midst of South African apartheid rule; a clandestine meeting was arranged during a time when the ruling government maintained a ban on contact with the African National Congress (ANC). Led by Franklin Thomas, then president of the Ford Foundation, a group of influential Afrikaners agreed to meet with a delegation of ANC leaders. The intent was to build bridges between two groups needing to find a way forward together. Beginnings can be treacherous, however, and this was no exception. At the first encounter, one of the ANC leaders leaped to his feet on sighting the chairman of the influential and secretive Afrikaners and shouted, "I'll shoot you, Broederbonder" (Sampson, 2000, p. 357).

What happened next was a remarkable example of the internal discipline required to welcome the emergent aspects of group life. One of the other ANC leaders, Mac Maharaj, did not refute his colleague but asked instead that there be consideration of the roots of his colleague's anger. What transpired was an emotionally meaningful exchange. The conference ended with the two men who met in confrontation embracing each other. Subsequently, a long private dinner was arranged between the Afrikaner chairman and another member of the ANC delegation, resulting in even further normalization of relationships.

The second example took place in Pecos, New Mexico. Lauren Artress, founder and creative director of a nonprofit group, Veriditas, convened a program called Theater of Enlightenment. The heart of the program was a labyrinth walk, which involved a local monastery and the larger community of Pecos. In the midst of the proceedings, unknown to anyone in the group, a man walked directly into the labyrinth and fell to his knees weeping and sobbing.

Artress intuitively understood that intervening too soon was inconsistent with the intent to promote the healing, meditative powers of the labyrinth. She grasped the connection between a leader's role of maintaining personal restraint and group transformation. "I think that's part of the issue about the magic and the mystery of the group—it is that you have to be really secure in yourself, to let whatever's going to live out, live out. And I call it holding the space, but you're holding your inner space too" (Briskin et al., 2009, p. 58).

At first the group from the monastic order just let the man be, but after a time they came toward him and began a ritual healing called "laying on of hands." For over forty-five minutes they held him in this way, until some measure of his pain subsided and he was able to cope again.

Artress later learned that the man had had a dream that he should come to this church without any prior knowledge of her program's existence. Those in the monastic order came to understand the metaphoric power of the "stranger" who came into their midst, reminding them of their own vulnerability and the deep searing pain of their larger community. Out of apparent chaos came a new order.

Stance 6: Trust in the Transcendent

Critical to all the other stances, *trust in the transcendent* demonstrates a respect for that which animates human agency, arouses our appreciation for nature and beauty, and reminds us of the spiritual dimension in all our activities. When we look out upon the world with awe and wonder, we are better able to see constructive possibilities rather than simply constricting limits. When inspiration might easily be relegated to the side in the midst of pitched political battles and declining resources, the transcendent element is necessary to articulate the larger purposes and moral nature of our efforts.

Too often this aspirational quality has been focused on the charismatic persona of the leader rather than the vitality of the group itself. Peter Senge, director of the Center for Organizational Learning, points out that the world is filled with stories of extraordinary individuals who exercised wisdom. Yet what is compelling about these stories is what emerged collectively. "Gandhi and Martin Luther King Jr. were not wise leaders just because of what they said but also because of the coordinated and consequential actions they helped inspire among millions" (Briskin et al., 2009, p. 58).

The stances of collective wisdom constitute a faith that we can re-create ourselves through dialogue, one that encourages critical thought while simultaneously being nourished by love, humility, and hope. It is a faith sorely tested. However, as Senge suggested, the faith in the group itself being the vehicle of transformation is a vastly underrated element in our current dialogue about leadership. We too rarely admit that our efforts for transformation are dependent on the consciousness of the group itself, not the skills, talents, and aspirations of the leader.

A powerful historical tale illustrates the nature of this dependent relationship. In 1935, Howard Thurman, the renowned African American theologian, was able to arrange a personal meeting with Mahatma Gandhi in India. It was more than a decade before India would gain independence from Britain and multiple decades before segregation in the United States would be systematically challenged. Gandhi was enthralled with what Thurman could tell him about the United States and racial relations but was insistent that he could not come to the United States until India had won its struggle with Britain. Thurman then asked Gandhi why they had failed to win their freedom from the British. As best as he could recall Gandhi's answer, Thurman (1979) wrote:

> The effectiveness of a creative ethical ideal such as nonviolence, ahimsa, or no killing depends upon the degree to which the masses of the people are able to embrace such a notion and have it become a working part of their total experience. It cannot be the unique property or experience of the leaders; it has to be rooted in the mass assent and creative push. The result is that when we first began our movement, it failed, and it will continue to fail until it is embraced by the masses of the people. I felt that they could not sustain this ethical ideal long enough for it to be effective because they did not have enough vitality. (pp. 132–133)

Gandhi's words particularly struck Thurman in their association of ethics and morality with physical vitality. The transcendent element of our purpose together on earth becomes the stored energy that, when released, galvanizes collective action. Current research on motivation confirms that along with a sense of autonomy and mastery, the sense of contribution to a greater purpose constitutes a critical variable of intrinsic motivation. We are individually vitalized and collectively galvanized when we can see and contribute to a transcendent purpose.

In 1944, with Gandhi's words still echoing in his ear, Thurman began the first integrated, intercultural, and interfaith congregation in the United States. A few years later, he became the first African American to become the dean of chapel at a majority-white institution, Boston University. It was there that he met and became the lifelong mentor to the son of a former colleague at Morehouse College. This young man's name was Martin Luther King Jr.

On the Nature of Transformation

The two words making up the word *transformation* are *trans* and *forma*. *Trans*, from Latin, means literally "to cross" or "go beyond" and *forma* indicates a form, shape, or mold, possibly derived from the Greek word *morphe*, indicating an outward appearance. For our purposes, transformational leadership indicates a person or persons crossing over into a new way of grasping collective action, including their own role in catalyzing sound judgment and harvesting the wisdom of groups.

Without the collective wisdom stances of deep listening, suspension of certainty, seeking diverse perspectives, group discernment, welcoming all that is arising, and trust in the transcendent, we are less likely to render new images of a positive future, less willing to experiment, and less likely to learn from our actions. Only in action, with appropriate reflection, can we find out if the change is superficial or deep. If not, we risk arguing about what is best in theory or simply react badly to the forced choices accelerating toward us. Alternatively, collective wisdom suggests a knowing that is already within us that can be cultivated with others and allowed to take on new forms. Each of us can choose to be a catalyst for this kind of change.

Howard Zinn (2007), who wrote of a "people's history," summarized beautifully this way of attending to the world, open to all of us, a perspective that allows us to see ourselves collectively, but simultaneously with individual agency:

What we choose to emphasize in this complex history will determine our lives. If we see only the worst, it destroys our capacity to do something. If we remember those times and places—and there are so many—where people have behaved magnificently, this gives us the energy to act, and at least the possibility of sending this spinning top of a world in a different direction.

And if we do act, in however small a way, we don't have to wait for some grand utopian future. The future is an infinite succession of presents, and to live now as we think human beings should live, in defiance of all that is bad around us, is itself a marvelous victory. (p. 270)

Alan Briskin, PhD, is an organizational consultant, a pioneer in the field of organizational learning, and cofounder of the Fetzer Institute–sponsored Collective Wisdom Initiative. His coauthored *The Power of Collective Wisdom: And the Trap of Collective Folly* was the winner of the Nautilus Award in the category of Conscious Business and Leadership. His other books include *The Stirring of Soul in the Workplace* and the coauthored *Daily Miracles*, which earned the *American Journal of Nursing*'s Book of the Year award in Public Interest and Creative Works. Alan is an adjunct faculty member at Saybrook University, where he helped found the doctoral program in systems and organizations. He also is a founding member of the Berrett-Koehler Author Cooperative and is an advisor to the Goi Peace Foundation in Tokyo, Japan.

| 15 |

New Approaches for Leadership

A Psychospiritual Model for Leadership
Development

Karin Jironet and Murray Stein

In the essay that follows, Karin Jironet and Murray Stein integrate ideas
related to dialogue processes with insights about how members of dyads
and groups can bond with one another more deeply. The authors bring
together Aizenstat's focus on going deep into the psyche with Briskin's
attention to broadening interaction through dialogue. Leaders can build
people's confidence by deep listening to the flashes of insight that
individuals and groups receive in dialogue informed by their own inner
listening. This mirroring reinforces new awareness. They also can help
groups reach a level of attunement that opens their spirits to realizations
and possibilities not known before. Jironet and Stein's essay provides a
"how to" for such deep listening and close attunement.

Globalization and the dramatic rise of information technology (such as
social media) have led to significant shifts in society and have radically
changed the contexts in which many organizations operate. Recent research indicates that collaboration, cocreation, and partnerships inside
and outside of organizations are the best means for achieving success in
the present environment and in the near and distant future (for various
perspectives on these changes, please see Brafman & Beckstrom, 2008;
Gobillot, 2009; Jironet, 2002, 2009, 2010; Li & Bernoff, 2008; Shirky,
2009). Successful leaders must create a heightened sense of their organization's potential for participating in an international landscape, create
space for individuals in their organizations to contribute to this vision,

and communicate the importance of this value throughout their organizations. See, for example, C. K. Prahalad, who concluded one of his
last works, a column in the April 2010 *Harvard Business Review*, with
this thought: "Executives are constrained not by resources but by their
imagination" (p. 33). R. Kaplan, together with D. Norton (1992), introduced the Balanced Scorecard, a strategic management tool used worldwide. *In Stop Overdoing Your Strengths*, Kaplan and Kaiser (2009) warn
that strengths taken too far become weaknesses and show that to strike
a balance between key leadership dualities, actions and motivations
must be clearly identified.

To meet this challenge successfully, leaders must not only become
conscious of their own personality traits and the impact these traits
have on others; they must also be competent at functioning in complex
and diverse environments (Jironet, 2010). Leadership now means skillfully interacting with others on an equal footing and in partnership,
while remaining solidly based within one's own psyche.

The Need for a New Level of Leadership Consciousness

Through our work with senior executives at large and medium-sized
companies in a variety of industries, we have become acutely aware of
the need for this new concept of leadership. Many executives find traditional leadership questions irrelevant. The head of a large financial institution, for example, asked: "What am I supposed to lead *toward* when
everything is up in the air and people under me are confused and mostly
just tending to their own personal business?" (Interview January 2011,
Amsterdam). A member of the board of directors of a large insurance
company said bluntly: "I don't see how I can tell others what to do if
I don't know what to do myself, and I don't hear anyone convincingly
pointing me in any direction." (Interview March 2011, Dublin). These
statements capture the general mood of disorientation and confusion
among many leaders today. In addition, many executives speak about
erratic and highly disruptive activities in their workplace that make
them feel either hyperactive or deprived of initiative. Numerous execu-

tives find it difficult to manage their own energies, let alone those of others, and lack realistic perspectives on how to move forward.

The time has come for a different approach in leadership development that enables leaders to face challenges with an internal sense of confidence. We call this a new level of leadership consciousness; it is an inner-transformation process to enable leaders to function comfortably in the challenging environments of today's complex world.

The Background of the Psychospiritual Approach

Drawing on our professional training and decades of experience, we created a psychospiritual model for leadership development that is derived primarily, but not exclusively, from the traditions of Sufism and analytical psychology.

We also have been influenced by the dialogues between quantum physicist David Bohm and the spiritual teacher Krishnamurti. In the early 1990s, Bohm and Krishnamurti formulated ideas on how to overcome the isolation, individualization, and fragmentation characteristic of modern societies and bring about a greater degree of wholeness, both individually and collectively. In *On Dialogue*, Bohm (1996) describes several methods that help create opportunities for positive change. He advocates that when engaging in free dialogue, two or more people with equal status observe the following principles: listen to each other with detachment, suspend opinion and judgment, allow the free flow of thought and feeling, and accept and appreciate differing beliefs or understanding. When followed, these principles allow for surprising agreement and unity to emerge from widely disparate positions. The theories established by Krishnamurti (Lutyens, 1975; Williams, 2002) and Bohm have influenced Appreciative Inquiry, and especially MIT's Center for Organizational Learning's work on dialogue. They have also formed the basis of the work of C. Otto Scharmer (2007) and the Presencing Institute in their method of *presencing* and on working toward social renewal through Theory U, a theoretical perspective indicating that the way we attend to a situation has an impact on that situation (see Hayashi, 2010).

Drawing on these and other well-known teachings, our model for leadership development is rooted in a specific practice of psychospiritual guidance that proceeds in three phases: deep listening, close attunement, and transformational shifts. The model teaches leaders how to use themselves as instruments for transformation and thus create and develop equal relationships between themselves and those around them, grasp and formulate surprising new outcomes and ideas, and manage the energies in groups of people as these emerge in free, open, and creative settings.

Deep Listening

When all your knowledge and resources for coping, planning a future, and leading others in a common enterprise prove insufficient, you need to look for alternative ways of thinking, acting, and living. This calls for a dramatic change, a fundamental transformation in attitude, a leap to another level of awareness and behavior, and a radical shucking-off of old habits of thought and behavior to make space for something new. Experiences from the past are deeply internalized, but an attempt must be made to put habitual patterns aside in order for new ones to emerge. Genuinely new and unprecedented insights and ideas can only materialize out of the dark background of consciousness, known as the unconscious. In the unconscious, there is a potential for awareness and insight that exists below the surface of ordinary consciousness. Psychologist Timothy D. Wilson (2001) writes about this as "discovering the nature of our adaptive unconscious" (p. 202). These new ideas tend to emerge suddenly, like flashes of insight. Scientists from many disciplines have reported such sudden insights after long and deep contemplation of a problem, falling asleep, and suddenly awakening with the solution in mind. August Kekulé, for instance, claimed that the notion of the structure of the benzene ring struck him during a daydream in which he saw an ouroboros, a snake swallowing its own tail (Benfey, 1958).

Deep listening is a technique for allowing insights to emerge into consciousness. This involves a subtle process of listening for a voice that speaks from the unconscious, from recesses below the habits of thinking and behavior that govern daily life. Deep listening seeks to turn up the volume of the inner voice and help the listener to accept intuitively the guidance that may come. The success of this method depends on the listener's capability to enter the realm of the unconscious and to develop an awareness of how to navigate there.

To turn your consciousness to the inner voice, sit down in a spot where you feel comfortable and relaxed. Close your eyes. Turn your attention to your breathing. Feel your breath moving in and out. Turn your attention to your feet and feel how the floor comes up and meets your feet. Breathe through your right foot into the center of the Earth. Breathe through your left foot into the center of the Earth. Make a connection there, and breathe up and down from your lower back straight into the center of the Earth. Breathe in and draw energy from the Earth into your body. Hold your breath and feel how you are filled with that energy. Then exhale with a sigh. Focus your attention on the energy vibrating in your body. Repeat three times. Turn your attention to your heart. Feel its energy reaching out and filling up the space around you. You are now in your own energy field.

- Gently touch the space around you with your attention. This is how you are in essence. Become aware of how that is. Let go of all images of yourself. Leave your perception of the world and your personal theory of life for a while.
- Close your ears with your thumbs, fingers pointing upward. Listen to the sounds inside your ears. Drop your hands in your lap and continue to listen to that sound. Become aware of how the sound fills the space around your head and shoulders. Keep listening. You feel a deep sense of peace. Let yourself become blank and open to receive what comes to you without it affecting you. Simply let it come to you. Just be aware, and all you need will be revealed through you.

By following these simple instructions, deep listening develops and the voice of the adaptive unconscious begins to become available in consciousness. By consistent practice, people become more and more proficient in the practice of deep listening. Leaders who work with deep listening allow for novel and unpredictable insights to emerge in themselves and are able to stimulate this same process in their peers and coworkers. Some report that merely thinking of sitting in deep listening activates the form of consciousness that it brings.

> One senior executive reported that although he had always relied on his sixth sense, he had never proactively searched for information through intuition, instead taking a reactive approach to whatever came through this doorway. After learning the method of deep listening, he now consults this voice deliberately and relies on the information he receives from it. As a result, he is better able to assess complex environments and situations and more profoundly trusts his intuition as a basis for decision making.

Close Attunement

Close attunement involves sharing the voice of the unconscious, one's own inner knowing, with another person or several persons. Close attunement is essential for strengthening the insights and solutions that arise from deep listening. It is a kind of intimate dialogue that is based on mutuality and deep trust. It is as though all the partners in this sharing are listening to the same inner voice. *Attunement* denotes synchronization of two or more psychic energy fields (Jung, 1966, para. 163). Attunement is also a term used in Sufi teachings to signify a form of concentration (Inayat Khan, 1960).

Close attunement takes place with the entry of two (or more) people into the same unconscious space simultaneously, as if jumping into a pool of water together. It is a shared moment in which the water entered is the same for all involved and those leaping into it are on the same journey. At the same time, this moment is individually experienced by each participant. Close attunement can be geared to address a particular dilemma, or toward the purpose of inspiration, or the building up of relationships among coworkers. For in-depth instructions on how to work with a group in close attunement, please see http://www.jironet .com and http://www.murraystein.com.

> Clients speak about how close attunement brings increased body-mind harmonization, more conscious living, greater command of energy, and a renewed spirit. One participant stated that she was finally able to take the steps that she had long been convinced would professionalize her entire organization, as well as benefiting her personally. The urge to take this personal transformation forward and seek renewal in the professional setting is a recurrent theme. The process is strengthened because it is shared and witnessed by the group.

In most groups, the participants report that a surprising potential answer comes to them during deep listening and close attunement. It appears first in the form of a visual image, a bodily sensation, or a mind-body combination. In the exchange-and-reflection stage, it becomes verbally articulated, and the beginnings of solutions to the dilemma are formulated as possibilities, prospects, or, sometimes, as promises. This can be a lot of fun, with laughter and moments of hilarity, or synchronicity. The intuitive answers proposed at this time represent only a potential and not the complete solution. This potential reaches concrete realization when there is an individual or a collective feeling of "Aha! This is it," which is typically mirrored by all in the group at the same time.

The process of close attunement ensures that all participants act as equal partners in finding and forming the resolution of the issue being dealt with or in solidifying a previous decision. This ensures that all are engaged and have a shared understanding, albeit individually experienced and arrived at.

Transformational Shifts

Transformational shifts occur when a new awareness is fully experienced, recognized as true and meaningful, and shared among all present. This experience constitutes a fundamental transformation of consciousness and changes the basic attitude and outlook on life of each individual and the group.

> Leaders who have experienced such transformational shifts speak of a growing sense of relatedness and a feeling of renewal, as well as a heightened sense of presence and of increased clarity as to what is

going on in complex organizational situations. This tends to create enhanced levels of detached involvement and tranquility, as well as a fuller sense of inner security and trust in the processes unfolding.

Implementation

For transformational outcomes to reach implementation and to spread beyond the group, two fundamental principles must be addressed. The previous exercises have set out the plan; now, this plan must be realized. A new narrative must be created that frames the intention and ensures that all dispersed energy—everything people do in the workplace—fits into and contributes to the new narrative.

It is important that the new narrative picks up the essential threads of the themes that emerged in the earlier steps, develops them into a story line that is connected to the social and organization realities, and is communicated to others. Together, the story is told and retold until all feel sure that, although they have their own stories, this is one that represents the solution that resolves the dilemma. The new narrative converts the ideas and energies released in deep listening and close attunement into a possible plan for action, but on a metaphorical level.

To start the narrative, ask yourself the following questions:

- *What is cooking?* Example: A group of senior leaders—politicians and financial experts—convene to discuss the way forward for Europe. A multitude of areas is addressed. There is no consensus about either a methodological approach or desired outcomes. The meeting is considered inspiring and inconclusive. To find out what is cooking, you need to realize what is going on behind the scenes and identify the main theme at play (space limitations prevent an elaboration of this technique). Generally there is one major theme, but there may be more. If you identify more than four or five themes, you are probably not distinguishing the core level from its elements, the soup from its ingredients. Bouillabaisse means more than just a list of its ingredients.
- *What is the germ?* The germ is what is hanging in the air, but not yet realized. Let us assume that the germ in the example above is

fear. If it manifests itself in fearful or defensive acts, it cannot be extinguished. A narrative will be your best way of countering, containing, and setting a framework in which fear (or any other germ) does not get out of hand. This creates a new attitude to whatever unspoken energy is in the air.

- *Who is drawn to it?* The narrative needs to be shared by communicating it. It is best to draw together a group of people who are interested in contributing. Together, the story is told and retold until the ambassadors feel sure that, although they have their own story, it is one that represents the shared narrative, which resolves whatever dilemma is at hand.

To manage the energy in large groups, it is critical that you are first aware of your own energy and how you regulate it. It is your responsibility to discover your own behavior and energy patterns, as well as being able to move in and out of these states at will. Second, you need to communicate effectively. Ensure that all the technical support and facilities are readily available to you and that information can flow freely to you. Be aware, however, that it is not possible to control communication conduits in the myriad of streams of the Internet. Drop the idea of managing communication. Think instead of what is cooking, and connect to yourself, and then to one or two more people in a shared conversation. Make a statement, whether in the form of an image, written text, or vocal statement. Post it, send it, share it with the world. Then wait.

When you receive responses, connect with the narrative before engaging in communication. Make sure you stay with your own story.

Conclusion

Leadership today is no longer just about directing people and energy toward solving problems. It is about creating settings and atmosphere that enables people to flourish, grow, and become leaders themselves. To create these spaces, leaders must begin with a new type of consciousness that enables them to create partnerships and lead transformation. They can attain this by the methods of deep listening and close attunement, which can lead them to gain insights and develop a vision by using the resources of their adaptive unconscious. They can then move toward assisting others to share their vision and work together for solutions by creating a narrative that furthers transformational shifts. Such leaders can address today's challenges with confidence and flexibility, while tapping directly into the creativity, knowledge, and awareness in themselves and others.

Karin Jironet, PhD, is a Jungian psychoanalyst and an international and interdisciplinary scholar. She studied art, medical science, and theology at Lund University and holds a doctoral degree in the psychology of religion from the University of Amsterdam. She works closely with individuals at the board level within leading Dutch financial institutions, including ABN AMRO Bank, ING Group, and the Dutch Central Bank. As head of the International Desk at de Baak VNO-NCW, a major Dutch leadership institute, Dr. Jironet serves as a catalyst for projects, bringing together representatives from European member states to improve approaches to corporate governance. She is the author of several books and articles related to leadership development. In 2010, her book *Female Leadership* was published by Routledge.

Murray Stein, PhD, is a Jungian psychoanalyst, the president of the International School of Analytical Psychology in Zurich (ISAPZurich), and a past president of the International Association for Analytical Psychology (2001–2004). He is the author of *In MidLife* (1983), *Jung's Map of the Soul* (1998), *The Principle of Individuation* (2006), and other books and the editor of many works, including *Psyche at Work*. He has consulted internationally with business leaders and has lectured and offered workshops on psychology in the workplace. He holds a doctorate from the University of Chicago in religion and psychological studies. Working together in the corporate sector, Karin Jironet and Murray Stein have created a methodology for transformational leadership development under the name Partners in Transformation. At psychospiritual retreats around the globe, they provide guidance to high-level executives. For more information, go to http://www.murraystein.com.

| 16 |

It's All a Dream

Depth Approaches to Understanding and
Withdrawing Projection

Jeremy Taylor

In Jironet and Stein's essay, unconscious wisdom is an asset leaders
tap to their advantage. However, the work of the unconscious also can
distance us from reality and undermine our relationships with others.
Sometimes we think we are listening, but really we are just projecting our
own ideas or fears onto situations and groups. People project onto others
all the time, particularly when stressed or fearful. As an example, at the
University of Maryland, where I taught, two different leadership classes of
executives unconsciously ascribed higher status to the second-semester
class, acting this out in rather exaggerated forms, even though they had
similar positions in the larger world and were only a semester apart in the
program. Clearly, they were projecting status differences onto one another
that were not based on fact, and it impeded their ability to share insights
collaboratively. In the essay that follows, Jeremy Taylor shares essential
knowledge about how to recognize and withdraw projection proactively so
that possibilities can emerge that allow problems to be solved, alliances
forged, and visions implemented.

Our world is increasingly divided by differences of culture, religion,
and ideology—differences and divisions that are ironically made all
the more intense and inescapable by our increasingly globalized economy and expanding information technologies. The intense struggles
between and among groups of mutually unacceptable others not only
jeopardize our collective growth and development, but also the wars
they generate imperil the economy, the environment, and the lives of

those touched—and potentially, when we consider widespread nuclear capability, our survival.

In the face of these realities, one of the most essential tasks of leadership at all levels today is to become more consciously aware of our instinctive, unconscious mistrust, fear, and dislike of these archetypical "others" and, in that process, to come to see both them and ourselves more clearly. This task becomes all the more urgent the more we engage in the globalization of business and shared security concerns.

Our reconciliation of these hostilities is directly linked to a greater self-awareness of our instinctive propensity to fear and reject the archetypal, unconscious "other" (the universal, ever-repeating, unconscious pattern Carl Jung termed "the Shadow"), and our ability to reconcile our own, previously unconscious, fears and longings. Our chances of survival and healthy development are increased dramatically when we look within—particularly at the parts of ourselves that seem other in our initial encounters with them.

The collective world of violent strife and global-ideological turmoil and the individual world of intimate personal struggle and disappointment in relationships may seem at first glance to be totally separate. But in fact, they are both generated by the same interior patterns of unreflective enmity, intolerance, and misunderstanding. At the unconscious level, the hidden factors that drive collective, international, political-ideological-economic-ecological strife are the same as the unconscious factors that twist and cripple our personal relationships and frustrate our individual longings and desires. We encounter the same unconscious thoughts, fears, and desires when we struggle with our personal dilemmas as we do when we try to confront the necessity of pacific change and reconciliation in the outer world. The same unconscious patterns of projection that we encounter in our individual, day-to-day lives drive and enflame our collective struggles with other nations and societies.

No matter how these conflicts are commonly conceived and presented, the violent, counterproductive, pain-filled situations we create at both the collective and personal levels are not the result of conscious choice and sober consideration. They are shaped by predominantly unconscious energies and patterns of projected perception. The seemingly separate realms of collective strife and personal struggle are united by the unconscious archetypal energies and patterns that energize and drive them both.

Our ubiquitous problems stemming from counterproductive communication and failed mutual understanding regularly lead us to horrible violence at both the personal and intercommunal levels. They are outward manifestations of internal, unconscious energies. The problem with the unconscious is that it really is unconscious. It influences and shapes our waking lives without our even knowing it in the moments when it's happening.

Leaders and those they lead may honestly believe that they are acting rationally, and that they have no other choice but to respond to particular circumstances with the decisive force of physical, emotional, economic, and religious violence. However, the deeper truth of the matter is that the situations that regularly lead us to these thoughts, and the destructive actions that grow from them, are the results of irrational interior processes that are regularly hidden from our conscious view.

In fact, the miseries of our personal lives—the hatred, fear, and failed relationships—as well as in the greater world—the ecological calamities, economic misfortunes, religious bigotry, political tyranny, military aggression, and cultural collapse—are all consequences of the ways our conscious relationships with the world are distorted and subverted by the projected perceptions of our own unconscious fears and desires.

All these repeating patterns of human activity, both individual and collective, are shaped by the inevitable process of unconscious projection—"inevitable" precisely because it is unconscious, and for that reason simply not subject to conscious scrutiny and rational decision making. For example, "seeing conspiracies everywhere" is, in itself, an unconscious, symbolic projection of the nagging, preconscious knowledge of being part of a great conspiracy ourselves—a not-fully-conscious conspiracy of unexamined assumptions and patterns of thoughts and feelings that reflect and perpetuate the status quo of our individual and collective lives.

Our current collective economic, political, and religious life rests upon and reflects the masculinist, rationalist, intellectual, antiemotional, nationalist, separatist, elitist, and isolationist way we live at both the personal and collective levels. These attitudes are so deeply ingrained that they are invisible to us. They surround us in childhood and, for the most part, remain below the horizon of rational awareness in adulthood. They form the unseen and unacknowledged background of our frustrations and anxieties and are an inescapable part of contemporary global and personal life.

The primary process that feeds, reifies, and perpetuates these unconscious patterns is projection. Projection is not just a neurotic "defense mechanism," of interest only to therapists and their clients when it assumes the forms of "transference" and "countertransference." It is a universal, unconscious pattern of evolving human awareness itself.

The key to understanding projection is this "evolutionary" significance. It is through projection that we gather our first consciously articulate awareness of previously unconscious aspects of our own being. We see in others that which is pressing to become more conscious in ourselves. We mistake these as objective descriptions of "others" and sincerely believe that these things we "see" in them have nothing to do with our own selves. The deeper truth of the matter is that we become aware of evolving aspects of our own interior lives initially in the form of the projections we make on others. As the current entertainment jargon has it: "If you spot it, you've got it!"

It seems to us as though we are looking objectively at other people and situations that exist independently and are exclusively outside ourselves, when in fact we are looking at our nascent awareness of aspects of our own individual and collective identity in this unconsciously projected form. These aspects of our own character and personality are initially always much easier to perceive in others than to identify and take conscious responsibility for as aspects of our own being.

These unconscious projections come in negative and positive "flavors." They are as visible in hero worship and love at first sight as they are in racism, sexism, and classism. Either way, these seemingly objective views of others around us are born out of our own propensities, which we have not yet consciously acknowledged as our own and for which we are not yet prepared to take conscious responsibility.

In this vitally important sense, the problems we unconsciously create for ourselves personally and globally are the result not so much of projection itself as of the refusal to examine our perceptions more carefully and withdraw the projections that could, should, or would help us become more consciously aware of our own awakening possibilities and propensities.

The universality of projection not only applies to the collective denial of human status to "our enemies"; it also applies directly to the repeating patterns of failed individual relationships and the spiritual search that characterize the lives of so many people today. It seems that a great number of us would rather believe that our personal frustrations and misfortunes are the result of other people consciously lying and conniving to betray us, than admit to even the possibility that these repeating patterns in our experience might be shaped by unconscious factors in which we ourselves play a decisive and unwitting role through projection.

As the decades roll by, it seems more and more clear: if we are to have any real hope of resolving our enmities and destructive rivalries—both personally and collectively—we must begin to take responsibility for our initial projections and turn our conscious attention, individually and collectively, to the symbolic nature and content of our own unconscious interior lives.

History can be understood as the record of the desperate, continuing race between education and disaster. We have vast and complex information about how to manipulate the physical world to satisfy our needs and desires and little information about the deep, unconscious, symbolic nature of those same unconscious needs and desires. We must begin to admit to ourselves how our own unconscious energies influence and shape our waking actions and beliefs, particularly through the "automatic," unexamined process of projection (again, "automatic" because it is not subject to conscious consideration, judgment, or control). If we are to survive, individually and collectively, we must make the effort necessary to plumb the depths of the metaphoric "darkness" of our own hidden lives.

To put it simply and bluntly: any plans of salvation (personal or collective, economic or political, scientific or religious) that ignore these unconscious factors are doomed to failure, no matter how sincere, well-motivated, carefully thought through, or seemingly practical they may appear to be.

Therefore, if we are to find "salvation" of any kind, we must find practical and reliable ways of becoming more consciously aware of our own and others' "hidden" unconscious lives. Unless leaders do so, they will unconsciously collude with those that follow them, not recognizing that they are leading the whole organization off the edge of a cliff. As long as both leaders and followers are trapped in the same unconscious projection, they will fail to see the world accurately, and racism, war, and environmental devastation will continue. They will inevitably get mired down in intensely involving but counterproductive turf wars in and between organizations, which only serve to feed our denial of the real issues facing us.

Shared Dream Work as a Strategy to Understand Projections

I began doing group dream work when I was a community organizer working to diffuse the powerful interracial projection and scapegoating that was making it impossible to cooperatively solve neighborhood problems.

Sharing dreams with others on some sort of regular basis is a practical means of bringing that which is previously unconscious up to the surface of awareness, so we can begin to take more conscious responsibility for our thoughts and actions. Moreover, hearing someone else's dreams helps them become a person to the listener—not just a body with a particular look and skin color to project upon. If you share your perception of another person's dream, you can also begin to notice that your reading of that dream may tell you more about yourself than them (i.e., we inevitably project our own issues onto other people's dreams, just as we do on their actions in everyday life).

One of the reasons why I am such a proponent of group projective dream work as a strategy for transforming individual and group enmities and misunderstandings is that all conversations about the deeper meanings and implications of dreams are so obvious and inescapably clear as projections. Even if I am a dyed-in-the-wool Freudian behaviorist and am sincerely convinced that all my knowledge and information about unconscious dreams is scientific and has been gathered by rational, objective research and study, I still have no way of applying this supposedly objective information to any particular dream other than by forming my own imagined version of the dreamer's original dream experience and moving forward from there.

There is no better exercise, in my experience, to bring people to a vivid (and occasionally uncomfortable) recognition of their own unconscious habits of projection than persuading them to share dreams with one another and to talk openly together about their possible meanings and interpretations. Sooner or later, the realization dawns with increasing clarity that what is true about discussing the possible meanings of dreams—namely that it is all projection—is also true of all discussions and about everything (including the big four topics of greatest tension and disagreement: sex, religion, politics, and child rearing).

The realization that it really is all projection is one of the foundational principles of exploring dreams with an eye to their deeper meaning and significance. It is also a very reliable foundation for searching for practical solutions to our shared problems, both personal and collective.

The greatest stumbling block in the exploration of our own and others' dreams is *mistaken literalism*. This is a particularly poignant and pervasive problem, since dreams do, from time to time, have literal levels of meaning and implication. If, for example, I dream that I am careening down a mountain road and the brakes fail, it is always a good idea to take my waking-life vehicle to my mechanic and get the brakes checked. If there is a nascent problem with my car's brakes that I sensed unconsciously and, therefore, dreamed about before I had any waking-life awareness that there was anything wrong with the brakes, so much the better. However, even if there is a level of literal warning about my actual brakes failing, there will also always be other simultaneous levels of meaning and significance referring symbolically to other areas of my life. It may, for example, point toward my tendency to "move too fast" and not "slow down when my (social and emotional) safety demands it." Or, perhaps, it metaphorically refers to the way I handle myself in relationships, or how I seek advancement and recognition in the workplace.

Simultaneously, at the collective level, there may be an implication of impending collective "crashes," particularly if the vehicle in the dream has other people in it and even more so if the vehicle in the dream is designed for collective transportation—like a bus or a train.

As we share and explore our dreams together, it is important to remember that only the original dreamer can "remember" what the dream was all about. And, of course, for the dreamer, the temptation to take the dream literally is far greater than for anyone listening to and imagining the dream. For the original dreamer, it seemed to be a literal experience. This is one of the primary reasons why sharing one's dreams with others and listening to their projections (born out of their own imagined versions of the dream) is such an interesting and potentially productive strategy for becoming more aware of one's own previously out-of-sight-and-out-of-mind unconscious life, deeper motivations, and creative energies.

When the effort to remember and better understand our dreams is shared with others, particularly in a context that consciously acknowledges the inevitability of unconscious projection in the process, it is an invaluable way to gain insight into the previously "hidden" factors that shape both our personal and collective experiences. As we gain more understanding of these previously unknown and unacknowledged unconscious patterns in our psyches, it becomes possible to change and transform even the most seemingly intractable repeating patterns of fear, frustration, and dissatisfaction in our lives.

It may be more difficult to see that all our social and relational interactions are also determined to the same profound and inescapable extent by unconscious projection, and yet it is the case. The experience of raising projections up into the light of consciousness in the course of exploring one another's dreams also leads to a dawning realization of the profound extent to which projections shape all our experiences, interactions, and decision-making processes, awake and asleep.

Withdrawing Projections in Other Ways

There are, of course, ways to be made aware of our projections. For example, many organizations, like many individuals, project positive qualities onto themselves and negative ones onto other organizations or individuals. Transformational leaders can develop the capacity to notice when members of their group are demonizing or feeling victimized by others, knowing that when people get particularly worked up over something, their own complexes are likely being tapped and projection is becoming rampant. Such leaders can slow things down, begin to investigate why there is such heat over the matter, and seek out the more objective facts of the situation.

Sometimes a marketing study, an employee satisfaction survey, or other objective data can begin to call into question such a dualistic view of things, enabling an organization to see itself more realistically. Similarly, in a political election, where one party has convinced itself of the diabolical nature of the other, finding out that the voters see things differently can begin to call one's certainty into question.

Leaders who can listen to and learn from input they do not necessarily want to hear have the capacity to assist others in doing so. Unfortunately, sometimes leaders who withdraw their projections and try to educate the rest of us to do so may be undercut by those who see vilifying opponents as a sign of strength. This sad fact shows how society can encourage projection and how a dualistic view of reality, no matter how skewed it might be, can masquerade as realism.

Leaders who understand the phenomenon of projection are sometimes able to notice what story they are telling, what archetypal narrative informs that story, and the results of living out that plot. For some, the simple act of telling six different stories about the same circumstances —especially if two or three of those stories are from the point of view of the person they regard as their enemy or opponent—can help them see where they are projecting and how they might withdraw that projection and view the situation differently.

Whether through psychotherapy, dream analysis, meditation, narrative analysis, deep listening, or simply a commitment to being fully honest with themselves, leaders can develop the capacity to recognize their projections and those of others and help individuals and groups withdraw those projections in the interest of solving common problems. These are the kind of leaders we need the most in the twenty-first century. Until such abilities become normal in groups and organizations, we will continue to fail to realize our dreams of peace, justice, and shared prosperity. However, were we all to learn to recognize and withdraw projections, those dreams would actually become possible.

Reverend Jeremy Taylor, DMin, SThD (hon.), is one of the original four founders and past president of the International Association for the Study of Dreams. He also is the founder and director of the Marin Institute for Projective Dream Work and the author of several books, articles, and poems—most recently including *The Wisdom of Your Dreams* (2009) and *World Tales and Mythic Narratives for Dreamers and Dream Workers* (2010). He is internationally known for his unique blending of archetypal analysis with a focus on social justice and pacific cultural change. For more information, go to http://www.jeremytaylor.com.

| 17 |

Hearing the Music

Leadership and the Inner Work of Art

John J. Cimino and Robert B. Denhardt

Building on Jironet and Stein's focus on fostering deep attunement, where two or more people find that their rhythms are suddenly in tune, John Cimino and Robert Denhardt explore musical analogies to help engender a level of group performance that is comfortably aligned and where individuality is applauded. They reveal how leaders can promote deeper connection with a group by attending to its rhythm, and how they can enhance group effectiveness by encouraging shared leadership that releases a sense of collective spontaneity and enjoyment, similar to what musicians experience in jazz improvisation. Similar to Taylor's focus on freeing our mind and spirits through withdrawing projection, they open the possibility that leaders like you can experience greater ease in their work through reimagining their roles as being similar to that of an orchestra conductor, a member of a jazz improvisation group, or any musician who helps people experience emotion or mirrors their experience in ways that inspire or heal.

> The man that hath no music in himself,
> Nor is not moved with concord of sweet sounds,
> Is fit for treasons, stratagems, and spoils.
> —William Shakespeare, *The Merchant of Venice*

Music and leadership are rarely considered side by side, much less as integral aspects of a more comprehensive way of understanding human thought and human action. But we hold that music and transformational leadership shape and are shaped by similar patterns of human experience and human energy, that the best leaders display a certain "musicality" that distinguishes them from others, and that actual musical expressions, skillfully facilitated, can be employed to tap and evoke significant aspects of the leadership experience and help to unveil its mysteries. In other words, our leadership can be enhanced by recognizing and drawing upon our aesthetic makeup. To turn our opening quotation from Shakespeare around, the best leaders do have "music in themselves" that moves them to think and to act, engaging emotion, imagination, and will. If this is the case, then locating and bringing forth the aesthetic element of leadership can be extremely helpful in the practice of leadership.

Transformational leaders engage others in a very special way, touching elements of desire, commitment, and possibility that are deeply seated in the inner lives of potential followers. They connect with us emotionally in a way that energizes us and moves us to act. In addition, these leaders provide the assurance that we often need to pursue important values. They facilitate a reshaping of human energy, restructure the narratives of human experience, and bring alive a new progression of possibilities, even in spite of ambiguity, complexity, and uncertainty (Denhardt & Denhardt, 2005).

Interestingly, this is similar to the role of music in our lives. Music connects with us emotionally and communicates a certain energy that resonates with one or another emotional state. It touches us physically, emotionally, even spiritually, and primes us for what might be called a *feeling-based exploration* of our personal condition. In this way, music relaxes us, reassures us, consoles us, inspires us, excites us, or calms us as its rhythms and harmonies interact with our own. In a very real way, we are moved from wherever we might have been to a new condition noticeably more in tune with something we value and definitely a couple of notches removed from any of our default states. The music's progressions and transitions—its changes in harmony, melody, and rhythm—become progressions and transitions in our own feeling states, and, indeed, over time we are primed for analogous progressions in other aspects of our lives, becoming more or less at ease with complexity, dissonance, ambiguity, dramatic emotion, and more.

Many have illustrated leadership by reference to the role of an orchestra conductor or the leader of a jazz ensemble. But leaders are rarely able to write and conduct a symphony that others play. More often they are called on to be fully integrated into the performance themselves, to play along with others, like the leader of a jazz ensemble improvising a tune.

> By establishing the theme, the leader of the ensemble . . . can chart the basic pattern and direction in which the performance will move. By setting the tone and the tempo, the leader gives focus to the spirit and energy of the group. By modeling effective and responsible performance in their own solos, leaders can energize and articulate the performance of others. But it is the performance of others that is critical. (Denhardt, 1993, pp. 180–181)

More important, leaders confront many of the same issues faced by musicians and do so in ways that go beyond metaphorical parallels. For example, leaders, like musicians, are concerned with rhythm and timing, and leaders can learn a great deal about rhythm and timing from musicians. Groups and organizations have rhythmic patterns and varying paces that organize the experience of those in the group. Many have experienced the chaos and frustration that occurs when a group accustomed to a particular rhythm in their work gets a new boss, someone with a completely different rhythm.

Both music and leadership are concerned with shaping human energy, energizing people, and encouraging them to new horizons. Both are concerned with summoning things into existence, with enlivening and deepening the human endeavor. In this way, both music and leadership participate in the same philosophical tradition, not the tradition of physical or empirical thought, but the tradition of aesthetic thought, that field of study concerned with the exploration of mind, body, and spirit in relation to art, beauty, and imagination—the world of possibility and potential.

Leadership

Leadership for us is not associated with positions or power, but rather with the act of leading. The one who leads is not necessarily the king, the queen, the boss, or the manager, but one who energizes others in a group, an organization, or a society. Leadership is not the result of hierarchical position, but of a human relationship between the potential leader and potential followers. Transformational leadership does not direct followers to do something, but engages with them in such a way that the full potential of the group is brought to bear on the choice of its future activities. While "management" may be concerned with agency and desired outcomes, transformational leadership is more concerned with creating a narrative that portrays the group's future and compels movement in that direction. In this, the leader doesn't exert power or control, but is more concerned with facilitating an ongoing dialogue that enables participants to explore possible values they might pursue and, when they find those values compelling, to act in their pursuit. In this way of thinking, leadership is not only about "getting things done" but also about developing meaning, insight, and choice.

Within this way of working, the potential leader must be keenly perceptive of the dynamics, traditions, and structures native to a particular group. He or she must engage the group at its own tempo, in its own language, and via its own mechanisms, channels, and structures. This is careful, measured, and intuitive work. It means living and working with large helpings of ambiguity, and shifting and often competing perspectives—the full panorama of human emotions, virtues, and frailties. Like an artist, the potential leader must excel at seeing what is in all its complexity and richness of context in order, gradually and painstakingly, to envision what might be. Like an artist, the potential leader must assimilate the structures, boundaries, and limits of the field of action, the better to know its potential for renovation, renewal, and creativity. The leader, like the artist, must sense this in his or her bones.

Leadership dialogue that is capable of birthing a group's emergent narrative is both time intensive and time sensitive. It is necessarily an affair of great patience, subtlety, and skill. It is almost always more about listening than it is about speaking, and more about feeling than it is about reasoning. The leader here is artist personified, music maker, and evoker of new visions and stories.

In April 2007, Michael Gold was asked to present his Jazz Impact program to a gathering of IBM's thought leaders who were exploring the relationship between transformational leadership, creativity, risk, and innovation. Jazz Impact held an appeal for a number of reasons. First, jazz is an art form based in the essentials of collaborative transformation: generative growth, integrating change, and the ability to sustain innovation. Second, jazz musicians know how to work with ambiguity, how to take action despite uncertainty, and how to challenge the status quo.

When the executives entered the meeting space, they were, of course, surprised to see a jazz ensemble. Before any words were spoken, the musicians engaged them with their music, prompting their minds in a way entirely unexpected. Incoming information in the form of music was captured and stored as *somatic experience*, coded into the body's senses and feeling states, with the result of intensifying its capacity for recall. Longer recall would also facilitate the possibility of integrating this new experience with deeply seated existing knowledge. Over the next two hours, the model of the jazz ensemble would push them further still, helping them to frame discussions of organizational dynamics difficult to address in ordinary language. Jazz, however, provided the perfect vehicle because it was made of the same stuff—our key point.

Gold placed the executives in what he liked to call *liminal situations* and challenged them to work creatively and collaboratively. The term *liminal* refers to the threshold between what we do and do not understand. In jazz, as in life, we are constantly moving back and forth across that threshold. We discover new knowledge and, via the cognitive process known as *transfer*, we integrate our new knowledge into our existing knowledge. The most useful integrations (those actually facilitating transformational change) take place only when our new knowledge has been retained in a deep and meaningful way—and for long-enough periods—to allow transfer to happen. This is why the experiential and somatic aspects of musical engagement, and jazz in particular, as well as other art forms if done correctly, are so important. They have the durability and potency to serve as catalysts for shifting our perspectives and our organizational cultures toward new states and, potentially, more flexible and sustainably innovative states.

When an ensemble is playing jazz successfully, we say that it "swings." Lovers of jazz will tell us this happens when the boundaries between the players and their roles appear to dissolve. We might say that leadership and support flow spontaneously among them. How can there be such clarity of shared intent, such collaborative definition of ideas, such momentum and passion, all without a score? In fact, there is a score; but it is not a literal one. The score is internalized by each of the musicians and works as a set of minimal guidelines for working toward, achieving, and then creatively sustaining the incredible balance that is swing. In jazz, as in leadership, the goal is the process, not the score, the process of finding and sustaining a high-functioning dynamic balance. The result is an ability to embrace ambiguity, interdependence, inner directedness, and an appreciation for unique ideas.

Creativity

Both music and leadership are concerned with summoning things into existence, with enlivening and deepening the human endeavor. This is, of course, the realm of creativity. But how does it happen? To begin with, creativity demands a level of mastery in a domain. Before one can be creative upon the violin, for example, one needs to learn quite a lot about it, but not just about it; one must, in truth, "learn the violin." Moreover, the great artists are not only masters of their technique, they are vulnerable before their art. They learn to risk everything to go right to the edge of what is possible and then just a bit farther, breathing life and their own life's blood into their creations and performances.

Creativity is clearly transformative for the artist. It is also transformative for the leader, and anyone who harnesses himself or herself to the task. Its demand for mastery is matched only by its demand for self-knowledge, risk taking, passion, constant challenge, and stimulation. Creativity is fed by imagination, new experiences, and new connections. Priming the mind for creativity means activating its capacities for connectivity and meaning making—connectivity in the realm of ideas, most certainly, but also in the realm of sensation. We must literally come to our senses in order to tap our creativity, senses both external and internal, sight both through the eye and in the mind's eye. Relentless attention to this formation and transformation of the self—the constant making and remaking of the eye, the mind, and the senses—is the artist's and leader's price of admission to the domain of creativity.

And as they look inward, they must also look outward to the world and its systems, structures, forms, and limits. The form or the genre, be it a sonnet or a multinational corporation, is the grounding bedrock for the creative impulse. The leader and the artist must be students of the world, the better to serve as vectors and catalysts for its future. The leader's dialogue with a group is precisely this: an exploration of existing values and commitments and a simultaneous and mutual process of building possibilities for the future. Like the artist, the transformational leader is midwife to the "not yet," bringing into concert the existing and the imagined, the mundane and the exciting, the old and the new.

Vision inward and wonder outward are, therefore, the sine qua non of transformation. Leaders and artists must be dedicated to this discipline: that knowledge of the world and self-knowledge are each critical and ultimately inseparable.

Miha Pogacnik is a concert violinist, entrepreneur, and cultural ambassador of the Republic of Slovenia. In the past twenty years, he has worked with the leadership of more than 100 world-brand companies, delving into the life force and inspiration of classical music masterpieces. Why? "Because they are archetypal, profoundly inspired higher productions of nature gone through the genius of the composer's individuality" (personal communication, July 12, 2010). But where's the connection to leadership? Pogacnik's answer is as straight as an arrow and just as penetrating. "Is not your life or your organization a potential masterpiece? This lifelong, unfinished product, with which we are all more or less consciously engaged?" Pogacnik is absolutely convinced that music, consciously experienced and keenly observed, offers us an ideal learning field for the exploration of what he calls "the biographical masterpiece." The musical masterpieces, he says, evoke emotions that he helps leaders recognize in their own lives, and, in the process, they have revelations about those moments of life when they have to puzzle their way through a maze of difficulties, perhaps seeing the truth of themselves in the mirror, or learning something new that may change them, or steeling their resolve to take charge and act with courage. In leading participants through this process, Pogacnik takes the journey with them, a journey that corresponds to Otto Scharmer's (2007) Theory U of transformational change. Inspired by Scharmer's work, Pogacnik, through music, assists leaders in going down the U into deeper and deeper understandings and then emerging on the other side with applications to their leadership context, cross-sector group cooperation, and the transformation not only of their organization, but of the wider world.

Resilience

One of the most important messages that music and leadership impart is their effect on the resilience of the human endeavor. Music has a special relationship to healing and restoration. In times of crisis or disaster, music can soothe the soul and restore the spirit. It can bring us back from the edge of chaos and energize us for future struggles, often making us stronger than we were in the beginning. Fresh energy courses through us, reconditioning and revalidating us. Music helps us recover.

Creative Leaps International is a nonprofit educational and consulting group known for its innovative use of the arts, most especially music, in leadership development and organizational renewal. Their work encourages creativity, vision, and imagination through experiential workshops and a uniquely designed Concert of Ideas. Two years after Hurricane Katrina, Creative Leaps, together with leadership experts from the George Washington University Institute for Crisis, Disaster, and Risk Management and the University of Maryland James MacGregor Burns Center for Leadership, were called upon to help the members of the Southeast Louisiana Chapter of the American Red Cross (SELA). The Red Cross group had been decimated, with members losing their own homes and loved ones to the storm. They had pushed themselves beyond the breaking point working for others and neglecting themselves. How to rebuild their spirits? How to rekindle hope and possibility for getting back on track for the new hurricane season just a couple of months away?

Following painstaking research, interviews, and archetypal inter-ventions by the experts from the two universities, the Creative Leaps team mounted a special Concert of Ideas, designed, in this instance, to honor heroic service, catalyze new thinking, and gently, but surely re-surface the emotional trauma of SELA's Katrina experience. The music mirrored the bravery of the SELA staff, substituting a self-image based on what they had accomplished for the trauma-induced frozen feelings and sense of powerlessness that had overwhelmed them. The music mirrored their heroism, as well as their sorrow, and loosened what was locked away. Tears flowed, glances raced from one to another, and smiles began to break out from tightly clasped lips. Within minutes, the room came alive and the journey with Creative Leaps International was begun. Workshops combining music with leadership lessons, habits of excellence, and deep sharing followed. Finally, on the last day, the SELA participants authored their own Harvest of Learnings, a performance event created and performed with just a bit of musical and theatrical assistance from their Creative Leaps colleagues. As they concluded their heartfelt performance, participants triumphantly exclaimed, "We're back!"—and the room shook with their life force.

What had happened? The feeling of what these Red Cross workers had been through was again palpable to them, but no longer paralyzing. The numbness (the anesthetic) had retreated, and the life impulse (the aesthetic) had returned. They had completed the inner work of art and could, once again, dare to imagine.

Conclusion

Music and leadership are easy to compare metaphorically, but we think there is much more to the relationship. We see music and leadership engaging in the same endeavor—to move us to think, to feel, and to act in new ways, ways that express the best possibilities of the human spirit. In this way, both music and leadership are elements of the aesthetic tradition, that tradition concerned with the exploration of mind, body, and spirit in relation to art, beauty, and imagination—explorations felt and sensed as well as cognitively processed.

We would argue that even in the absence of musical performance, aspiring leaders who recognize and tap into the aesthetic dimension of their work likely will be more effective in reshaping human energy. The leader who recognizes and draws upon the "music within" will be the most effective in shaping the "energy without," and that is the essence of effective and transformational leadership.

John J. Cimino is president and CEO of Creative Leaps International and the Learning Arts. As a champion of the arts in business and professional life, Cimino has brought his Concerts of Ideas and other innovative programs into projects of the White House, the Center for Creative Leadership, WDC's Center for Excellence in Municipal Management, and the leadership programs of dozens of Fortune 500 companies. Current projects include Partners for a New Beginning with the U.S. State Department and Aspen Institute, the 50 + 20 Project on the future of management education in conjunction with the United Nations, and consultancies with numerous universities.

Robert B. Denhardt is Regents Professor Emeritus and former director of the School of Public Affairs at Arizona State University. A past president of the American Society for Public Administration and a fellow of the National Academy of Public Administration, Professor Denhardt is the author of over a hundred articles in professional journals and has published twenty-four books, including *The Dance of Leadership* and *The New Public Service*. A popular motivational speaker, Denhardt specializes in leadership and organizational change.

| 18 |

Unleashing Possibilities

Leadership and the Third Space

Zachary Green, Omowale Elson, and Anjet van Linge

In the previous essay, Cimino and Denhardt demonstrated how leaders foster connections and relationships in groups through music and rhythm. The final essay in Part Three, by Zachary Green, Omowale Elson, and Anjet van Linge, moves our attention to recognizing and identifying with such larger patterns—the whole, not the parts—by thinking structurally. They explain that we can benefit by differentiating the various parts of ourselves, and the cultural and other groups outside ourselves, so as not to minimize unique needs and perspectives. As Colman and Ubalijoro identify the "third thing" in the resolution of internal and external tensions, these authors provide a similar idea of the Third Space as existing beyond our differences in the relationships within, between, and among us. This essay offers a perspective that can help you gain the capacity to recognize and understand your own complexity as well as of that of the other living systems of which you are a part.

It is common for many of us to say that as humanity, we are one. This statement suggests that we share a capacity to see the underlying unity of life. It also means that there is a tacit acknowledgment of our differences. When we are born, we encounter our first duality. It is affirmed in that first moment of life when someone says, "It's a girl." By definition, it is determined that this new life is of one identity, but not another—not a boy. Soon thereafter, a form may ask for another designation of this child—a race. Along with whatever name the parents give to their newborn, other ways of naming are also present. We are classified into a number of categories or identities: gender, race, social class, nationality, (dis)ability, and so forth.

Our narrow distinctions become ways to differentiate ourselves from one another. Our gender, race, age, and nationality are but a few attributes we use to mark our uniqueness and claim a first space of identity. As individuals and as larger societies we use these same attributes to separate ourselves into "us" and "them" categories. What was one becomes two. In other words, what was our common humanity readily becomes lived as duality (Friedman, 2007). The result is that we have male and female, black and white, older and younger, native and foreign where before there was simply the fundamental unity of our common humanity. From the very beginning, we come into a world of yes/no, either/or, and black/white. If we are lucky, we rediscover the both-and-also that was there before our duality training began.

Once there is the duality of two and the emphasis on difference, there is also the beginning of tension and struggle for dominance—we are better than you. There is no longer only the differences in attributes, but a very human push to create hierarchy (Elson, 2002). Others label us and often we ourselves embrace a "we," when in a couple or when we are seen as being part of a group. However, while classifying others in a group is easy, being labeled as being in a group is more difficult. We then have a common, almost immediate reaction to differentiate ourselves from this we-ness, because we feel we lose who the "I" is. Duality then is expressed not only by an "us-and-them," but also by a "we-and-I." There is, however, merit to looking deeper into what it means to belong to a "we." The "we" invites us to be responsible for who we are together and honor the tension, destruction, and creation that go with that. It invites us to take responsibility for the "we" and carry our part in the collective leadership.

The challenge comes when we want to have our "we" recognized as more powerful than another "we." The desire for dominance separates us from our common humanity. Paradoxically, duality becomes a retreat from the unity in humanity and needs a Third Space to bring us back to one.

The Third Space

The Third Space is known to us, though we are likely more familiar and practiced in thinking in dualities. Whether we are considering divisions within self-identity, individuals with one another, individuals with groups, or groups with other groups, the Third Space occurs when we move out of an identification with any of the parts (including our own ego orientation) to see a bigger picture, a structural view, or the relationship that links the parts together. Doing so almost always opens up possibilities that could not be recognized in any other way.

The theory was derived from the work of Bhabha (1994), who noticed how identity arising out of the struggle of colonized people with oppressive authority created a third, blended identity. He went on to suggest that the tension in the power relationships between the oppressor and the oppressed created a space where those new forms of identity were negotiated and emerged. In postcolonial contemporary societies, the Third Space can be seen in a generation whose parents worked in multiple international posts or experienced numerous military deployments. The children, commonly referred to as Third Culture Kids, shared a sense of identity formed by the variety of points in the world where they lived. They often felt alienated in their early development with no firmly fixed sense of identity. As adults, they became known for their flexibility and adaptability to cope with a wide range of the human condition (Pollack & Van Reken, 2001).

The leadership implication of the Third Space, as being evidenced by these children, is hope for moving beyond protracted and seemingly intractable human conflicts. The Third Space demonstrates that identity can be other than the regressed and known familiarity of duality (Starosta & Olorunnisola, 1995).

In terms of leadership, the Third Space is the location of the tension, negotiation, creation, and emergence of the new. Initially, three points form it: the leaders, the followers, and the relationship between the two. When we remain fixed on leadership strictly in terms of leaders and followers (Burns, 1978), our thinking is linear and locked in duality. The Third Space invites us to consider leadership as a process and system of interactions with infinite potential points of action and networked dimensionality. In this way, the Third Space is a location from which leadership as transformation begins. Leadership in this perspective can be seen as a function of the group (a view also held in the group relations tradition). In other words, what we call leadership is more of a calling forth of what the group as a collective requires at any given moment (Bion, 1961). While a "moment" may be as little as the few seconds it takes to deal with an immediate crisis, or a millennium in the case of some faith traditions, in any instance it is the group that has a significant role in what leadership arises and how it is sustained. The importance of the Third Space is that it recognizes the importance of time in the development of what leadership becomes. When we move out of static positions into the world of dynamic relationships, everything is in motion, all the parts are affecting one another, and new possibilities emerge.

Leadership and the Third Space: A Model

Leadership and the Third Space are evidenced when a plane of potential is created between one and another. Rather than the tug-of-war of dynamic tension between one person and another, or one group and another, or even one nation and another, a third is coconceived. It is more common to think about a battle between two forces. The human tendency for thinking in "either/or" terms helps reduce anxiety and complexity when people engage one another (Heifetz & Linsky, 2002). Thinking in these kinds of dualities is rather a default position. Indeed, "us-and-them" tensions may be a necessary first step before the Third Space can be seen. The leadership challenge is for groups to move beyond the kind of embattled "double consciousness" that was presented by DuBois (1903) to describe the experience of African Americans: "One ever feels his two-ness—an American, a Negro; two souls, two thoughts, two unreconciled strivings; two warring ideals in one dark body, whose dogged strength alone keeps it from being torn asunder" (p. 255).

This process is readily recognized in people in the United States who identify often as "hyphenated" Americans, but it is actually more universal. For example, a person who is Asian American or African American identifies with a place of racial and cultural origin, as well as with the land of their nationality. Each side of the hyphen is a discrete identity with its own nature, mores, values, and socially constructed meaning. The Third Space holds what the two identities create when viewed as one. Simply put, the nature and meaning of being Asian or American is perceived and is likely to be experienced as different from being Asian and American at the same time. Yet we are our nation, culture, race, and gender all at once. What we make discrete in dualities is a retreat from the Third Space and from the promise of unity in our humanity.

Thus, it is only in our Western Christian (and more so in our post-Descartes) times that we are invited to invest in choosing between one of two aspects within ourselves and, therefore, identifying two in the first place. Doing so helps us contain our anxiety of a more complex "we" that also exists (Heifetz & Linsky, 2002). When we invite ourselves to think of two points (previously thought of as opposing or dual) as markers in a field, we can see the field emerge between them.

Modern science is slowly unpacking verifiable aspects of this "we," uncovering how things can be both a particle and a wave, and that what it is depends on how we choose to measure it—when we measure for particles that is what we find; when we measure for waves, it will be that. We have not yet discovered a way to measure and, thus, prove the simultaneous existence of both states (Heisenberg, 1927/1983).

As a model for leadership, the Third Space invites us to consistently explore not only who the "other" is (the other group, the other department, country, or religion, or the other side of self), but also what might be the Third Space that can be cocreated with this other, as a field in which the different perspectives held by both parties can serve as anchors for what is new that may need to emerge.

Transforming Leadership and the Third Space

If we think of this field as a space that is always present, yet rarely accessed, we open ourselves to new ways of thinking about leadership.

One can think of the youth movements that created the Arab Spring to see the Third Space in operation. Through acts of collective will by the group, the existing formal leadership responded and created a different kind of relationship—sometimes revolutionary and sometimes reactionary—with repressive crackdowns. The potential of what is held in the Third Space was activated, and it created the conditions for transformation. E-tools facilitated the emergence of this Third Space by connecting thousands of people and tapping into their energy and desire for change.

In a similar fashion, an increasingly global Internet provides an increasing percentage of the world population with greater instantaneous access to the triumphs and tragedies of human life than even a generation ago (Friedman, 2007). The network of communication means that the nature of authority is also shifting. Social uprisings against repressive and autocratic states are broadcast via videos made on mobile phones. Bloggers and social networkers offer their commentaries on the issues of the day with the capacity for immediate potential transformation when messages reach millions in moments. These experiences mean that we each have available to us encounters with a space apart from our own, often unconscious, fixed notions of identity. While such "e-proximity" hardly assures connection, the potential for it is now infinite. Without leaving one's home, other worlds are readily present to explore and experience. Through these various modes of media, massive migration, and other means, the other is more often nearby, existing in another kind of Third Space. Yet those same e-tools enable us also to retreat into a this-is-not-me space, because we are offered easy access to everything that happens in the world and, when feeling low, may seek to explore other people's misery to feel better. We have been trained to think it takes courage to live in this "we." That is how invested we are in maintaining the struggle of duality (Rutherford, 1990), or the see-me-be-brave venturing out into the Third Space as an act of courage (rather than, perhaps, our natural state).

Leadership that emerges from this field does not necessarily divide the world into leaders and followers. It may describe the field as held by people in various roles at various times (Hayden & Molenkamp, 2004).

It invites actors in that field to think about the roles they take and how they relate to others in the field. New media enable us to make that field visible more swiftly. The Obama presidential candidacy may be one example of how in such a Third Space, in such a field, new leadership can emerge, held by many, yet claimed by no one in particular. A man who is biracial, who is a product of different faith traditions, who lived in other cultures, who was termed by some the "first viable female" candidate (Linsky, 2008), and who spoke of a common American identity— actually embodies the Third Space. However, as soon as he was in office, his ability to evoke a larger Third Space was undermined by partisan culture wars.

The Third Space Applied

It is rather easy to find evidence of where Third Space thinking is not applied and practiced. In the political discourse of the United States, in the ongoing struggles for dominance in more than a few sub-Saharan African nations, and in the seemingly interminable and intractable Israeli-Palestinian negotiations there is an apparent collective propensity to operate in dualities that easily regress into polarities. The familiar nature of these discords reflects an apparent larger need by human groups to be reductionist about complex questions of identity, governance, and change. As a consequence, slogans, catchwords, sound bites, and coded language replace dialogue that could produce deeper meaning and compassion between different others (Isaacs, 1999). Rather than becoming the apex of dimensionality, the practice is more akin to a tug-of-war with clear winners and losers. While this kind of linearity offers a facile black-and-white reflection of the world, it does not create the developed consciousness needed for leadership that is truly transforming.

There are a few examples in recent human history when the Third Space could be seen. One of the most compelling examples was in post-apartheid South Africa. While issues of poverty and inequality still abounded, the fact that the country did not collapse into civil war or retro-oppression was a function of the leadership that was demonstrated at the moment of the historic shift in power from a white minority government to one of the whole, as represented in the presidency of Nelson Mandela. In the development of the Truth and Reconciliation Commission (TRC), the horrors of the apartheid era were given a forum for expression. Those who were perpetrators and victims of atrocities during those dark days were given time to tell their stories, be heard, and experience a degree of healing not possible within the realm of simpler right-wrong duality. Though many cried for a familiar brand of justice in which individuals were expected to pay for their crimes, the TRC offered a third way (Tutu, 2000).

Another less known event is Women in Black, where in Israel, for example, Palestinian and Israeli women traverse rigid polarized boundaries to meet at a common space at intervals to share their common grief for their lost sons, husbands, and relatives in a seemingly endless war (Baillie, 2002).

Implications

In the years to come, leadership that is authentically transforming may well require competence in traversing the Third Space. While systems ranging from couples, to communities, to corporations, to countries may continue to operate in dualistic reductionism, greater success in addressing the host of challenges of tomorrow may be through what can be created in the Third Space. It is in the individual courage to see, hold, and act upon what feels like the "other" within that a process begins that leads to leadership. Until we can experience the Third Space within ourselves, it is difficult to experience it with others. Once known, the reflection of the process beyond the bounds of self can be seen first in our relationships with those closest to us and then, much later, in those whom we experience as different, alien, and, perhaps, even disdainful. It is in the recognition that these others are also ourselves that the Third Space becomes not only an expression of a different kind of leadership, but also a source of compassion for our fellow humans—as one.

When leadership begins to take on a texture of more dimensionality— when those who hold the roles of directors and decision makers of various forms and forums see the potential that exists beyond polarity—then there is the Third Space and the emergence of a world anew.

Zachary Green, an executive leadership coach for the World Bank, is a member of the founding circle of Group Relations International. He currently is a visiting professor in leadership studies at the University of San Diego.

Omowale Elson is on the graduate faculty of Trinity Washington University. He is also an A. K. Rice Institute board member and managing principal of Elson Consulting Group, LLC.

Anjet van Linge is also a founder of Group Relations International. A leadership consultant operating from Bureau Zee in the Netherlands, she devotes most of her time to stone carving and writing.

| Conclusion |

Reinforcing Change through Transformational Communication

The three major sections of this book have been designed to help present and would-be transforming leaders be more effective in today's world by enhancing their ability to analyze situations, deepen their consciousness so as to embody presence and evoke trust, and develop their relationship-building and communication skills in order to influence complex adaptive human systems to produce transformational outcomes. The sequence is important, because each section builds on the previous one. Being different starts with thinking differently. Relating in empowering ways depends on authenticity and integrity.

Each major part of this book has implications for how we talk. Part One, for instance, encourages us to shift our attention from problems to vision; from what is lacking to noticing strengths; from blaming individuals to fostering structural and relational solutions; and from looking to others to make a difference to fully claiming our own responsibility for doing so. To the degree that our communication reflects these shifts of perspective, we reinforce them in ourselves and others.

Part Two challenges us to acknowledge that we are not just human capital pursuing careers for status and material gain. Instead, it encourages us to recognize that we are ensouled creatures, who can respond to a call or sense of vocation that has meaning beyond just a way to get ahead. We do not have to be confined by the limitations of our fears and anxieties, emotionalism, narrow rationality, or how things have always

you can remove yourself from a setting where a destructive drama is being played out, that is ideal. If you cannot, you can experiment with acting a different part in that story to see if the whole drama shifts; or you can imagine a number of other stories you could tell about the situation, live into one of them, and see what opens up for you over time.

In many circumstances, asking "What story do I want to live?" simply reminds us of what we actually desire, so that our immediate feelings do not pull us into a drama we do not want to be in. For example, when I'm angry with a colleague and feel like going for the jugular, I might remember that my goal is to work well with him. So I tone down my Warrior archetype impulse and try to express my concerns in a more reasonable (Sage) or loving (Lover) way. Or, if I find I am wimping out on an issue important to me, I might want to live consciously into a Warrior story and fight for what I think is right.

Leadership communication that comes from a clear understanding of our stories and what narratives we want to live is honest and unafraid to acknowledge uncomfortable realities. But it is also, as much as possible, appreciative and positive. While honoring the legacy of the past, it holds an inspiring vision of what can be. It is most effective, moreover, when its messages are archetypal and hence reveal deeper truths of the human heart than mere facts can ever do. Archetypal images and narratives connect to realities the soul already has access to; the very term *archetype* means that these are eternal and available to people regardless of their cultures or individual differences (Pearson & Marr, 2006). Archetypal branding can act as a call to the people who need or want the qualities the archetypal story of your enterprise fosters. For example, Apple Computer's Revolutionary archetype identity (a tag like Think Different, a logo that has an apple with a bite out of it as in the Garden of Eden, a reputation for game-changing innovation) attracts customers who want to be ahead of the curve.

One of the leadership quandaries mentioned by my students (see the general introduction) concerns the degree to which strategic planning is effective in a context of global interdependence, unpredictability, and fast change. To engage in strategic planning as if it were possible to set specific objectives and goals and consistently meet them communicates the unrealistic belief that the future can and should be controlled. Today, such plans, while helpful, are merely statements of what is desired at a particular moment in time. Thus, many leaders and organizations are adopting scenario planning as an alternative or complement to strategic plans. How does scenario planning work? Try to imagine all the different possibilities that could happen, then tell stories about how you might handle them to achieve a positive result, while also noting likely results you would like to avoid. Does this accurately predict the future? Maybe not, but it develops creativity and flexibility in the thinking of those involved, which can be useful whatever transpires. In addition, it raises the questions: What stories do we collectively want to live, and what images and plot regressions resonate with us?

As leaders, the metaphors and images we use, and the narrative structures we employ, frequently determine both how we are seen by others and the degree to which they trust us. Inevitably, this will have an impact on the results achieved, for good or ill. The stories you tell in your role as a leader are likely to be enacted, so it is important to think about where this narrative is likely to lead. If you tell Warrior stories, you predictably will have enemies. If you constantly complain about how bad things are (an Orphan story), they are likely to get worse as people around you become more and more dispirited.

A key task of transformational leaders is to reframe situations by sharing narratives that provide a clear, felt sense of what is right to do in any situation, or that awaken openness to trying out new possibilities. Sometimes sharing an image that arises in your mind can reframe reality in a clarifying way. Fetzer participant and executive coach Rene Molenkamp (2011) wrote about a client who complained that he had become desperately unhappy at work. An image suddenly formed in Molenkamp's mind of "a very solid ship that used to be in calm waters, but now found itself in the midst of a severe storm and there was no end in sight." This image struck a chord in his client, who upon reflection realized that he was strong, but not strong enough to weather what was going on in his company. He recognized that it was time to seek other options.

Many famous quotations reframe reality in ways that open up possibilities, for example, Franklin Delano Roosevelt's "The only thing we have to fear is fear itself"; John F. Kennedy's "Ask not what your country can do for you—ask what you can do for your country"; and Marianne Williamson's "Our deepest fear is not that we are inadequate. Our deepest fear is that we are powerful beyond measure. It is our light, not our darkness, that most frightens us."

But reframing does not always have to be so serious. Sometimes humor can be just as helpful. It lightens the mood, so people can regain perspective. One of my favorites is, "If at first you don't succeed, then skydiving is not for you" (variously attributed). Humor also can help people laugh while accepting realities that otherwise might feel sobering, such as, "We must all hang together, or assuredly we shall all hang separately" (Benjamin Franklin), which during the Revolutionary War was literally true, or the more everyday reality any of us might experience, captured in Maya Angelou's quip, "Achievement brings its own anticlimax." Humor also can be a way to defuse hostility and turn the tables to one's advantage. For example, President Ronald Reagan, during a 1984 campaign debate with Walter Mondale, neutralized concern about his age with a quip: "I want you to know that . . . I will not make age an issue of this campaign. I am not going to exploit, for political purposes, my opponent's youth and inexperience."

The purpose of *The Transforming Leader* is to reframe the challenge of leading in today's interdependent, unpredictable world. Its message is that if we update our thinking, enhance the quality of our being, deepen our sense of relatedness with the ecology of our natural and social worlds, and practice transformational communication—then things don't have to be so hard.

You each are transforming the world every moment by the choices you make. The more conscious you are, even about your own thinking and communication, the more likely it is that this transformation is moving in a positive direction, not only for the world, but also for yourself. If enough of us are responsible and aware, we will create a critical mass that can produce the tipping point that puts the world back on a positive path and, hence, a positive legacy for all the generations that follow in our footsteps. This choice is now yours, and mine, to make—every day.

| Appendix A |

Application Exercises

The exercises that follow are designed to apply concepts from the three parts and the conclusion of this book to your leadership practice. They provide a disciplined method for strategic analysis around specific situations you may be facing. In every case, begin with a specific situation and answer the questions in relationship to it. When you have gone through these exercises once, remember that you can return to them to help you think through other issues you may encounter in a contemporary, transformational way.

If you have difficulty completing any of these analyses, you can refer back to the relevant essay (capacity numbers correspond to chapter numbers), to Appendix B, or to the reference lists at the end of each chapter.

It may be helpful to keep a notebook or journal to record your reflections over time and/or share them with a partner, coach, or peer support group. If you are a leadership coach, mentor, or advisor, you may also want to use this strategic analysis model with leaders you are developing.

A: Applications for Thinking through What to Do

Step One: Describe a Challenging Situation

Choose a situation that provides an adaptive challenge, not just a technical one. Ideally, it should be a situation that requires some changes in structures, attitudes, and relationships, not just a problem that can easily be solved by applying standard procedures or otherwise operating in habitual ways. Then describe, ideally in narrative form, how you view this situation, including what you are now doing and what results you are getting.

Step Two: Develop Transformational Thinking as a Leadership Capacity

Explore the six major capacities in the categories below, addressing the numbered ways of thinking that inform each. Of course, feel free to omit those that do not seem relevant to the situation you have described, but be sure to consider all six capacities, as it is a human tendency to discount approaches that do not yet come naturally to us.

As you respond to the questions and analytical strategies listed below, your first task is to apply your answers to the particular situation you have described and then to your leadership challenges more broadly.

CAPACITY 1: TRUST THAT TRANSFORMATIONAL LEADERSHIP WORKS IN PRACTICE

1. Identify where you have witnessed leadership that inspires with a win-win vision, initiates a process that brings out the best in the people involved (including yourself), and produces results that are genuinely transformational in impact.
2. Describe where, in any part of your life, you have been involved in such a successful transformation effort. What did you take away from that experience?
3. Imagine what a transformational process might look like in situations you face, working on this until you have some sense of confidence that it just might succeed.

CAPACITY 2: HAVE A CLEAR IMAGE OF WHAT
TRANSFORMATIONAL LEADERSHIP LOOKS LIKE

1. Now flesh out your vision of a win-win, positive outcome to this situation, one that can be shared with others. Work on describing this vision in a compelling way as a big dream that can release energy for change.
2. Determine who needs to be involved with you in creating a transformational outcome. Consider how you might inspire enthusiasm in a transformational team or network, enlist outside supporters, defuse resistance, and use transactional means to buy off adversaries if you cannot engage their cooperation in a transformational way.
3. Clarify how the process of working together will elevate you and all those involved by connecting your efforts with shared values and dreams.

CAPACITY 3: KNOW HOW TO INFLUENCE SOCIAL
NETWORKS

1. Moving away from hierarchical networks, analyze the social networks within your group and/or organization. Explore how these social networks interconnect with people in other groups, organizations, communities of practice, movements, and so on.
2. Identify individuals within these networks who are in a position to influence others. This can, of course, include people with positional power, but also those with great popularity, prestige, or facilitation or brokerage capabilities.
3. Identify what kind of power you have to influence the larger networks (positional power, popularity, prestige, facilitation or brokerage skills, etc.) and determine how you can use this power for transformational effect.

CAPACITY 4: REINFORCE THE POSITIVE TO BUILD
CONFIDENCE AND HOPE

1. Using an appreciative approach, identify the positive strengths, qualities, and values you possess that can help you be a transforming leader.
2. Identify the positive strengths, qualities, and values you see in other individuals who can assist in your efforts. Help them recognize what is positive and strong in them and how those qualities can aid you in addressing your situation. Use this knowledge of distributed talents to build strong teams and networked approaches to utilizing the combined capacity of multiple strengths.
3. Explore what is positive, past and present, in the group or groups (or the entire organization) involved and how these qualities can contribute to the realization of a consensual positive future vision.

CAPACITY 5: APPLY CONTEMPORARY SCIENTIFIC WAYS
OF THINKING TO YOUR LEADERSHIP

1. Build on your analysis of how to influence individuals and release their energy by exploring how you can free up energy in the systems involved by fostering relationships between key individuals or groups.
2. Listen closely to what appears to be resistance from others to gain important information about issues that need to be addressed (such as human fears, possible unanticipated side effects of the change effort, ways these efforts may be disempowering for some involved, serious values conflicts that need to be resolved, etc.). Explore how to refine your strategy as necessary to integrate solutions to such legitimate concerns respectfully.
3. Build a plan for influencing the larger field (considering fields as complex, dynamic, and constantly shaped by self-organizing activities). In doing so, begin by observing what problems may be in the process of being solved, and visions realized, in what is already happening. Then determine where you need to assist or

redirect energies and where you can help most by getting out of the way.

CAPACITY 6: ACCEPT RESPONSIBILITY FOR MAKING A
DIFFERENCE

1. Instead of viewing conflict or change as problems, cultivate an attitude that recognizes turbulence as normal (like weather) and how it destabilizes and promotes self-organization in human systems. See yourself as a fractal, an attractor that influences what happens by what you embody, say, and do. Consider how this mode of thinking might affect your attitude toward the situation you described.
2. Brainstorm ways to bring out the genius in others and in systems. (As a metaphor for this, imagine a butterfly when you see a cocoon.) To further transitions already in process, provide as much transparency as possible; share information so that everyone knows what they need to know to see the big picture; and be sure that people have the resources they need to do their part to achieve a collective vision.
3. Make time to read literature and to view movies, plays, and good television dramas to develop your capacity for vicariously experiencing the realities of people who seem different from you. Doing so develops your capacity for empathy.

Step Three: Create Strategic Narratives and Plans

Now look back at how you originally described the situation you want to transform. Applying the analysis above, describe any new insights about your situation and what it might require of you.

You also might find it helpful and enjoyable to write a new story, or narrative, about the situation you described, or your leadership more generally, that begins in the present and concludes with a happy and transformational ending. Good stories always have character development. Let your story show your development and that of other major players, and how that development allows you together to realize a happy ending.

B: Applications for Becoming the Change You Wish to See

Step One: Define the Situation

You can describe a new situation or keep working with the situation you described in the Part One application section. It is best to choose a situation for this exercise that evokes a sense of anxiety, fear, sadness, being overwhelmed, or other difficult feelings, and that, on reflection, you think might require you to develop a new capacity or enhance an existing one (staying calmer under stress, being more open to change, letting go of control in a context of interdependence, dealing more effectively with a difficult person, engendering more respect or confidence in others, etc.). In this case, describe not only the situation, but also the feelings it induces in you and anything you know about the inner capacity you need or want to develop to meet this challenge.

Step Two: Engage in the Journey of Inner Development to Acquire New Capacities

In addressing these questions and practices, it is desirable to apply them first to the situation you described and second to your leadership more generally.

CAPACITY 7: RESPONDING TO THE WORLD'S NEED
AS THE CALL TO LEAD

1. Define the need in your group, organization, or community, or the world in general, that calls you to leadership. How do you feel this need in your body's response to it?
2. To what degree do you have access to what is required to address this need (for example, ease in working with change, addressing conflict, letting go of control, or speaking the truth when it feels dangerous to do so)?
3. Consider other places in your life where you have risen to similar challenges and how you might translate those abilities to new ones; role models you might emulate to do so; and people who might provide support for faking it until you develop a needed capacity in yourself to respond in the way that is necessary now.

4. Reflect on whether your current call requires you to make conscious shadow elements in your psyche. (For example, if you find yourself obsessively judging someone, you might work on finding what in you is like them or where you might be repressing qualities that might be helpful to you if you did not disdain them.) Determine how to get the help you need to do so.

5. Unless your struggle is clearly yours alone, recognize that others in the system likely feel similar things. Provide assistance and support in the larger system for promoting the resilience and flexibility needed to develop underdeveloped and perhaps even unwanted abilities that are required by the situation you have described.

CAPACITY 8: BECOMING ACQUAINTED WITH YOUR
INNER TOOLBOX

1. If you believe your leadership in the situation you described to be a spiritual practice, what might this suggest you do? (If you are religious, you might apply the beliefs and precepts of your religion. If you are not religious, think about how leadership is a path of service for you.)

2. Identify elements of your inner toolbox and their gifts to you, especially your ego, soul, and spirit; your mind, heart, and body; and your conscious and unconscious minds. Consider how each might assist you in the situation you described.

3. Consider how you might engage in presencing by identifying the highest future possibility and committing to bringing it into the now. Describe what this would look and feel like for you.

4. Hone your leadership efficacy by acting on the freedom to choose your own attitude toward leadership challenges, even though you cannot control what you will encounter.

5. Notice whether making decisions from your heart opens up possibilities, and how this might aid you in making choices. Notice also how doing so helps you empathize with others and respect their points of view.

CAPACITY 9: LEADING WITH MINDFULNESS AND
EQUANIMITY

1. Notice whether you are hindered in addressing the situation
   you have described by the ego's need to look good, to maintain
   control, to be right, to worry constantly about how to avoid
   anticipated problems, and so on. If this is the case, describe how
   the ego may be getting in the way of leadership success.
2. To calm anxiety or any of the ego's obsessive concerns, practice
   bringing your attention to your physical body, to sensing the
   world around you and the feeling of your breath coming in and
   going out. You may do this as a sitting meditation or as you go
   through the activities of your day. When the mind is stilled,
   make note of any insight that trickles up into awareness without
   so much effort.
3. Cultivate an observing mind that recognizes all the events
   around you without getting into their drama. Work to accept
   reality as reality while not fighting it. (A friend once told me to
   just regard it as weather; sometimes the sun shines, sometimes it
   rains, and sometimes there are storms. They all come and go.)
   Notice how you know better what to do in any situation if you are
   not in resistance to whatever occurs.

CAPACITY 10: HARVESTING WISDOM FROM EXPERIENCE

1. Describe what it would, or does, mean for you to think of your
   leadership as a vocation. How does it differ from thinking about
   it as a career?
2. Remember when in your life so far you have experienced Via
   Positiva, Negativa, Creativa, and/or Transformativa. How has
   living these paths developed your character and capacities and
   made you a more transformational leader?
3. Describe how you might use awareness of these archetypal paths
   in your leadership by helping yourself and others identify what
   path they are on and what it asks of them in the context of
   challenging situations you and they face.

CAPACITY 11: HEALING YOURSELF, OTHERS, AND
SOCIAL SYSTEMS

1. Who in your life can listen empathically and mirror back to you both your deeper, wiser self and where you might be caught in a complex (our psychological issues), unaware of the impact you are having on others and yourself? Where might you, or do you, provide this support for others?

2. How have your learnings from painful experiences deepened your consciousness in ways that can help you lead others through similar circumstances? Are there any ways that unresolved issues of loss and pain might be limiting your leadership effectiveness? If so, how might you resolve them?

3. Have you been scapegoated or do you fear being scapegoated in the situation you have described? How might you protect yourself from this fate? How can facing such fears develop in you a deeper level of courage and commitment than you have experienced before?

4. Whose suffering calls to you at present? What is required of you to address, ease, or heal that suffering?

CAPACITY 12: LEADING CONTINUOUS CREATIVITY AND
INNOVATION

1. Grounded in your self-knowledge of your gifts, values, and uniqueness, think of how you can respond to challenging events in ways that are authentic and that meet the needs before you.

2. Think about how you may have to shapeshift in your leadership. Begin this practice by noting how qualities and capacities you demonstrate in other parts of your life, or ones that show up in your fantasy life, could be useful in your leadership, and then experiment with bringing them into play in how you actually lead.

3. Brainstorm playfully with others multiple innovative ways to address new challenges, including some that may seem very far out. Then choose some options to consider trying.

4. Imagine yourself modeling an attitude of curiosity, enjoying the wild ride of change, viewing the task of reinventing anything and everything as fun, and reveling in the uncertainty of liminal space as the womb of rebirth. Then work to live into this vision in real time.

5. Foster an environment that supports innovation and experimentation not only in creating new products or services but also in how things are run.

Step Three: Conclusion: Create a Leadership Development Narrative and Plan

Apply what you have learned to how you ideally would *be* in order to address the situation you have described with confidence and ease. Also, identify any capacities you might want to continue to develop in doing so.

You also may want to write a narrative about this situation or about your broader leadership journey that identifies through character development the capacities that journey has fostered and how you wish to continue to deepen and mature to gain the transformational mastery you aspire to embody. (To create a future narrative, it may be helpful to read a biography or autobiography of a role model who exemplifies the qualities that you want to embody. Such a narrative can give you ideas for thinking through the process of becoming your own unique, more mature, and developed you—not another them.)

You also can create a personal development plan, based on your responses to the questions and experiences with the practices, identifying which capacities you have mastered, which require more attention, and what you want to do to further mature and develop as a person and a leader.

C: Applications for the Art of Transforming Groups

Step One: Identify Your Transformational Aspirations for a Specific Group

1. Determine what team, group, organization, community, or network you want to influence to become more transformational.

2. Describe this group, how it functions, and how the members relate.
3. Imagine how you would like the group to function and relate.
4. Sketch out some ideas about what you might do to achieve this goal.

After completing these exercises, tell a brief story about how this group reached the goal and experienced a happy ending.

Step Two: Lead Groups from a Connected and Relational Stance

While our collective challenge requires transformation at large system levels, change begins in smaller groups and organizations. The following exercises therefore are focused on relating within such groups. However, the same principles apply to large-group transformation, using somewhat different, analogous strategies.

CAPACITY 13: LEAD FROM INNER GUIDANCE AND SOUND ANALYSIS

1. Reflect on the dreams and visions that inspire you to do the hard work of leadership. Engage with others involved in your enterprise by sharing such dreams and seeking out theirs as well, moving to weave them together into a collective dream.
2. When you wake up, recall the images and situations in your dreams. These can provide messages from your unconscious that can be understood metaphorically and can contribute compensatory information to balance your waking analysis of any given situation or the inner workings of a group.
3. Create space and time to open to intuitive understandings and make it safe for those around you to share their dreams, intuitive insights, hunches, and gut feelings as important information from the unconscious that can be considered along with rational analysis. Notice synchronistic events that tell you to go for it or stop and reconsider. Encourage discussion of observations, integrating such awareness with a businesslike strategic analysis.

4. Take time to listen to *anima mundi*, the soul of the world; consider the good of the planet in making decisions.

CAPACITY 14: USE DIALOGUE TO HARVEST GROUP WIS-
DOM

In a group context, sit in a circle with the goal of moving to a deeper collective understanding or vision. Model and encourage the following practices:

1. Practice deep listening, which requires suspending what you want to say, to hear with your mind and heart what a person is saying and the emotion and experiences behind what is said. Remember that your goal is to harvest group wisdom, not sell your ideas.

2. Suspend certainty in order to be open enough to hear and take in what others are sharing. When you are unclear about what they are saying, or if you initially disagree, ask questions to help yourself stay receptive to new perspectives and information.

3. Engage your objective, observing mind to notice the systemic and interactional patterns before you, tracking the whole, not just the parts. Encourage an attitude of seeking the good of the whole enterprise, not just getting one's way.

4. Make showing respect for the discernment of individuals and groups a discipline; practice it even when you do not feel like it. To do this, it is necessary to practice emotional intelligence in working with your transference issues and use mindfulness practice to quiet your mind (see Part Two).

5. Understanding synchronicity and trusting the transcendent at work can help you welcome whatever happens, assuming that even if it is annoying or painful, if addressed well it will provide the new insights and growth the group needs.

CAPACITY 15: BE OPEN TO RECEIVING COLLECTIVE
INTUITIVE GUIDANCE

1. Enhance the ability of group members to practice deep listening by literally closing off other stimuli.

2. Foster the practice of close attunement, in which two or more people connect so deeply that a sense of safety and intimacy is established. This enables a profound level of sharing, so much so that new insights are discovered, leading to transformational shifts in individuals, the dyads, or the larger group's sense of things.
3. Weave together such transformational insights into new narratives by answering these questions: What's cooking? What is the germ of the new understanding? Who is drawn to it?
4. Tell and retell the new narratives to encourage a collective vision, a stronger sense of the meaning of the shared enterprise, and a capacity for healthy collaboration.

CAPACITY 16: WITHDRAW PROJECTIONS TO ENHANCE CLARITY AND COOPERATION

1. Notice when individuals or groups are blaming others rather than taking responsibility for what they need to be doing and are making it difficult to work with those so judged. Explore the projection that is occurring and look for where the mirror image of the judged person or group is in the judger. Breaking down the us/them dichotomy in this way can empower people and groups and restore the ability to collaborate with others who initially may seem alien and threatening.
2. Be alert to prejudice and stereotyping within a group or in a group's relationship with others. Foster education and experiences that work to dispel harmful forms of projection and work to protect the victims of such attitudes. Also, ensure that it is okay for people to have made a mistake based on such projections if they are open and willing to treat everyone with respect as they work to let go of their preconceptions.
3. Find ways to help group members recognize that we are always projecting our mental frameworks and narratives onto others and events. Have members separately respond to an inkblot or to pictures that can be seen in at least two ways. Thinking individually about a workplace situation, sharing their analysis, and then

teasing out the different assumptions behind that analysis can have a similar effect, except when the group is afflicted with groupthink.

4. Sharing dreams in a group can help its members both open to intuitive awareness (as in Capability 1) and recognize the power of projection as they see how differently each person interprets the dream based on his or her own experience and ways of making meaning of life.

5. Be sure to do your own work to recognize and withdraw projection, since you cannot take others where you have not gone or are not willing to go.

CAPACITY 17: FOSTER EMOTIONAL CONNECTION
TO ENHANCE PERFORMANCE

1. Imagine your leadership as being similar to a conductor leading an orchestra. Think of the task people are engaged with as being like a particular piece of music they are playing. Then note what feelings are evoked by the various notes, phrases, and timing and the emotions engendered by their interaction with one another. How might you lead by actions as subtle as small movements of a baton to indicate more of this, less of that, and to enhance some emotions and dampen others?

2. Notice the rhythm of a group you want to influence by watching their body movements and how they are, or are not, synchronized. Match your body movements to the group if they are synchronized or, if not, move in a way that could connect with the speed and tempo of all or most of the group, helping through your movements to synchronize theirs. If the group rhythm is synchronized in a pattern that is not conducive to the task, model movements and use language that rev them up or calm them down, as needed.

3. As musicians evoke feelings, think about how you might promote feelings in a group to optimize its functioning—feelings such as enthusiasm, a sense of safety and contentment, or the intense passion of engaging in a full-court press to achieve a desired goal.

Make it clear that it is appropriate for group members to acknowledge feelings and receive appropriate sympathy, congratulations, or other feeling responses without unduly distracting from the work at hand.

4. When groups have experienced hardship, trauma, or defeat, mirror back to them what has been positive in their efforts, with the goal of restoring dignity, self-esteem, and hope. The goal is to heal through artistic reframing, compassion, and seeing the beauty within a deeply human and soulful situation.

CAPACITY 18: CONNECT WITH THE BIGGER PICTURE,
THE ECOLOGY OF THE WHOLE

1. Notice the various components of your sense of identity, such as one or more ethnic, national, or regional identities, your identification with various groups (such as sports teams, schools, political parties, etc.), your gender and sexual orientation, and the ways you may think and feel. Describe how all these various parts come together to provide a sense of you as a whole being. Are there any important parts that you exile, so that they are split off from the rest? If so, can you find a way to integrate such a part into the whole?

2. Identify any relationship that is difficult for you. Consider the relationship between you and the other person as a third space where possibilities lie for transforming what happens between you. Experiment with how thinking this way can open possibilities for relating with greater ease. Help others in difficult relationships find this generative space where change can happen.

3. Work with groups in conflict to recognize the story they each tell about the other. Then explore the third space in the relationship between the groups that allows for a new collective story to emerge. Practicing dialogue in ways that involve representatives from various groups can foster this practice, as can recognizing and withdrawing projections.

5. Find the third space in your relationship with groups or individuals that you lead, recognizing that your work entails building

better relationships at every level of a community or organization.

6. Recognize that all groups function within larger Third Space fields, that members are intertwined with family, community, religious, political, social, and other groups. Such traditional networks now are augmented by social media that provide access to people and ideas from all around the world, which means that a leader's influence is only one of many in a person's life. However, this larger field also provides a fertile ground to seed new, innovative ideas, so it is wise to harvest the wisdom and new ideas generated from this larger Third Space.

Conclusion: Creating a Connected Leadership Narrative and Plan

Decide what from the previous exercises is helpful in building healthy and transformational teams in touch with unconscious as well as conscious insights. Revise the story you wrote in Step One to reflect these new options for developing a transformational group.

Create a plan or checklist for what you might want to do differently in your relationships with groups you lead or influence as well as with other groups that affect your ability to implement a transformational vision.

Step One: Sum Up Where You Are and Where You Want to Go

Take responsibility for leading from where you are and where you want to go by integrating what you have learned. In the application sections for Parts One, Two, and Three, you were encouraged to write narratives that reflect how you want to think, what you want to embody, and how you want to relate to others. Look back at your answers to these exercises and sum up what you have learned.

Step Two: Revisit the Narratives

Revisit the narratives you have written to identify the themes and plot progressions that would make sense for you to share with others in formal and informal communications. You also may want to contemplate how to encourage others to rethink their communication in similar ways, perhaps helping them to develop the capacities outlined in this book and to reflect these in how they communicate (not only in what they say, but in what they measure, reward, and reinforce by other means). Make notes of what you want to say to whom, in what forms and settings, highlighting what themes you want to address.

Step Three: Write about Your Success

Craft one final narrative about your success as a great communicator and how you have transformed the communication patterns of those you influence in ways that reinforce new leadership thinking, being, and relating. Although you are writing about what you hope to achieve, write it as if it had already happened and you were looking back on it.

| Appendix B |

Additional Resources

Organizations and Associations

- The International Leadership Association (ILA) promotes access to new ideas and movements in the leadership field. ILA hosts an annual conference and numerous virtual interactive opportunities (http://www.ila-net.org).
- The Fetzer Institute supports ideas such as those found in this book—ideas that contribute to our ability to foster peace, generosity, love, and forgiveness in the world (http://www.fetzer .org).
- Pacifica Graduate Institute provides public programs and graduate degree programs with a focus on depth psychology, mythology, and organizational and community leadership (http://www .pacifica.edu).
- The Society for Organizational Learning (SOL) is one of the few organizations that has a strong focus on understanding both complex external structures and the inner development of leaders (featuring work by Peter Senge, Otto Scharmer, Betty Sue Flowers, and others) (http://www.solonline.org).
- The International Coach Federation promotes inner work fostered by coaching and mentoring (http://www.coachfederation.org).

Foundational Theory Sets

- Psychiatrist C. G. Jung developed foundational theories about many of the concepts raised in this book, including archetypes, projection, shadow, synchronicity, and the importance of listening to the wisdom of the unconscious as revealed in dreams and active imagination. He also wrote about how what he called the transcendent function kicks in when we are willing to hold the tension within ourselves or with others of opposed views and desires long enough that a third option suddenly is revealed. This breakthrough often is communicated to us through a dream, image, or bodily sensation of just knowing. Jung's concept informs the idea of a third thing or third option utilized in several essays in this volume. For more information, go to Pacifica Graduate Institute (http://www.pacifica.edu) or do a search to find the many Jungian resources accessible online and institutes and resources available in your area.
- The work of *The Transforming Leader* editor, Carol S. Pearson, explores depth psychological approaches to individual and leadership development, authentic archetypal branding, organizational development, and individual and cultural assessment (http://www.herowithin.com).

Leadership and Personal Development Instrumentation

- For a variety of leadership assessment strategies and assessments, go to the Center for Creative Leadership (http://www.ccl.org /leadership).
- For information on the Myers-Briggs Type Indicator™ and/or the Pearson-Marr Archetype Indicator™ (which assess psychological type and archetypes in individuals, respectively), go to the Center for Applications of Psychological Type (http://www.capt.org).
- For information on Gallup's StrengthsFinder™, which assesses leadership strengths, go to its website (http://www.strengthsfinder .com).

- For the Kenexa Cultural Insight Survey™, go to Kenexa (http://www.kenexa.com).
- For various surveys to assess emotional intelligence, go to Daniel Goleman's home page (http://www.danielgoleman.info).

Additional Communities of Practice

- For values clarification, go to the Courage to Lead Project, based on Parker Palmer's work on group support for leadership wholeness (http://www.couragetoleadnp.org).
- For developing abilities in connected ways of leading and the work of Jean Lipman Blumen and associates, go to the Connective Leadership Institute (http://www.achievingstyles.com).
- For communication skills, go to the Harvard Negotiation Project (http://www.pon.harvard.edu/category/research_projects/harvard-negotiation-project).
- For assistance in the more formal area of leadership speaking, consult the work of Stephen Denning, particularly *The Leader's Guide to Storytelling* (http://www.stevedenning.com).
- For releasing energy blocks in the body, go to the Strozzi Institute (http://www.strozziinstitute.com).

See also the author biographies for information about the community of practice represented.

REFERENCES

Part One

Burns, J. M. (1970a). *Leadership.* New York, NY: Harper & Row.

Burns, J. M. (1970b). *Roosevelt: The soldier of freedom: 1940–1945.* New York, NY: Harcourt Brace Jovanovich.

Burns, J. M. (2003). *Transforming leadership: A new pursuit of happiness.* New York, NY: Atlantic Monthly Press.

Maslow, A. H. (1943). A theory of human motivation. *Psychological Review, 50*(4), 370–396.

Smith, A. (1759). *The theory of moral sentiments.* London, UK: A. Millar.

Chapter One

Berger, J., Fisek, M. H., Norman, R. Z., & Zelditch, M., Jr. (1977). *Status characteristics and social interaction.* New York, NY: Elsevier.

Burns, J. M. (1978). *Leadership.* New York, NY: Harper & Row.

Carnegie, D. (1981). *How to win friends and influence people.* New York, NY: Dale Carnegie.

Deci, E. L., & Ryan, R. M. (1985). *Intrinsic motivation and self-determination in human behavior.* New York, NY: Plenum.

Emerson, R. M. (1962). Power-dependence relations. *American Sociological Review, 27,* 21–41.

Emerson, R. M. (1972). Exchange theory, part II: Exchange relations and networks. In J. Berger, M. Zelditch Jr., & B. Anderson (Eds.), *Sociological theories in progress* (Vol. 2; pp. 58–87). Boston, MA: Houghton-Mifflin.

French, J. R. P., Jr., & Raven, B. (1959). The bases of social power. In D. Cartwright (Ed.), *Studies in social power* (pp. 150–167). Ann Arbor: University of Michigan Press.

Lovaglia, M. J. (1995). Power and status: Exchange, attribution and expectation states. *Small Group Research, 26,* 400–426.

Lovaglia, M. J., Mannix, E. A., Samuelson, C. D., Sell, J., & Wilson, R. K. (2005). Conflict, power, and status in groups. In M. S. Poole & A. B. Hollingshead (Eds.), *Theories of small groups: Interdisciplinary perspectives* (pp. 139–184). Thousand Oaks, CA: SAGE.

Lucas, J. W. (1999). Behavioral and emotional outcomes of leadership in task groups. *Social Forces, 78,* 747–778.

Parsons, T. (1963). On the concept of political power. *Proceedings of the American Philosophical Society, 107,* 232–262.

Pink, D. H. (2009). *Drive: The surprising truth about what motivates us.* New York, NY: Riverhead.

Rashotte, L. S. (2006). Social influence. In G. Ritzer & J. M. Ryan (Eds.), *The Blackwell encyclopedia of sociology* (pp. 4426–4429). Oxford, UK: Blackwell.

Raven, B. H., & French, J. R. P., Jr. (1958). Legitimate power, coercive power, and observability in social influence. *Sociometry, 21,* 83–97.

Review of *Drive.* (2010, January 14). The *Economist,* 62.

Rogalin, C. L., Soboroff, S. D., & Lovaglia, M. (2007). Power, status, and affect control. *Sociological Focus, 40,* 202–220.

Skvoretz, J., Willer, D., & Fararo, T. J. (1993). Toward models of power development in exchange networks. *Sociological Perspectives, 36,* 95–115.

Weber, M. (1968). *Economy and society: An outline of interpretive sociology.* New York, NY: Bedminster Press.

Willer, D., Lovaglia, M. J., & Markovsky, B. (1997). Power and influence. *Social Forces, 76,* 571–603.

Chapter Two

Califano, J. A. (2008, May 19). *Seeing is believing: The enduring legacy of Lyndon Johnson* [Keynote address for the Centennial Celebration for President Lyndon Baines Johnson]. Austin, TX: LBJ Library.

Johnson, L. B. (1966). Special message to the Congress on conservation and restoration of natural beauty, February 8, 1965. *Public papers of the presidents of the United States: Lyndon B. Johnson, 1965* (Vol. 1, Entry 54, pp. 155–165). Washington, DC: U.S. Government Printing Office. http://www.lbjlibrary.org/collec tions/selected-speeches/1965/02-08-1965.html

Johnson, L. B. (1966). Special message to the Congress: The American promise, March 15, 1965. *Public papers of the presidents of the United States: Lyndon B. Johnson, 1966* (Vol. 1, Entry 107, pp. 281–287). Washington, DC: U.S. Government Printing Office. http://www.lbjlibrary.org/collections/selected-speeches /1965/03-15-1965.html

Johnson, L. B., & Bundy, M. (1964, May 27). Recording of telephone conversation between Lyndon B. Johnson and McGeorge Bundy, May 27, 1964, 11:24 a.m. (Citation #3522). *Recordings and transcripts of conversations and meetings.* Austin, TX: LBJ Library.

Johnson, L. B., & Dirksen, E. (1964, May 13). Recording of telephone conversation between Lyndon B. Johnson and E. Dirksen, May 13, 1964, 4:30 p.m. (Citation #3437). *Recordings and transcripts of conversations and meetings.* Austin, TX: LBJ Library.

Johnson, T. (2009). Taken from the manuscript of the op-ed "What LBJ Would Do" (2009). Bob Schieffer used a condensed version on CBS "Face The Nation." Other versions appeared in several blogs, including *The Daily Beast.* http:// www.thedailybeast.com/contributors/tom-johnson.html

Kotz, N. (2005). *Judgment days: Lyndon Baines Johnson, Martin Luther King Jr., and the laws that changed America.* New York, NY: Houghton Mifflin.

"Media and the Voting Rights Act of 1965" (October 20, 2008), a symposium cosponsored by the LBJ Library and the Paley Center for Media: http://www. paleycenter.org/media-and-the-voting-rights-act-of-1965

Reagan, R. (1988). State of the Union address. http://janda.org/politxts/State%20of %20Union%20Addresses/1981-1988%20Reagan/rwr88.html

Rosenberg, J., & Karabell, Z. (2003). *Kennedy, Johnson, and the quest for justice: The civil rights tapes.* New York, NY: W. W. Norton.

Smith, E. (2008, August). "Texas Monthly Talks" [interview]. *Texas Monthly.* Retrieved from http://www.texasmonthly.com/2008-08-01/talks.php.

Valenti, J. (1975). *A very human president.* New York, NY: W. W. Norton.

Young, A. (2008, October 20). *Media and the Voting Rights Act of 1965.* Symposium cosponsored by the LBJ Library and the Paley Center for Media. Retrieved from http://www.paleycenter.org/media-and-the-voting-rights-act-of -1965

Chapter Three

Balkundi, P., Barsness, Z., & Michael, J. H. (2009). Unlocking the influence of leadership network structures on team conflict and viability. *Journal of Organizational Behavior, 40*(3), 301–322.

Balkundi, P., & Harris, D. (2006). Ties, leaders, and time in teams: Strong inference about network structure's effects on team viability and performance. *Academy of Management Journal, 49*(1), 49–68.

Balkundi, P., & Kilduff, M. (2005). The ties that lead: A social network approach to leadership. *Leadership Quarterly, 16*, 941–961.

Balkundi, P., Kilduff, M., Barsness, Z. I., & Michael, J. H. (2007). Demographic antecedents and performance consequences of structural holes in work teams. *Journal of Organizational Behavior, 28*, 241–260.

Bonacich, P. (1987). Power and centrality: A family of measures. *American Sociological Review, 92*, 1170–1182.

Bonacich, P., & Lloyd, P. (2001). Eigenvector-like measures of centrality for asymmetric relations. *Social Networks, 23*, 191–201.

Brass, D. J. (1992). Power in organizations: A social network perspective. In G. Moore & J. A. Whitt (Eds.), *Research in politics and society* (pp. 295–323). Greenwich, CT: JAI Press.

Burt, R. (1992). *Structural holes: The social structure of competition.* Cambridge, MA: Harvard University Press.

Cross, R., & Parker, A. (2004). *The hidden power of social networks: Understanding how work really gets done in organizations.* Boston, MA: Harvard Business School.

Fielder, F. E. (1955). The influence of leader-keyman relations on combat crew effectiveness. *Journal of Abnormal and Social Psychology, 51*, 227–235.

Freeman, L. C., Roeder, D., & Mulholland, R. R. (1979/1980). Centrality in social networks II: Experimental results. *Social Networks, 2*, 119–141.

Krackhardt, D. (1990). Assessing the political landscape: Structure, cognition, and power in organizations. *Administrative Science Quarterly, 35*, 342–369.

Meyer, M. W. (1975). Leadership and organizational structure. *American Journal of Sociology, 81*(3), 514–542.

Moody, J., McFarland, D. A., & Bender-DeMoll, S. (2005). Dynamic network visualization. *American Journal of Sociology, 110*, 1206–1241.

Chapter Four

Buckingham, M., & Clifton, D. O. (2001). *Now discover your strengths*. New York, NY: Free Press.

Cooperrider, D. (2001). Positive image, positive action: The affirmative basis of organizing. In D. Cooperrider, P. Sonensen, T. Yaeger, & D. Whitney (Eds.), *Appreciative inquiry: An emerging direction for organization development* (pp. 31–55). Champaign, IL: Stipes.

Cooperrider, D., & Whitney, D. (2005). *Appreciative inquiry: A positive revolution in change*. San Francisco, CA: Berrett-Koehler.

Fialkov, C., & Haddad, D. (2010). *Appreciative supervision*. Unpublished manuscript.

Fredrickson, B. L. (2003). The value of positive emotions. *American Scientist, 91*(4), 300–335.

Fredrickson, B. L. (2009). *Positivity*. New York, NY: Crown.

Gottman, J. (1995). *Why Marriages Fail*. New York, NY: Simon & Schuster.

Losada, M. (1999). The complex dynamics of high-performance teams. *Mathematical and Computer Modeling, 30*(9–10), 179–192.

Peterson, C., & Seligman, M. (2004). *Character strengths and virtues: A handbook and classification*. New York, NY: Oxford University Press.

Seligman, M. (1998). *Learned optimism: How to change your mind and your life*. New York, NY: Simon & Schuster.

Whitney, D., & Trosten-Bloom, A. (2010). *The power of appreciative inquiry*. San Francisco, CA: Berrett-Koehler.

Whitney, D., Trosten-Bloom, A., Cherney, J., & Fry, R. (2004). *Appreciative team building*. Lincoln, NE: iUniverse.

Whitney, D., Trosten-Bloom, A., & Rader, K. (2010). *Appreciative leadership: Focus on what works to drive winning performance and build a thriving organization*. New York, NY: McGraw-Hill.

Chapter Five

Allen, K. A., & Cherrey, C. (2000). *Systemic leadership: Enriching the meaning of our work*. Lanham, MD: University Press of America.

Benyus, J. M. (2002). *Biomimicry: Innovations inspired by nature*. New York, NY: HarperCollins.

Brown, A. (2008). In the future, the best will be better than perfect: The new biology paradigm. *The Futurists, 42*(5), 25–28.

Capra, F. (1975). *The Tao of physics*. Boston, MA: Shambhala.

Capra, F. (1992). Changes in management—management of change: The systemic approach. *World Business Academy Perspectives, 6*(3), 7–17.

Capra, F. (1996). *The web of life*. New York, NY: Anchor Books Doubleday.

Clark, D. L. (1985). Emerging paradigms in organizational theory and research. In Y. S. Lincoln (Ed.), *Organizational theory and inquiry: The paradigm revolution* (pp. 43–79). Beverly Hills, CA: SAGE.

Deming, W. E. (1986). *Out of the crisis*. Boston, MA: MIT Press.

Glieck, J. (1987). *Chaos: Making a new science*. New York, NY: Penguin.

Handy, C. (1994). *The age of paradox*. Cambridge, MA: Harvard Business Press.

Hazy, J. K., Goldstein, J. A., & Lichtenstein, B. B. (Eds.). (2007). *Complex systems leadership theory: New perspectives from complexity science on social and organizational effectiveness*. Mansfield, MA: ISCE.

Jennings, P. L., & Dooley, K. J. (2007). An emerging complexity paradigm in leadership research. In J. K. Hazy, J. A. Goldstein, & B. B. Lichtenstein (Eds.), *Complex systems leadership theory: New perspectives from complexity science on social and organizational effectiveness* (pp. 17–34). Mansfield, MA: ISCE.

Lynch, D., & Kordis, P. L. (1988). *Strategy of the dolphin: Scoring a win in a chaotic world*. New York, NY: William Morrow.

Olson, E. E., & Eoyang, G. H. (2001). *Facilitating organization change: Lessons from complexity science*. San Francisco, CA: Jossey-Bass.

Schwandt, D. R., & Szabla, D. B. (2007). Systems and leadership: Coevolution or mutual evolution towards complexity? In J. K. Hazy, J. A. Goldstein, & B. B. Lichtenstein (Eds.), *Complex systems leadership theory: New perspectives from complexity science on social and organizational effectiveness* (pp. 35–60). Mansfield, MA: ISCE.

Stacey, R. (1992). *Managing the unknowable: Strategic boundaries between order and chaos in organizations*. San Francisco, CA: Jossey-Bass.

Wacker, W., & Taylor, J. (2000). *The visionary's handbook: Nine paradoxes that will shape the future of your business*. New York, NY: HarperCollins.

Wheatley, M. (1992). *Leadership and the new science: Learning about organization from an orderly universe*. San Francisco, CA: Berrett-Koehler.

Wheatley, M., & Frieze, D. (2009). Taking social innovation to scale. *Oxford Leadership Journal, 1*(1), 1–5.

Zohar, D. (1997). *Rewiring the corporate brain: Using the new science to rethink how we structure and lead organizations*. San Francisco, CA: Berrett-Koehler.

Chapter Six

Baum, F. (1987). *The wonderful wizard of Oz.* New York, NY: HarperCollins.

Dickinson, E. (1998). *The poems of Emily Dickinson: Reading edition* (R. W. Franklin, Ed.). Cambridge, MA: Harvard University Press.

Einstein, A. (1950). United Nations radio interview [recorded in Einstein's study]. Princeton, NJ. Letter of 1950, as quoted in the *New York Times* (29 March 1972) and the *New York Post* (28 November 1972).

Emerson, R. W. (1983). *Essays: First series: Essays and lectures.* New York, NY: Library of America.

Hugo, V. (1996). *Les miserables.* New York, NY: Random House.

Mossberg, B. (2001a). Achieving progress without losing tilt. In *Presidents in action, strategies for effective leadership: The presidency.* The Presidency, American Council on Education, October 1, 2001. http://www.highbeam.com/doc/1P3-88547973.html

Mossberg, B. (2001b). Leadership's natural ally: Applying chaos and complexity theories to academe. In M. Cutright (Ed.), *Chaos theory and higher education: Leadership, planning, and policy* (pp. 203–249). New York, NY: Peter Lang.

Mossberg, B. (2006). *Teaching as leadership, love, and forgiveness: Through the lens of comedy, tragedy, and chaos theory, the joy of teaching.* In *The Joy of Teaching: A Chorus of Voices* (J. C. Falsa & L. Anderson, Eds.). Lanham, MD: University Press of America.

Sophocles. (1996). *The Oedipus plays of Sophocles: Oedipus the King, Oedipus at Colonus, Antigone* (Paul Roche, Ed.). New York, NY: Penguin.

Tennyson, A. (1990). *The classic hundred poems* (W. Harmon, Ed.). New York, NY: Columbia University Press.

Twain, M. (2010). *Twain's autobiography* (Vol. 1). Berkeley: University of California Press.

Zimmerman, M. (2003). In Gary Tischler, "There's Something about Mary Zimmerman," the *Georgetowner,* February 9, 2011 (and as part of theater program, Arena Stage, Washington DC).

Part Two

Gandhi, M. (1958). General knowledge about health. In *The collected works of M. K. Gandhi* (Vol. 13). New Delhi, India: Government of India Publications Division. (Original work published 1913)

Kegan, R. (1994). *In over our heads: The mental demands of modern life.* Cambridge, MA: Harvard University Press.

Kegan, R., & Lahey, L. L. (2009). *Immunity to change: How to overcome it and unlock the potential in yourself and your organization.* Boston, MA: Harvard Business Press.

Senge, P., Scharmer, C. O., Jaworski, J., & Flowers, B. S. (2004). *Presence: An exploration of profound change in people, organizations, and society.* New York, NY: Doubleday.

Chapter Seven

Arendt, H. (2006). *Between past and future.* New York, NY: Penguin.

Bryum, R. (2010, October 1). Personal communication with Ki ThoughtBridge.

Johnson, R. (1986). *Inner work.* San Francisco, CA: HarperCollins.

Sanford, J. (1994). *Evil: The Shadow Side of Reality.* New York, NY: Crossroad
   Press.

Chapter Eight

Aurobindo, S. (2000). *The life divine* (2nd American ed.). Twin Lakes, WI: Lotus Press.

Beauregard, M., & Paquette, V. (2006). Neural correlates of a mystical experience in Carmelite nuns. *Neuroscience Letters, 405*(3), 186–190.

Beauregard, M., & Paquette, V. (2008). EEG activity in Carmelite nuns during a mystical experience. *Neuroscience Letters, 444*(1), 1–4.

Bell, J. (1964). On the Einstein Podolsky Rosen paradox. *Physics, 1*, 195–200.

Bohm, D. (1980). *Wholeness and the implicate order.* London: Routledge.

Bohm, D. (1992). *Thought as a system.* London: Routledge.

Bradley, R. (2007). The psychophysiology of intuition: A quantum-holographic theory of nonlocal communication. *World Futures, 63*, 61–97.

Carey, M. (1992). Transformational leadership and the fundamental option for self-transcendence. *Leadership Quarterly, 3*(3), 217–236.

Deikman, A. (1996). "I" = awareness. *Journal of Consciousness Studies 3*(4), 350–356.

Frankl, V. (1992). *Man's search for meaning: An introduction to logotherapy* (4th ed.). Boston, MA: Beacon Square.

Gebser, J. (1985). *The ever-present origin* (N. Barstad, Trans.). Athens: Ohio University Press.

Goleman, D. (1995). *Emotional intelligence: Why it can matter more than IQ for character, health and lifelong achievement.* New York, NY: Bantam.

Goleman, D., Boyatzis, R., & McKee, A. (2002). *Primal leadership: Realizing the power of emotional intelligence.* Cambridge, MA: Harvard Business School Press.

Graves, C. (1974). Human nature prepares for a momentous leap. *Futurist, 8*(2), 72–87.

Hillman, J. (1996). *The soul's code: In search of character and calling.* New York, NY: Warner.

Isen, H., & Kline, P. (1999). *The genesis principle: A journey into the source of creativity and leadership.* Arlington, VA: Great Ocean.

Kegan, R. (1994). *In over our heads: The mental demands of modern life.* Cambridge, MA: Harvard University Press.

Klemp, H. (2002). *The spiritual laws of life.* Minneapolis, MN: Eckankar.

Kriger, M., & Seng, Y. (2005). Leadership with inner meaning: A contingency theory of leadership based on worldviews of five religions. *Leadership Quarterly, 16*, 771–806.

Laszlo, E. (2007). *Science and the akashic field: An integral theory of everything* (2nd rev. ed.). Rochester, VT: Inner Traditions.

McCraty, R., Atkinson, M., & Bradley, R. (2004). Electrophysiological evidence of intuition: Part 2. *Journal of Alternative and Complementary Medicine, 10*(2), 325–336.

Chapter Eight (continued)

McCraty, R., Atkinson, M., Tomasino, B., & Bradley, R. (2009). The coherent heart: Heart-brain interactions, psychophysiological coherence, and the emergence of system wide order. *Integral Review, 5*(2), 4–107.

Newton, M. (1994). *Journey of souls: Case studies of life between lives.* Woodbury, MN: Llewellyn.

Newton, M. (2000). *Destiny of souls: New case studies of life between lives.* Woodbury, MN: Llewellyn.

Owen, H. (2000). *The power of spirit: How organizations transform.* San Francisco, CA: Berrett-Koehler.

Palmer, P. (1993). *To know as we are known: Education as a spiritual journey.* San Francisco, CA: HarperSanFrancisco.

Palmer, P. (1997). *The courage to teach: Exploring the inner landscape of a teacher's life.* San Francisco, CA: Jossey-Bass.

Pattakos, A. (2004). *Prisoners of our thoughts.* San Francisco, CA: Berrett-Koehler.

Plato. (1992). *Republic* (C. Reeve, Ed., & G. Grube, Trans.). Indianapolis, IN: Hackett.

Ray, M. (2004). *The highest goal: The secret that sustains you in every moment.* San Francisco, CA: Berrett-Koehler.

Scharmer, C. O. (2007). *Theory U: Leading from the future as it emerges: The social technology of presencing.* Cambridge, MA: Society for Organizational Learning.

Torbert, W., & Associates. (2004). *Action inquiry: The secret of timely and transforming leadership.* San Francisco, CA: Berrett-Koehler.

Wilber, K. (1996). *A brief history of everything.* Boston, MA: Shambhala.

Wilber, K. (2000). *Integral psychology: Consciousness, spirit, psychology, therapy.* Boston, MA: Shambhala.

Chapter Nine

Rock, D. (2009). *Your brain at work: Strategies for overcoming distraction, regaining focus, and working smarter all day long.* New York, NY: Harper-Collins.

Trungpa, C. (1991). *The heart of the Buddha.* Boston, MA: Shambhala.

Chapter Ten

Fox, M. (1983). *Meditations with Meister Eckhart.* Santa Fe, NM: Bear & Co.

Fox, M. (1999). *A spirituality named compassion* (Chapter 2). Rochester, VT: Inner Traditions.

Fox, M. (2000). *Original blessing.* New York, NY: Jeremy Tarcher/Putnam.

Fox, M. (2001). *Prayer: A radical response to life.* New York, NY: Jeremy Tarcher/Putnam.

Fox, M. (2004). *The reinvention of work.* San Francisco, CA: HarperSanFrancisco.

Fox, M. (2008). *The hidden spirituality of men: Ten metaphors to awaken the sacred masculine.* Novato, CA: New World Library.

Fox, M. (2011). *Christian mystics.* Novato, CA: New World Library.

Herrmann, S. (2009). *William Everson: The shaman's call.* New York, NY: Eloquent Books.

Chapter Eleven

Chouinard, Y. (2005). *Let my people go surfing: The education of a reluctant businessman.* New York, NY: Penguin.

Colman, A. D. (1995). *Up from scapegoating: Awakening consciousness in groups.* Evanston, IL: Chiron.

Colman, A. D. (1997, November). *In the final analysis.* Paper presented at the Mexican Association for the Study of Depth Psychology in Mexico City, Mexico. Retrieved from http://www.arthurcolman.com/final.html

Eastwood, C. (Producer & Director), & Peckham, A. (Writer). (2009). *Invictus* [Motion picture]. U.S.: Warner Bros. Pictures, Spyglass Entertainment, and Revelations Entertainment.

Edinger, E. F. (1972). *Ego and archetype.* New York, NY: Penguin.

Harvey, A. (2008). Sacred activism. Retrieved from http://www.andrewharvey .net/sacred_activism.php

Jung, C. G. (1963). Mysterium coniunctionis: An inquiry into the separation and synthesis of psychic opposites in alchemy. In H. Read, M. Fordham, & G. Adler (Eds.) & R. F. C. Hull (Trans.), *The collected works of C. G. Jung* (Vol. 14). New York, NY: Bollinger Foundation. (Original work published 1955–1956)

Kacou, E. (2009). Archimedes' formidable dare. In M. Fairbanks, M. Fal, M. Escobari-Rose, & E. Hooper (Eds.), *In the river they swim* (p. 249). West Conshohocken, PA: Templeton Press.

Maathai, W. (2009). *The challenge for Africa.* Toronto, ON: Pantheon.

Marcel, G. (1949). *Being and having* (K. Farrer, Trans.). Westminster, UK: Dacre Press. (Original work published 1935)

Montero, P., & Colman, A. D. (2000). Collective consciousness and the psychology of human interconnectedness. *Group, 24*(2/3), 203–219. doi: 10.1023/A: 1007540101096

Chapter Twelve

Avolio, B. J., & Gardner, W. L. (2005). Authentic leadership development: Getting to the root of positive forms of leadership. *Leadership Quarterly, 16*, 315–338.

Avolio, B. J., Gardner, W. L., Walumbwa, F. O., Luthans, F., & May, D. R. (2004). Unlocking the mask: A look at the process by which authentic leaders impact follower attitudes and behaviors. *Leadership Quarterly, 15*, 801–823.

Beck, D. E., & Cowan, C. C. (1996). *Spiral dynamics: Mastering values, leadership, and change.* Malden, MA: Blackwell.

Burns, J. M. (2003). *Transforming leadership.* New York, NY: Grove.

Combs, A., & Holland, M. (2001). *Synchronicity: Through the eyes of science, myth and the trickster.* New York, NY: Marlowe.

Denhardt, R. B., & Denhardt, J. V. (2006). *The dance of leadership: The art of leading in business, government, and society.* New York, NY: M. E. Sharpe.

De Pree, M. (1995). Leadership jazz. In J. T. Wren (Ed.), *The leader's companion: Insights on leadership through the ages* (pp. 453–455). New York, NY: Free Press.

Endrissat, N., Muller, W. R., & Kaudela-Baum, S. (2007). En route to an empirically-based understanding of authentic leadership. *European Management Journal, 25*, 207–220.

Gardner, H. (2006). *Five minds for the future.* Boston, MA: Harvard Business Press.

Gardner, W. L., Avolio, B. J., Luthans, F., May, D. R., & Walumbwa, F. (2005). "Can you see the real me?" A self-based model of authentic leader and follower development. *Leadership Quarterly, 16*, 343–372.

Gardner, W. L., Fischer, D., & Hunt, J. (2009). Emotional labor and leadership: A threat to authenticity? *Leadership Quarterly, 20*, 466–482.

George, W. (2003). *Authentic leadership: Rediscovering the secrets to creating lasting value.* San Francisco, CA: Jossey-Bass.

George, W. (2007). *True north: Discover your authentic leadership self.* San Francisco, CA: Jossey-Bass.

Hyde, L. (1998). *Trickster makes this world: Mischief, myth, and art.* New York, NY: Farrar, Straus and Giroux.

Jung, C. (1976). *The portable Jung* (J. Campbell, Trans.). New York, NY: Viking Penguin.

Keller, H. (1903). *The story of my life* (J. A. Macy, Ed., Kindle ed.). New York, NY: Doubleday.

Kouzes, J. M., & Posner, B. Z. (1995). *The leadership challenge.* San Francisco, CA: Jossey-Bass.

Lakoff, G. (2009). *The political mind: A cognitive scientist's guide to your brain and its politics.* New York, NY: Penguin.

Lovgren, S. (2006, October 13). Nobel Peace Prize goes to micro-loan pioneers. *National Geographic News.* Retrieved from http://news.nationalgeographic.com/news/2006/10/061013-nobel-peace.html

Chapter Twelve (continued)

McFarland, L. J., Senn, L. E., & Childress, J. R. (1995). Redefining leadership for the next century. In J. T. Wren (Ed.), *The leader's companion: Insights on leadership through the ages* (pp. 456–463). New York, NY: Free Press.

Pearson, C. S., & Seivert, S. (1995). *Magic at work: A guide to releasing your highest creative powers*. New York, NY: Doubleday.

Tippett, K. (2010). *Einstein's God: Conversations about science and the human spirit*. New York, NY: Penguin.

Yunus, M. (2010). *Building social business: The new kind of capitalism that serves humanity's most pressing needs*. New York, NY: Public Affairs.

Part Three

Brooks, D. (2011). *The social animal: Hidden sources of love, character, and achievement.* New York, NY: Random House.

Gladwell, M. (2000). *The tipping point: How little things can make a big difference.* Boston, MA: Little, Brown.

Gladwell, M. (2005). *Blink: The power of thinking without thinking.* Boston, MA: Little, Brown.

Jaworski, J. (1996). *Synchronicity: The inner path of leadership.* San Francisco, CA: Berrett-Koehler.

Senge, P. (1996). Telling a story. In J. Jaworski, *Synchronicity: The inner path of leadership.* San Francisco, CA: Berrett-Koehler.

Chapter Fourteen

Bion, W. (1965). *Transformations*. London, UK: H. Karnac.

Briskin, A., Erickson, S., Ott, J., & Callanan, T. (2009). *The power of collective wisdom*. San Francisco, CA: Berrett-Koehler.

Sampson, A. (2000). *Mandela: The authorized biography*. New York, NY: Vintage.

Surowiecki, J. (2004). *The wisdom of crowds: Why the many are smarter than the few and how collective wisdom shapes business, economies, societies and nations*. New York, NY: Anchor.

Thurman, H. (1979). *With head and heart: The autobiography of Howard Thurman*. New York, NY: Harvest.

Tucker, J. (2010, January 27). Huge cut for S.F. schools detailed. *San Francisco Chronicle*.

Zinn, H. (2007). *A Power Government Cannot Suppress*. San Francisco, CA: City Lights Books.

Chapter Fifteen

Benfey, O. T. (1958). "August Kekulé and the Birth of Structural Theory of Organic Chemistry in 1858. *Journal of Chemical Education, 35,* 21–23.

Bohm, D. (1996). *On dialogue* (L. Nichol, Ed.). London, UK: Routledge.

Brafman, O., & Beckstrom, R. A. (2008). *The starfish and the spider: The unstoppable power of leaderless organizations.* New York, NY: Portfolio Trade.

Gobillot, E. (2009). *Leadershift: Reinventing leadership for the age of mass collaboration.* London, UK: Kogan Page.

Hayashi, A. (2010). Feminine principle and Theory U. *Oxford Leadership Journal, 1*(2).

Inayat Khan, H. (1960). *The Sufi message of Hazrat Inayat Khan* (Vol. 2): *The mysticism of sound: Music, the power of the word, cosmic language.* New Delhi, India: Motilal Banarsidass.

Jironet, K. (2002). *The image of spiritual liberty in the Western Sufi movement following Hazrat Inayat Khan.* Leuven, Belgium: Peeters.

Jironet, K. (2009). *Sufi mysticism into the West: Life and leadership of Hazrat Inayat Khan's brothers 1927–1967.* Leuven, Belgium: Peeters.

Jironet, K. (2010). *Female leadership: Management, Jungian psychology, spirituality and the global journey through purgatory.* London, UK: Routledge.

Jung, C. G. (1966). Some aspects of modern psychotherapy. In H. Read, M. Fordham, & G. Adler (Eds.) & R. F. C. Hull (Trans.), *The collected works of C. G. Jung* (Vol. 16, pp. 29–35). Princeton, NJ: Princeton University Press. (Original work published 1930)

Kaplan, R. S., & Norton, D. P. (1992, January–February). The balanced scorecard: Measures that drive performance. *Harvard Business Review* (reprint #92105). Retrieved from http://www.stevens-tech.edu/MSISCourses/450 /Articles/ValueOfIT/TheBalancedScoreCard .pdf

Kaplan, R., & Kaiser, R. (2009). Stop overdoing your strengths. *Harvard Business Review, 87*(2), 100–103.

Li, C., & Bernoff, J. (2008). *Groundswell: Winning in a world transformed by social technologies.* Boston, MA: Harvard Business Press.

Lutyens, M. (1975). *Krishnamurti: The years of awakening.* London, UK: John Murray.

Prahalad, C. K. (2010). Best practices get you only so far. *Harvard Business Review, 88*(4), 32–33.

Scharmer, C. O. (2007). *Theory U: Leading from the future as it emerges.* Cambridge, MA: SoL.

Shirky, C. (2009). *Here comes everybody: The power of organizing without organizations.* London, UK: Penguin.

Stein, M. (1998). *Jung's map of the soul.* Chicago, IL: Open Court.

Stein, M. (2006). *The principle of individuation: Toward the development of human consciousness.* Wilmette, IL: Chiron.

Chapter Fifteen (continued)

Williams, C. V. (2002). *Jiddu Krishnamurti: World philosopher (1895–1986): His life and thoughts.* Delhi, India: Motilal Banarsidass.

Wilson, T. D. (2001). *Strangers to ourselves: Discovering the adaptive unconscious.* Cambridge, MA: Belknap.

Chapter Seventeen

Denhardt, R. B. (1993). *The pursuit of significance: Strategies for managerial success in public organizations.* Belmont, CA: Wadsworth.

Denhardt, R. B., & Denhardt, J. V. (2005). *The dance of leadership.* Armonk, NY: M. E. Sharpe.

Scharmer, C. O. (2007). *Theory U: Leading from the future as it emerges.* Cambridge, MA: SoL.

Chapter Eighteen

Baillie, D. (Producer). (2002). *Women in Black* [motion picture]. Israel/Palestine: Journeyman Pictures.

Bhabha, H. (1994). *The location of culture*. New York, NY: Routledge.

Bion, W. (1961). *Experiences in groups*. London, UK: Tavistock.

Burns, J. M. (1978). *Leadership*. New York, NY: Harper Torchbooks.

DuBois, W. E. B. (1903). *The souls of black folks: Essays and sketches*. Chicago, IL: A. C. McClurg.

Elson, O. (2002). Communicating gender agency and structuration in the organizing of the Spiritual Baptist Church of Barbados. *Goliath Knowledge on Demand*. Retrieved from http://goliath.ecnext.com/comsite5

Friedman, T. (2007). *The world is flat: A brief history of the twenty-first century*. New York, NY: Picador/Farrar, Straus and Giroux.

Hayden, C., & Molenkamp, R. (2004). *Group relations reader 3* (D. Noumair & S. Cytrynbaum, Eds.). Jupiter, FL: AK Rice Institute.

Heifetz, R. A., & Linsky, M. (2002). *Leadership on the line: Staying alive through the dangers of leading*. Boston, MA: Harvard Business Press.

Heisenberg, W. (1983). *Über den anschaulichen Inhalt der quantentheoretischen Kinematik und Mechanik* [Quantum theory and measurement] (J. A. Wheeler & H. Zurek, Trans.). Princeton, NJ: Princeton University Press. (Original work published 1927)

Isaacs, W. (1999). *Dialogue: The art of thinking together*. New York, NY: Currency.

Linsky, M. (2008, February 26). First woman president? *Newsweek*.

Pollack, D. C., & Van Reken, R. (2001). *Third culture kids: Growing up among worlds*. Yarmouth, ME: Intercultural Press.

Rutherford, J. (1990). The third space: Interview with Homi Bhabha. In J. Rutherford (Ed.), *Identity: Community, culture, difference* (pp. 207–221). London, UK: Lawrence & Wishart.

Starosta, W., & Olorunnisola, A. (1995). *A meta-model for third culture development*. Paper presented at the annual meeting of Eastern Communication Association, Pittsburgh, PA.

Tutu, D. (2000). *No future without forgiveness*. New York, NY: Image Books.

Conclusion

Mark, M., & Pearson, C. S. (2001). *The hero and the outlaw: Building extraordinary brands through the power of archetypes*. New York, NY: McGraw-Hill.

Molenkamp, R. (2011). *A picture is worth a thousand words*. Unpublished manuscript, Leadership for Transformation Project.

Pearson, C. S., & Marr, H. (2006). *What story are you living?* Gainesville, FL: Center for Applications of Psychological Type.

LEADERSHIP FOR
TRANSFORMATION BIBLIOGRAPHY

This list includes books selected for their worth and timeliness, as well as to support and complement material in the essays. Please also see the author biographies at the end of the essays, as many of these authors also have written very fine and timely books. In addition, other excellent books and articles are included in the reference lists.

Publications generated by the Fetzer Institute Leadership for Transformation Project (in addition to *The Transforming Leader*)

Brown, J. (2012). *The art and spirit of leadership*. Indianapolis, IN: Trafford Publishing. A book on transformational practices by Judy Brown, coinvestigator on the Leadership for Transformation Project.

Hickman, G., & Barbour, J. (Eds.). (2011). *Leadership for transformation*. San Francisco, CA: Jossey-Bass. A volume in the International Leadership Series, Building Leadership Bridges, that emerged from the Fetzer Institute–sponsored 2009 conference, Leadership for Global Transformation.

Twenty-First-Century Transformational Leadership Books

Ackerman-Anderson, L. (2010). *The change leader's roadmap: How to navigate your organization's transformation* (2nd ed.). San Francisco, CA: Wiley.

Derungs-Ruhier, I. (2010). *Trans-cultural leadership for transformation*. Basingstoke, UK: Palgrave Macmillan.

Dobbs, R. (2010). *Transformational leadership: A blueprint for real organizational change*. Little Rock, AR: Parkhurst Brothers.

Harris, G. (2009). *The art of quantum planning: Lessons from quantum physics for breakthrough strategy, innovation, and leadership.* San Francisco, CA: Berrett-Koehler.

Hickman, G. (2010). *Leading organizations: Perspectives for a new era* (2nd ed.). Thousand Oaks, CA: SAGE.

Kuhn, L. (2009). *Adventures in complexity: For organizations near the edge of chaos.* Axminster, UK: Triarchy Press.

Martin, R. (2009). *The opposable mind: How successful leaders win through integrative thinking.* Boston, MA: Harvard Business Press.

Nohria, N., & Khurana, R. (Eds.). (2010). *Handbook of leadership theory and practice: A Harvard Business School centennial colloquium.* Boston, MA: Harvard Business Press.

Palmer, P. (2011). *Healing the heart of democracy: The courage to create a politics worthy of the human spirit.* San Francisco, CA: Jossey-Bass.

Pearson, C. S., & Corlett, J. G. (2003). *Mapping the organizational psyche: A Jungian theory of organizational dynamics and change.* Gainesville, FL: Center for Applications of Psychological Type.

Popper, M. (2005). *Leaders who transform society: What drives them and why we are attracted.* Westport, CT: Praeger.

Scharmer, C. O., & Society for Organizational Learning. (2009). *Theory U: Leading from the future as it emerges: The social technology of presencing.* San Francisco, CA: Berrett-Koehler.

Sosik, J. (2006). *Leading with character: Stories of valor and virtue and the principles they teach.* Greenwich, CT: Information Age.

Torbert, B. (2011). *Action inquiry: The secret of timely and transforming leadership.* San Francisco, CA: Berrett-Koehler.

Weinstein, S. (2004). *Transformational leadership: Vision, persuasion, and team building for the development professional: New directions for philanthropic fundraising.* Hoboken, NJ: Jossey-Bass.

Classic Works on Transformational Leadership and Organizational Change

Bass, B., & Avolio, B. (Eds.). (1994). *Improving organizational effectiveness through transformational leadership.* Thousand Oaks, CA: SAGE.

Bass, B., & Riggio, R. (2006). *Transformational leadership* (2nd ed.). Mahwah, NJ: Lawrence Erlbaum.

Burns, J. M. (1978). *Leadership.* New York, NY: Harper & Row.

Northouse, P. (2010). *Leadership: Theory and practice* (5th ed.). Thousand Oaks, CA: SAGE.

Schein, E. (1992). *Organizational culture and leadership.* San Francisco, CA: Jossey-Bass.

Senge, P. (1990). *The fifth discipline: The art and practice of the learning organization.* New York, NY: Doubleday/Currency.

Senge, P., Scharmer, C. O., Jaworski, J., & Flowers, B. S. (2005). *Presence: An exploration of profound change in people, organizations and society.* New York, NY: Doubleday/Currency.

Stein, M., & Hollwitz, J. (1995). *Psyche at work: Workplace applications of Jungian analytical psychology.* Wilmette, IL: Chiron.

Wheatley, M. (2006). *Leadership and the new science: Discovering order in a chaotic world.* San Francisco, CA: Berrett-Koehler.

Books on Inner Work and Transformational Psychologies

Apter, M. (Ed.). (2001). *Motivational styles in everyday life: A guide to reversal theory.* Washington, DC: American Psychological Association.

Apter, M. (2006). *Reversal theory: The dynamics of motivation, emotion and personality* (2nd ed.). London, UK: Oneworld.

Colman, A., & Geller, M. (Eds.). (1985). *Group relations reader 2.* Washington, DC: A. K. Rice Institute.

Goleman, D. (1995). *Emotional intelligence: Why it can matter more than IQ.* New York, NY: Bantam.

Johnson, R. (1986). *Inner work: Using dreams and active imagination for personal growth.* San Francisco, CA: HarperSanFrancisco.

Kegan, R. (1994). *In over our heads: The mental demands of modern life.* Cambridge, MA: Harvard University Press.

King, V. (1998). *Soul play: Turning your daily dramas into divine comedies.* Georgetown, MA: Ant Hill Press.

Palmer, P. (2004). *A hidden wholeness: The journey toward an undivided life.* San Francisco, CA: Jossey-Bass.

Pearson, C. S. (1991). *Awakening the heroes within: Twelve archetypes to help us find ourselves and transform our world.* San Francisco, CA: HarperSanFrancisco.

Pierman, R. (1998). *Hard-wired leadership: Unleashing the power of personality to become a new millennium leader.* Palo Alto, CA: Davies-Black.

GRATITUDES

I first want to thank the Fetzer Institute for funding and being a true partner for the Leadership for Transformation Project, out of which this book arose, and for supporting the publication of this book along with its publisher, Berrett-Koehler. I enjoyed working with Berrett-Koehler editor Neal Maillet and managing editor Javeen Sivasubramaniam, as well as the rest of their supportive and professional staff, and I admire the high quality of their innovative publications. In addition, I'd like to thank the School of Public Policy at the University of Maryland and the James MacGregor Burns Academy of Leadership, where this project began. Finally, but most importantly, I want to thank James MacGregor Burns for providing foundational theory about transformational leadership and for supporting the academy, and me as its director, over the years.

Second, it is important to honor the people who partnered in the development of the Leadership for Transformation Project. Judy Brown, who wrote a separate book inspired by this project, *The Art and Spirit of Leadership* (Trafford Publishing, 2012), was my primary partner in the early phases of its design and implementation, and has been an incredible friend, colleague, and thinking partner, not only in planning and hosting the dialogues, but also in my life and work more generally. I am extraordinarily grateful to the participants in the Fetzer Institute's Leadership for Transformation dialogues for generously sharing their wisdom, experience, and practices and the essay authors, whose words and ideas have enriched this book. The Leadership for Transformation Stewardship Team collaborated so harmoniously and well that retreat participants began to see us as exemplifying what we were writing about. It was an enormous pleasure working with its members: Judy Brown; Fetzer Institute program officer Mark Nepo and director of programs Deborah Higgins; International Leadership Association president Cynthia Cherrey, director Shelly Wilsey, and board member Gil Hickman; consultant Michael Jones, and editor Megan Scribner. A special thanks goes to Deborah Higgins, who stayed on as my program officer during the preparation of this manuscript, enlisting and coordinating the institute's continued support of it and providing the foreword to the book.

I also had a great support team, without which, given my responsibilities at Pacifica Graduate Institute, I could not have completed the book in the appropriate time frame. My deep appreciation and thanks go to Megan Scribner for the amazing job she did as the editor of the writing throughout. We had an abundance of rich material to work with, and I don't know what I would have done without her help in reducing the length of the essays and refining my introductions. She demonstrated a sculptor's craft in revealing the essential art within the rock.

At Pacifica Graduate Institute, many thanks to Lauren Lastra for her highly competent and professional logistical and formatting assistance, to reference librarian Mark Kelly for discovering the best source for many quotations and for his beaming smile, to Toni D'Anca and her staff for planning and implementing a workshop prior to the book's publication and a subsequent conference to highlight the importance of this work, and to Erik Davis for his help in publicizing these events.

On the personal level, I want to acknowledge Wisdom University and the Creation Spirituality Community, and especially Carol Vaccariello and Judith Yost, for their contributions to my own growth as a leader, and for studies helping me to develop my leadership as a spiritual practice. And finally, thanks to my husband, David Merkowitz, for his support during vacations and weekends while I was hunkered down working on this project, and for providing helpful feedback on my ideas and fine editing of my writing. It is my sincere hope, David, that you will not be called upon to do this again in the future, and that our next vacation actually will be one.

INDEX

About the Editor

Carol S. Pearson, PhD, is the president of Pacifica Graduate Institute, an accredited graduate school located in the Santa Barbara, California, area offering master's and doctoral degree programs in clinical psychology, counseling psychology, depth psychology (with specializations in somatics and in community, liberation, and ecopsychology), mythology, and the humanities—and currently developing a program in organizational leadership. Visit http://www.pacifica.edu.

The Transforming Leader builds on themes that have informed many of her earlier books: *The Hero Within: Six Archetypes We Live By; Awakening the Heroes Within: Twelve Archetypes to Help Us Find Ourselves and Transform Our World*, and *What Story Are You Living?* (coauthor Hugh Marr), as well as the Pearson-Marr Archetype Indicator, which readers can use to assess the archetypes active in their lives and which provides information, not included in this book, on how readers can access a wider range of leadership capacities through enhancing their awareness of archetypal energies within and around them.

Dr. Pearson's work on identifying archetypes in group and organizational cultures provides a means to articulate the unwritten rules and taboos of an organization's culture by naming the archetypal energies within it. Doing so can assist in integrated approaches to authentic brand identity development; organizational development and change management; and recruitment, retention, and leadership development efforts. Such aligned approaches make it easier for organizations to deliver on their branding promises because these practices build on the genuine values, motivations, and strengths of an organization. As part of this effort, Dr. Pearson published (with coauthor Margaret Mark) *The Hero and the Outlaw: Building Extraordinary Brands through the Power of Archetypes* and *Mapping the Organizational Psyche: A Jungian Theory of Organizational Dynamics and Change* (with coauthor John G. Corlett) and developed and tested the Kenexa Cultural Insight Survey™, which assesses the archetypes active in an organizational culture.

Dr. Pearson has long studied and practiced leadership in the interest of human development and liberation. She was an American Council on Education Fellow in Academic Administration, a program designed to develop higher education leaders, and subsequently held faculty and administrative positions in several colleges and universities. Prior to taking a position at Pacifica Graduate Institute, she directed the James MacGregor Burns Academy of Leadership in the School of Public Policy at the University of Maryland. The Academy at that time was the home of the International Leadership Association.

Dr. Pearson is now interested in how identifying the larger (Third Space) mythic stories in situations of conflict and strife can help us imagine ways to shift to more positive narratives, thus enabling new possibilities to emerge. From this concern, she recently published a monograph through the Fetzer Institute American Dream Series titled *Maturing the American Dream: Archetypal Narratives Meet the Twenty-First Century.* Moving from conflictual relationships to collaboration around solutions, she believes, also can be furthered through holding in our minds and hearts the image of our planet viewed from outer space, looking both so beautiful and so fragile. Such an image evokes the realization that we are all in this together and can challenge us to let our minds, hearts, and souls grow big enough to embrace the whole, thus finding an evolving Third Space where all is possible.

For more information about Dr. Pearson and the Pearson Archetypal System, go to http://www.herowithin.com.

About the Fetzer Institute

Leadership for Transformation Project Funder and Partner

The Fetzer Institute is a nonprofit, private operating foundation whose mission is to foster awareness of the power of love and forgiveness in the emerging global community. Our work is grounded in a conviction that the connection between the inner life of spirit and outer life of service and action in the world holds the key to lasting change. All of our activities—past, present, and future—are united by a desire to help improve the human condition by increasing conscious awareness of the relationship between this inner and outer life. This desire is central to the world's religious and wisdom traditions. Established by broadcast pioneer John E. Fetzer (1901–1991) and located in Kalamazoo, Michigan, the institute uses its philanthropic resources to create programs in support of its mission. With an endowment of $380 million, the institute dedicates approximately $20 million annually toward its programming efforts. For more information, visit http://www.fetzer.org.

About the International Leadership Association

Leadership for Transformation Project Partner

Established at the turn of the century, the International Leadership Association (ILA) is the global organization for those with a stake in leadership.

The ILA embodies leadership for the twenty-first century with the following features:

- Multinational membership base and conference attendance bringing together perspectives from seventy-plus countries and cultures
- Multidisciplinary approach to leadership and followership leading to unique insights and innovative connections
- Multisector networking between those who study, teach, develop, and exercise leadership, resulting in research-based, field-tested best practices

With thousands of members across the globe, the ILA is transforming leadership for the greater good of communities worldwide. Learn more or join us at http://www.ila-net.org.

About Pacifica Graduate Institute

Pacifica Graduate Institute is an accredited graduate school offering master's and doctoral degree programs. The mission of Pacifica Graduate Institute is to foster creative learning and research in the fields of psychology and mythological studies, framed in the traditions of depth psychology. By creating an educational environment with a spirit of free and open inquiry, consistent with the recognized values of academic freedom, Pacifica is dedicated to cultivating and harvesting the gifts of the human imagination. So that these insights may influence the personal, cultural, and planetary concerns of our era, this dedication is contained in its motto: *Animae mundi colendae gratia*—for the sake of tending soul in and of the world. For more information, visit http://www.pacifica.edu.

Berrett–Koehler
BK Publishers

Berrett-Koehler is an independent publisher dedicated to an ambitious mission: *Creating a World That Works for All*.

We believe that to truly create a better world, action is needed at all levels—individual, organizational, and societal. At the individual level, our publications help people align their lives with their values and with their aspirations for a better world. At the organizational level, our publications promote progressive leadership and management practices, socially responsible approaches to business, and humane and effective organizations. At the societal level, our publications advance social and economic justice, shared prosperity, sustainability, and new solutions to national and global issues.

A major theme of our publications is "Opening Up New Space." Berrett-Koehler titles challenge conventional thinking, introduce new ideas, and foster positive change. Their common quest is changing the underlying beliefs, mindsets, institutions, and structures that keep generating the same cycles of problems, no matter who our leaders are or what improvement programs we adopt.

We strive to practice what we preach—to operate our publishing company in line with the ideas in our books. At the core of our approach is stewardship, which we define as a deep sense of responsibility to administer the company for the benefit of all of our "stakeholder" groups: authors, customers, employees, investors, service providers, and the communities and environment around us.

We are grateful to the thousands of readers, authors, and other friends of the company who consider themselves to be part of the "BK Community." We hope that you, too, will join us in our mission.

A BK Business Book

This book is part of our BK Business series. BK Business titles pioneer new and progressive leadership and management practices in all types of public, private, and nonprofit organizations. They promote socially responsible approaches to business, innovative organizational change methods, and more humane and effective organizations.

Berrett–Koehler
Publishers

A community dedicated to creating
a world that works for all

Visit Our Website: www.bkconnection.com

Read book excerpts, see author videos and Internet movies, read our authors' blogs, join discussion groups, download book apps, find out about the BK Affiliate Network, browse subject-area libraries of books, get special discounts, and more!

Subscribe to Our Free E-Newsletter, the *BK Communiqué*

Be the first to hear about new publications, special discount offers, exclusive articles, news about bestsellers, and more! Get on the list for our free e-newsletter by going to **www.bkconnection.com**.

Get Quantity Discounts

Berrett-Koehler books are available at quantity discounts for orders of ten or more copies. Please call us toll-free at (800) 929-2929 or email us at **bkp.orders@aidcvt.com**.

Join the BK Community

BKcommunity.com is a virtual meeting place where people from around the world can engage with kindred spirits to create a world that works for all. BKcommunity.com members may create their own profiles, blog, start and participate in forums and discussion groups, post photos and videos, answer surveys, announce and register for upcoming events, and chat with others online in real time. Please join the conversation!